6 Janvier 89

Dîner

Salades Variées

Grand Cassoulet
au Canard, porc
et Saucisses

Fromages

Crème Caramel Sce au Rhum

Biscotti

Pain au Son Maison
• Mondavi Chardonnay
Ducru-Beaucaillou
magnum 73 • Rauzan Gassies 82
OFFLEY 1972 SOAVETA VINTAGE PORT

Retour
7 Juin
Radis de
et J

Lapin côté à la
Jardinière de
Salade de Epinar
l'huile vierge
fromages
Brownies (glacie?)
café

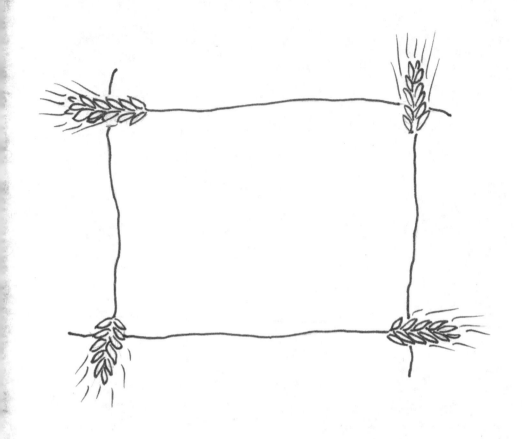

THE APPRENTICE

THE Apprentice

MY LIFE IN THE KITCHEN

Jacques Pépin

HOUGHTON MIFFLIN COMPANY

BOSTON   NEW YORK   2003

Copyright © 2003 by Jacques Pépin
Illustrations copyright © 2003 by Jacques Pépin
All rights reserved

For information about permission to reproduce selections from
this book, write to Permissions, Houghton Mifflin Company,
215 Park Avenue South, New York, New York 10003.

Visit our Web site: www.houghtonmifflinbooks.com.

Library of Congress Cataloging-in-Publication Data

Pépin, Jacques.
The apprentice : my life in the kitchen / Jacques Pépin.
p. cm.
Includes index.
ISBN 0-618-19737-0
1. Pépin, Jacques—Biography. 2. Cookery. I. Title.
TX649.P47A3 2003
641.5'092—dc21
[B] 2002192158

Book design by Anne Chalmers
Typefaces: New Baskerville, Dalliance, Copperplate

Printed in the United States of America

DOC 10 9 8 7 6 5 4 3 2

Unless otherwise credited,
all photographs are reprinted courtesy of the author.

I DEDICATE THIS BOOK TO MY TWO BROTHERS,

ROLAND AND BICHON,

WHOSE LOVE OF GOOD FOOD, OF WINE, OF FAMILY,
AND ESPECIALLY OF LIFE IS REFLECTED IN THIS BOOK.
THEY DEPARTED TOO EARLY BUT WILL
ALWAYS BE PART OF MY LIFE.

Acknowledgments

At the time that this book was going to print, I had the great misfortune of losing my older brother, Roland, to lung cancer, the same sickness that took my younger brother, Bichon, five years ago. Both of them are very much a part of this book and very much in my heart, and I want to acknowledge their important influence on my life.

This book would not have been possible without the help of Barry Estabrook. I started writing essays about my apprenticeship more than fifteen years ago, and always in the back of my mind I thought I would shape them into a book someday. I wrote about my experiences in the kitchen as a child in France, my years in Paris, my life after coming to the States, the way cuisine changed during those years, and what I acquired and learned along the way. Eventually, I had a pile of little stories and anecdotes going back over four decades, but I needed help to shape my rough manuscript into a book. This involved and complex task resulted in hours of lively discussions between Barry and me. I benefited mightily from his clear insights and his grasp and knowledge of good storytelling. His professionalism, unassuming approach, and gentle manner made him a pleasure to work with. He brought the material to life without ever imposing his style of writing or his ideas on me, insisting always on keeping my voice first and foremost, and for this I will forever be gratefully indebted.

I also want to thank Doe Coover, my agent, who not only organized the sale of this book to the right publisher and the right editor, but also suggested Barry.

I want to acknowledge Anne Chalmers, the art director, for the appealing layout of the book and the good use she made of my drawings and pictures.

I particularly want to thank Rux Martin, my editor, whose incisive mind, clear vision, and sharp scissors purposefully improved the manuscript. Her initial confidence never deviated, and her enthusiasm for the project only increased as we got further along.

I thank Norma Galehouse, my assistant, who was involved with this book from its earliest inception. A one-woman business office, Norma does my scheduling and tracks my invoices and expenses. She knows pretty much which assignments I should and should not take, she advises me, and she corrects my mistakes. She has become a trusted friend. She learned to decipher my handwriting and can now read it better than I can. When friends call, asking where I am or when I will be home, my wife, Gloria, usually replies, "Ask Norma." Norma freed me to concentrate on what I do best: cook.

I thank my daughter, Claudine, for her work with me during those years on television, and particularly I thank Gloria, for her love and her understanding, for sticking with me through the ups and downs for so many years, and for the unconditional faith she has always had in me.

Finally, I thank all the people who have been part of my life for the past half-century for their help, support, and love.

Contents

THE APPRENTICE

1

The
War Years

MY MOTHER made it sound like a great adventure.

"Tati," she said, using the nickname my brother had given me as a toddler, "you are going to a marvelous place. A farm. A real farm."

My six-year-old's imagination filled in the rest of the details. Enormous plow horses. Fat, grunting pigs. Dairy cows with sharp horns and swollen, swaying udders. All manner of fowl: chickens, ducks, geese. Dogs and cats. In short, heaven.

Maman had more practical reasons for sending me to a farm. School had ended, and I would be on summer vacation for the next two and a half months. In towns and cities, food was always scarce in France during the Second World War. In the countryside, farmers may not have had two sous to rub together, but gardens produced vegetables, corn grew in fields, pigs became fat, chickens laid eggs, and cows gave milk that was turned into cream, butter, and cheese. Out of kindness, rural folk would take in the children of townspeople, giving room and board in exchange for chores. Although hearty, the food at the farms was simple and straightforward, coarse and without variety. A gratin of squash with cream, homemade cheeses, roasted or boiled potatoes, and cured pork held in barrels from the previous year were the most common dishes. Occasionally on Sundays, farm families ate roast chicken or rabbit, followed by plum or apple tarts. Nothing fancy, but compared to what we ate in town, this was feasting. In the fall, the children would return home tanner, stronger, and fatter.

The big day came. Maman prepared a picnic lunch. I hopped into a trailer that she towed behind her bike, and together we set off through a landscape of hills, valleys, vineyards, fields, and roadsides shaded by the leafy branches of plane trees. Late that afternoon, we arrived in Foissiat, a hamlet in the center of the rich agricultural region of La Bresse. We pulled into the courtyard of a farmhouse identical to any of a hundred Maman had already pedaled past. It was fashioned from blond-colored mud and round stones and had a red tile roof, plain except for being topped by the ornate and vaguely Middle Eastern–style Saracen chimney. Just as I had imagined, chickens, ducks, and a pair of majestic geese squabbled, quacked, and honked in the courtyard, and a stinky, mud-caked pig grunted in one corner. It was exciting and a bit scary to be that close to real farm animals.

The farmer's wife greeted us, ruffling my hair and cooing. It was a surprising sound, given its source: the tallest, roughest-looking, and most powerfully built woman I had ever laid eyes on. She had a bright red face and wore the traditional peasant's bonnet.

While she and my mother went into the house, the farmer, a big man with a great moustache that curled up at the corners, took me to the barn, which was even more exhilarating than the courtyard. Although I had seen plenty of cows in my day, I had never stood close to one. In that shadowy building, where the sweet scent of hay and raw milk mingled with the acidity of manure and urine, a dozen broad, wet noses turned in my direction. The closest cow, an enormous beast, lifted her tail and hunched her back. I jumped away just in time to avoid being splattered by the resulting mess. That was my first act as an apprentice cowherd.

We returned just as the farmer's wife heaped dinner on the table — literally. She slopped spoonfuls of a yellowish brown porridge, called *gaudes,* not onto plates or bowls, as we ate it at home, but directly into hollows carved into the wooden tabletop. We gathered around as the farmer's wife poured cool, raw milk over our *gaudes.* With no further ceremony, we all sat down and dug in. The *gaudes* were thick and smooth and had the salty, slightly nutty taste of the roasted corn flour from which they had been made. The best part of dinner was getting to eat with my elbows on the table and not even being asked whether I had washed my hands. What a summer this was shaping up to be!

But as soon as the last oil lamp was blown out that night, my excitement vanished, replaced by a hollow sense of emptiness and abandonment, sadness and fear. The farmer's wife had done her best to provide what comforts her home offered. I was given a tall bed beside the wall. For warmth, she tucked an eiderdown around me, and I curled up beneath its homespun cover. It smelled of the fields and outdoors, a foreign scent to a six-year-old boy who, until that night, had always fallen asleep in his own bed in a second-floor apartment in a busy little town. Lying there with a *coeur gros,* a heavy heart, I thought of my family. Papa, a jovial bear of a man. Zizi, or Roland, eighteen months my senior, a mentor, constant companion, and best friend, so much more than a big brother. Richard, known as Bichon, just a baby. And, most of all, my beautiful, effervescent mother, who had slipped away without my even knowing.

My pillow was still damp from tears when I woke up the next morning to begin the routine that would set the tone of my summer days. At first light, after a breakfast of café au lait and bread and jam, the farmer led me into the barn and presented me with a wooden staff. The other component of my cowherd's uniform was a pair of wooden shoes stuffed with hay. I was also introduced to my work mate, a big black mutt. Our job was to escort the cows out into the fields in the morning, watch over them during the day, and see that they returned safely to the barn in the evening. Although I fancied myself very important and hardworking, the truth is that the cows and their canine overseer knew what was expected of them far better than I did.

Still, there have been few prouder dairymen than I as I trailed home behind my twelve charges that evening. Inside the barn, the woman sat me on a stool beneath one of the animals, which caused me some nervousness, given the size of the beast and my close call the previous day. She took my fingers gently in her callused hand and placed them on the cow's teat, showing me how to pinch the top with my thumb and forefinger and then pull down, squeezing with my palm. To my delight, milk squirted noisily into the pail, more each time I repeated the motion, until it brimmed with creamy, frothy milk. The woman took down a small bowl and filled it.

"It's yours, *mon petit*," she said, handing me the bowl.

The milk was foamy and slightly tepid, with a rich, buttery flavor.

She had no way of knowing it, but that plain country woman, whose name I have long forgotten, taught me one of the most important lessons of my life: food could be much more than mere sustenance.

That night, I didn't cry.

I WAS BORN on the eighteenth of December, 1935, in the town Bourg-en-Bresse, about thirty miles northeast of Lyon, the second of three sons of Jeanne and Jean-Victor Pépin. Weighing only two and one half pounds, I nearly died at birth. The midwife lined a shoebox with dishtowels and put me inside, placing the makeshift incubator between two bricks that had been warmed on the stove.

Like his grandfather, father, and older brother before him, Papa was a cabinetmaker, an *ébéniste*, from the word for "ebony." He specialized in period furniture such as the *table en chiffonnier*, a narrow dresser made of cherry wood, with three drawers and elegant curved legs carved in the Louis XV Provençal style. It was precise work, more art than craft. In his workshop, he had a can of *colle de bois,* or wood glue, that he kept hot on a small wood stove. It had an awful smell. He told me it was made from mistletoe berries. I was fascinated by the idea of those little white berries turning into that darkish, thick, sticky, and smelly mixture.

In contrast to my small, energetic mother, my father was big, barrel-chested, and jovial — a happy guy, a man's man, more like one extra overgrown kid under our roof than an authority figure. He'd throw us in the air and catch us, bounce us on our beds, and wrestle with us, and he was always up for a game of soccer or rugby, a sport at which he excelled. He loved to drink wine in the company of his many friends. It always put him in a cheery mood, and when he had a few too many glasses of Côtes du Rhône, he would sometimes remove his shirt and dance on a table, La Bresse's answer to Zorba the Greek. When fooling around like this, he would show off by hurling walnuts against the outside windows of the café with the accuracy of a major league pitcher. The nuts shattered each time but never broke the glass. It was his private trick, and he got a kick out of seeing our puzzled faces. No one ever found out how he did it. My mother, who tried it once, broke the window, and Roland and I never dared to attempt it.

But like virtually all young Frenchmen, Papa, then twenty-nine, was drafted when war was declared against Germany. Nine months later, the French army was routed and a period of confusion and disarray called *la débâcle* began. We had no idea where my father was, whether he was safe among the hordes of retreating soldiers who clogged the roadways trying to get home, whether he was suffering in some military hospital, or whether he, like thousands of young French soldiers, lay dead in the mud of what was once the invincible Maginot Line. But by then, those of us at home had our own war to fight.

～～～

AT FIRST they were quiet, like wind moaning through branches or the howling of distant dogs. But they became louder, like the whistle of an approaching locomotive.

I awoke, sitting up.

Maman was already there with Bichon in her arms.

"Hurry, Zizi, Tati," she said to Roland and me.

We hopped out of bed, still in our pajamas, and ran outside behind her. We crossed the street and dove beneath a railroad underpass, where some of the neighbors had already gathered. Maman wrapped us in blankets, and we waited.

The sky lit up. A second later we heard thuds and felt the ground vibrate. Then silence. The adults whispered among themselves. After the consultation, Maman turned to us and said, "We can go back now."

Our home was part of a small apartment complex near a key bridge leading to Lyon and next to a railroad sorting depot. Because of the depot and bridge, it was a strategic area frequently targeted by bombers. After the first raid, we never knew whether or not we'd get a full night's sleep. Night after night, siren wails awakened me, and I ran from the house with my mother and brothers.

The responsibility of keeping three young boys safe and fed during this time fell solely to my mother, then only in her mid-twenties. Maman was strikingly beautiful, with proud, erect posture, high cheekbones, large brown eyes, and masses of black curls swept back from her forehead. She was a tiny, wrenlike bundle of energy, always on the move.

She earned money by working all day as a waitress at L'Hôtel de Bourgogne in Bourg-en-Bresse. In the evenings, she sewed every article of clothing the family wore. And on her one day off from the restaurant each week, she shopped for our food, though hers was hardly your typical grocery run. Early in the morning, she would put on one of her Provençal-style floral dresses and wrap her dark curls in a scarf before mounting an old bicycle with solid rubber tires (no inner tubes), pedaling down our street onto the main road and out to the dusty byways of the countryside. With her slim, muscular legs, she pedaled thirty-five or forty miles, going from farm to farm, filling the wicker basket strapped on the back of her bicycle with bread, eggs, meat, chicken, honey — anything that she could find that would help feed us.

Somehow she managed, and we ate every day, but necessity exposed my taste buds to some unconventional recipes. In lieu of sugar, which wasn't available, Maman made a wartime sweetener by cooking beets in water on her wood stove for hours, straining the mixture, and then reducing the syrup to a thick brownish liquid. It filled the entire apartment with an earthy, slightly caramelized sweet scent — an aroma every bit as appealing to me as the inside of a pastry shop. I loved the stuff almost as much as I hated another one of our staples, Jerusalem artichokes, which we consumed "natural," with no butter, oil, or cream. Their smell made me gag. But when I grimaced and said, "I don't like these," Maman would say, "Too bad, Tati, that's all we have." And I would eat them, though I haven't put a Jerusalem artichoke in my mouth since.

At the end of each meal, our plates were sparkling clean, so clean that we would turn them over, and the small circle in the center of the underside would serve as a dessert plate. Usually, when we had dessert at all, it consisted of a few tablespoons of jam or fruit purée that Maman had made, bartered for at a farm, or purchased on the black market.

When she had the ingredients, Maman made something she called *coque*, or *matefaim*, roughly translated as "hunger quencher," a kind of French toast. For this, she used eggs that she had preserved in a whitish, slimy mixture of lime and water, which made the shells very brittle and rough. She mixed the eggs with flour and water, or milk, if available, creating a thick, unsophisticated crêpe batter, in which she soaked slices of dark, tough, dry bread. To produce the *coque*, she cooked the soaked bread and some of the batter in a skillet coated with a little rapeseed oil. Not exactly French toast, but it did quench our hunger.

Another unlikely favorite of mine was *mou au vin rouge:* cubes of beef or veal lungs cooked with onion and the sediment left in the bottom of a red wine barrel. Before cutting them into cubes,

Maman inflated the lungs by blowing into the trachea. I once witnessed the disastrous results of omitting this step. The lung pieces expanded in the cooking liquid, tripling or quadrupling in size, until the lid of the vessel suddenly lifted and pieces of lung spewed out of the pot like volcanic lava. Maman never had such problems with her *mou* and served it several times a month. Even though the spongy texture of the lungs and the acidity of the sauce would not thrill a gourmet, I loved *mou au vin rouge*. In a perverse way, I still do.

Occasionally, my mother got a few pounds of butter, which she would cook and salt to preserve in jars. The darkened scum that rose to the top of the butter and stuck in a ring to the sides of the pot as the butter cooked was *la crasse du beurre,* or "butter's dirt." Despite the name, it had a deep, nutty taste that turned a stale piece of bread into a culinary triumph that ranked right up there with *mou.*

To supplement what my mother acquired on her excursions through the countryside, we had a plot in a community garden about a half-mile from home. Roland and I were assigned to push a homemade cart and clean up behind a large Percheron horse that made grocery deliveries through the neighborhood. Often competing with other local boys, we rushed in and shoveled up the malodorous but precious "piles of gold." Our garden was truly organic. And, thanks to us, the streets of Bourg were kept impeccably clean.

The few crops we grew in our plot were precious: potatoes, radishes, onions, leeks, parsley, zucchini, beans, and, especially, salad greens. One day, Roland and I were instructed to get salad from the garden. But when we arrived there, we were confused. Which plants were we supposed to pick? After some discussion, we chose the tender young greens aligned in well-cultivated rows, by far the most appetizing specimens and also the easiest to pick, although gathering enough for a salad required the uprooting of three entire rows. We proudly bore our harvest home, only to be greeted by a shriek from Maman. Those seedlings had been transplanted from the cold frame only days before. Although baby greens may be all the rage today, size often trumped quality on the tables of wartime France.

One afternoon, during the peak of Mussolini's bombing of Bourg-en-Bresse, Maman was off waitressing. Roland, Grandmother, and I were weeding the garden, while Bichon napped in his carriage at the end of a row. By then, the howls of air raid sirens and the thuds of exploding bombs had become so common that we barely looked up from our chores when a loud blast went off nearby. It wasn't until we turned the corner at the top of our street on our way home that we saw the destruction. In front of our building, the landlord's car had been reduced to a blackened, smoldering tangle of metal. Much of the ground floor had been blown away. Protruding above, completely windowless and minus its balcony and the exterior staircase that provided access, was the apartment that had been the only home I had known.

Everyone was gathering what belongings they could and fleeing from the advancing German columns. We lacked a car, but my aunt, La Marraine, said we could get out of Bourg with her. Nothing could have delighted me more. La Marraine was the mother of my favorite cousin, Robert, who was a teenage version of Papa. Traveling with him would make Robert just like another brother.

But to my disappointment, La Marraine informed me that Robert wouldn't be going with us. He had joined the army, and La Marraine said that he had disappeared. We climbed into my uncle's old Citroën; he had also gone to war. La Marraine, who did not drive, drove. Crowded into that car, which smelled of gasoline fumes, old leather, and Uncle's tobacco, we struck out toward the mountains of the massif Central, near the Auvergne region. Our progress was anything but smooth. La Marraine worked the shift like an uncooperative pump handle, and the gears crunched and grated before engaging, jolting the car forward. Just as often, it jerked to a stall. During those interludes when La Marraine got us moving in the right direction, she drove at full throttle, swerving from side to side like someone who'd enjoyed one too many glasses of wine at lunch. We might never have survived that journey had we not passed a young soldier wandering the road. La Marraine stomped the brake.

"Where are you going?" she asked.

The soldier shrugged. "I don't know. I've lost my regiment."

"Well, you do know how to drive, don't you?"

He nodded.

"Good, it's yours," she said, sliding over so he could take the wheel.

A few kilometers later, he spotted a couple of trucks filled with French soldiers along the side of the road. Hoping to get some information about his regiment, our driver stopped and called out. Immediately, a young man in the dark blue uniform of the French army jumped from the truck and embraced him. La Marraine screamed. Incredibly, it was Robert. He took over the driving, and we ended up in a small hamlet called Baribas, where we found lodging in a farm for a few weeks. Eventually, we moved back into our home on rue de l'École normale. One morning I woke up and there, seated at the table as if not a day had passed, was Papa.

Unfortunately, this period of tranquility turned out to be but a moment of peace in the eye of the storm. In late 1943 and early 1944, the Germans began gathering able-bodied men at random and coercing them into forced labor for their war machine. Many men, moved by patriotism as well as unwillingness to participate in a German labor camp, joined the French underground, known as *le maquis,* the term applied to the tight, impenetrable bush regions of Corsica, where bandits would hide from the law.

One day my father was strolling down avenue Alsace-Lorraine, the main street of Bourg, when a German officer accosted him, accusing him of being part of *le maquis.* The soldiers lined up Papa and seven other townsmen against a wall outside the Préfecture de police, a seventeenth-century castle-like building at the bottom of the street, and held them there all day at gunpoint. In the late afternoon, the soldiers dragged two of the men away and summarily shot them. The Germans returned. Instead of taking more victims, however, they told the survivors to go home. Shortly afterward, Papa moved to the mountains and joined some of his friends in the Resistance.

For a second extended period, he was gone. But this time, he would occasionally slip home, often at night when my brothers and I slept. We would not even know he had been there until the next morning when Maman, wearing a faint smile, told us that our father had visited. He often left behind small gifts of food. For a while, we were awash in sardines. Papa had brought us a few dozen tins that he had gotten from parachuted goods, compliments of the American air force. I still love canned sardines, served simply on top of salad with finely sliced onion and a sprinkling of red wine vinegar.

SUMMER CAME, and once again I was going to leave home to spend a few months on a farm. This time, much to my delight, Roland and I went together. There were tears on my cheeks when Maman left us at the train station in Lyon, but they dried quickly as the train, filled with other young boys, chugged toward Chambéry, a town in the Savoy area known for its vermouth, pasta, and fish from nearby lac du Bourget. We spent the night in an army barracks in Chambéry and the next day boarded a small shuttle train to complete our journey to St.-Jean-de-Maurienne, a small town in the foothills of the Alps.

Standing on the platform, I heard a voice calling, "Pépin! *Les frères* Pépin!"

Roland and I separated ourselves from the crowd.

A priest with a rough, leathery outdoorsman's complexion and clad in an old-fashioned ground-length black soutane was calling. We presented ourselves, and without much more conversation, this most unpriestly-looking priest led us to a distinctly un-priestly conveyance: a two-wheeled cart to which a small donkey was hitched. The priest climbed aboard, indicating that we were to sit beside each other on a bench that faced backward. From that vantage point, I had my first encounter with big mountains, immense peaks glowing in the bright sun of that early June day.

The priest and his donkey headed up a dirt road, bordered by the abrupt wall of the mountain on one side and the gaping abyss of the valley on the other. Finally, we arrived in the village of Montvernier. I was hoping that Roland and I would stay in the same house that summer, but the priest took me alone to the home of the family where I would stay, leaving Roland on the cart. Mme. Mercier was waiting for us in the large, central — and only — room of the farmhouse. After a few minutes of conversation, the priest left with my brother, facing backward, waving goodbye to me. Once again, I was alone.

Every couple of weeks, Mme. Mercier undertook the formidable task of making bread, a staple for the family. Preparation started two to three days ahead of time. She began with a leftover hunk of dough about the size of a plucked chicken, which she kept covered with water in an earthen jar in the cool cellar under the house. To that, she added flour, water, and salt to form a soft mixture, like slurry, in the *pétrin,* or kneading vessel. The *pétrin* was made of carved hardwood and resembled a coffin in size and appearance. Proudly displayed, with its beautiful carved lid, it functioned as a table or sideboard when not in use for bread baking.

Making the dough was backbreaking work. The first slurry would be left to ferment and rise a little, usually overnight. In the morning, the fermentation would have run its course, and Mme. Mercier added fresh flour and water to the mixture to give it new life. She left the dough again for a few hours to activate and ferment, repeating this process, called a *rafraîchi,* or a refreshing, several times over the course of three days. Eventually, her dough became strong, elastic, and filled with pockets of air, which would burst and produce a wonderfully aromatic, yeasty fragrance that permeated the farmhouse. On the final day, Mme. Mercier shaped the dough into round loaves, saving a piece to store in the cellar as a starter for the next batch of bread.

Like every other household in Montvernier, the Merciers lacked an oven large enough to bake the dough Mme. Mercier had so laboriously prepared. Instead, the people of the town shared a massive common baking oven with the residents of a nearby village called Montbrunal. Bread-baking day had all the excitement of a carnival. Villagers greeted each other loudly and gossiped in small clusters. Kids ran about and played. I was standing forlornly on the outskirts when Roland appeared.

He was staying with a family in Montbrunal, which meant that I would not only see him on baking days but on Sundays as well, since the villages also shared a single church. Montvernier and Montbrunal were so close together that we could even walk to visit each other during the week when our farm duties permitted.

The oven seemed as large as a house, and together Roland and I watched the baker-farmer feed it with the pile of wood needed to bring it to the proper temperature. The smell of so much baking bread was enthralling. We stood there for hours. One after the other, farmers arrived with their loaves, two dozen or so each, and the baker would take over. At the end of the day, some farmers brought casserole dishes, containing anything from beans to cabbage, to be cooked overnight in the heat retained by the oven.

Back at the farm, Mme. Mercier arranged her loaves like decorative plates on the high, narrow shelves running along two entire walls of the room. Every night for dinner, she brought down a new loaf. Seated at the head of the table, M. Mercier held the loaf on its edge and marked a cross on its underside with his folding wood-handled knife. This was intended as a sign of respect for the bread and an offering to God, although it was more a ritual of food than a religious observance. Only then would he cut the bread into large chunks and distribute it around the table.

An unusual custom dictated that cheeses, made in the village, were always to be consumed with bread at the start of the meal. One of these was a wonderful cheese called Beaufort, rich, dense, and nutty, similar to a Gruyère. Another Savoy cheese, *Tomme de Savoie,* was harder and more pungent than the Beaufort. Sometimes we ate the Beaufort by itself. Other times Mme. Mercier grated it into soups, gratins, soufflés, and stuffings, but the *Tomme* was always eaten on its own. Mme. Mercier's meals always ended with a soup — precisely the opposite order that I had been used to. We also ate homemade cured, dried ham, redolent of the hay in the summer fields. For dessert we had plum tarts made with sugary yellow mirabelle plums about the size of cherry tomatoes.

Montvernier offered plenty of experiences for a young city boy: the glorious peaks of the Alps, the frightening chasms bordering the narrow mountain roads, the powerful and intoxicating smell of the summer hay that we spent hours cutting and gathering, the hair-raising rides perched on bales of hay in a cart pulled by a donkey that occasionally slipped as he headed down treacherous paths on his way to the barn. But for me the most impressive thing about the Alps was that wood-fired bread oven and the way it not only nourished but also brought together the people of two remote mountain communities.

~

I HAD REASON to dread the end of summer. Although I was officially too young to attend, Roland was already enrolled in Lycée St. Louis, a boarding school in Bourg. Between her six-day-a-week job and her day-off food-gathering expeditions, not to mention caring for Bichon, who'd grown into a big, active toddler, Maman did not have time to watch over me. The solution was to see if she could prevail upon the Jesuit priests who ran Lycée St. Louis to grant me what amounted to early admission.

She, Roland, and I approached the somber stone edifice that housed the *lycée.* We were shown into a dark reception room. A door shut behind us, and we waited. At length *le directeur* entered.

He was a tall, austere priest whose pure white hair made him seem old enough to be on speaking terms with St. Peter himself. He took a seat behind his desk and glowered.

"What is it you want?" he said to Maman.

Normally not easily cowed or at a loss for words, she stammered, "My husband is away."

This merited only a faint snort from the exceptionally long nose of *le directeur.*

"And I have a job, and a baby to take care of, and since Jacques's older brother is already enrolled . . ."

Le directeur did not so much as cast a glance at or in any way acknowledge the presence of Roland and me. Children, clearly, were beneath this man's contempt.

"The boy is not of age," he said.

"But, please . . ."

The adult conversation continued for a long time. I'm not sure what she said, but somehow she accomplished a minor miracle: she got *le directeur* to change his mind and, more impressive, to bend one of Lycée St. Louis's strict rules.

I immediately learned that one of the most important of those numerous rules was that students were forbidden to talk. A policy of silence prevailed unless we were addressed directly by a priest or given explicit permission to speak. A natural chatterbox like all Pépins, I ran afoul of that rule early in my studies. The priest who was teaching our class said something that I couldn't hear from my desk in the back of the room, so I asked a neighboring student to repeat it for me. I spoke in my quietest whisper, but the Jesuits of Lycée St. Louis, aged though they may have been, possessed superhuman hearing.

"Pépin!" he roared, before I'd gotten out two syllables.

I snapped to attention bedside my desk.

"Come to the front of the room."

I came forward and was ordered to get down on my knees in front of the class and extend my arms to the side, palms up. On each palm, the priest placed a heavy book. He forced me to hold those books until my arms burned with pain. Whenever I lowered them, even by an inch, he ordered me to get them back up.

Thursday provided us with a day off from classes, but not from discipline and rules. The priests' idea of letting boys play in the woods was to make us form a single-file line, with a priest at its head and another at its end, and march us along in that manner. The forest had been the scene of some fighting, and the priests warned us not to touch any military ordnance that we might see lying around. I resisted until near the end of our "play" session, when I spotted a brilliant gleam of brass under a leaf. I checked behind me. The priest bringing up the rear was behind some trees, out of sight. The lead priest was looking the other way. I made a swipe. It was a spent cartridge casing, sleek and beautiful, a treasure beyond compare to a boy whose father was off in the mountains fighting with *le maquis,* wearing an ammunition belt studded with shells just like that one. I pocketed it.

When we emerged from the forest, the priests stood before us. One demanded, "Did any of you pick anything up in there?"

I was too frightened to confess, even if I had wanted to, so I stood there shaking, my prize clutched in a sweating palm deep in my pocket.

"No?" the priest asked.

We all remained silent.

"If you have anything, drop it immediately."

Nothing hit the ground.

"Pépin!" he said. "Hands out of your pockets."

I did as told, leaving the cartridge in my pocket.

He strolled over to me and frisked the outside of my pants. Before I could speak, he smacked me twice, as hard as he could across the face.

Corporal punishment was swift, certain, and harsh at Lycée St. Louis, but it was an era when stern discipline was the norm, even at home, and to their credit, the priests meted it out equally. I got used to it. But the same cannot be said for the food, which was simply inedible. On my first morning there, an older student told me that for breakfast, we were having *le caca de René*. René was the infant son of the female cook, and *caca* being . . . well . . . if you've ever changed a soiled diaper, you understand. In the dining hall my bowl was filled with some ignoble gruel, whitish and thick. It turned out that we were served — and required to eat — *le caca de René* several times a week. The slop lived up to its name in every way. Although we were hungry and nearly starving, we would even pay fellow students to consume our servings of that vile concoction.

Things started looking up after breakfast, however. As we filed out of the dining room after the meal, we were each allowed to take one piece of black bread out of a basket. The bread was hard and stale, but it had to be better than *le caca de René*. I was about to gnaw off a chunk when my new friend cautioned me to stop. Taking his own piece, he struck it on the corner of the table. Several flea-like insects fell out and began scurrying for freedom. In time, this step became routine.

Many of the boarders were farmers' kids who from time to time received parcels of goodies, honey or salted lard or sausages, items that city kids like us never got. I became excellent at bartering, and for a few marbles or a roll of string, I would wangle all kinds of food. When I had nothing to trade with, I cajoled and pleaded. One day I convinced a farm boy to spread some of his jam on my dry piece of bread. I was just about to bite into this delicacy when I glanced down the table and saw that another boy was dipping his knife into a strong-smelling purée of salted fish. I deftly turned my slice of bread jam side down, so only the bare side was visible, and begged the other boy for a smear of his purée. Assuming that the only thing I had to eat was a piece of dry bread, he took mercy. I thoroughly enjoyed my some-bites-sweet, some-bites-fishy open-face sandwich.

During the winter, the dorm was cold enough at night to

freeze the water in the trough where we were supposed to wash. My feet stayed cold for so long that they grew red, raw, cracked, and painfully itchy with chilblains. Finally, spring came, and with it the prospect of a great celebration. Roland was to have his first communion. All the family, including La Marraine and my cousins from Bourg, even Robert, were going to gather at our apartment on rue de l'École normale. My mother would be cooking.

I needed to acquire a suitable gift for Roland, and I finally decided that the perfect thing would be the dry salami sausage called *saucisson*. Every member of our family loved *saucisson*, especially Roland, particularly after six months of *le caca de René*. In war-rationed France, acquiring a *saucisson* was difficult, and for a boy confined to Lycée St. Louis, it was attempting the impossible. But I was determined.

At school I knew a farm kid whose father kept cattle and pigs and was also adept at sausage making. The boy, well aware of the value of decent food at St. Louis, flatly refused to get me a *saucisson*. I bartered with him for days. First I put my collection of marbles on the table. He shook his head. I asked him what he wanted. What possession of mine could be more valuable than my beautiful cat's-eyes and puries?

"Your knife," he said.

My prized pocketknife. That was too much.

"Absolutely not," I told him.

For a time we each stood our ground. Finally, with only a week to go until the big day, I approached him and told him he could have the knife. It was a major sacrifice, but this was, after all, Roland's first communion.

"And your marbles," the farm boy said.

We sealed the deal, and I placed the precious *saucisson* in my *casier personel*, the small locker each student had, which was as close as we got to having private space at that school. Hopefully, it would be safe from other hungry students. I couldn't resist checking on my prize two or three times a day to see if it was still there. Each time I looked at it, my mouth watered and my hand reached out toward it. Eventually, I gave in to temptation and bit into the end of the sausage, just to taste it. After that, I continued to gnaw at my *saucisson*. Luckily, with a couple of days to go before that special Sunday, I had nibbled only about a half-inch off the end and was pleased that I had managed to keep the original shape of the sausage intact.

As the weekend approached, my anxiety increased. I couldn't wait to see the look on Roland's face. My mind was not focused on my studies, a bad idea at any time at Lycée St. Louis, but especially so when asking for dispensation to attend a special event. So maybe I was a few seconds behind the rest of the students in lining up before morning classes.

"You're late, Pépin," said a priest, a notorious stickler for punctuality who had never much cared for me anyway. The same priest later made me stand up in class and explain aloud to one and all why I was gazing out the window instead of reading my lessons. What was I to say? That I was daydreaming about the apartment on rue de l'École normale filled with relatives and friends there for Roland's party? I apologized, and I guess I murmured something under my breath as I sat down after receiving my public humiliation.

"That's it, Pépin," said the priest. "We'll see if you learn to behave after being grounded for the weekend."

My mother pleaded with *le directeur,* but he did not relent; I was to be restricted to school during that weekend. On Sunday after church and before the big meal, the whole family came to visit and comfort me. I handed my *saucisson* to my mother as they left and went up to the empty dorm. There was no one there to hear me crying.

But it has always been hard for me to stay unhappy for long. Time passed. Papa continued to visit occasionally in the night, leaving exotic treats like bananas and oranges. Word reached Bourg that the Allies had landed on the beaches of Normandy. Paris was liberated. Our home was bombed again, this time compliments of the retreating Germans, but no one was hurt, and we soon returned. Then one afternoon, people poured into the streets, yelling, "They're coming! They're coming!" Roland and I joined the crowds standing in the sunshine along avenue Alsace-Lorraine. In the distance there was a rumble, clearly different from the familiar drone of Italian and German bombers. Certainly no car, not even La Marraine's ancient Citroën, ever produced such a racket. The noise got louder, and then its source appeared: an Allied army tank.

Roland and I burst from the crowd and, along with every other kid in Bourg-en-Bresse, began running behind the tank. The soldiers — Americans! — laughed and tossed goodies to us. Roland and I managed to catch gum, something entirely new and such a luxury that we kept it for days, passing it between us; I'd chew it for a while and then Roland would.

The soldiers also threw candy bars. Running behind the tank, I caught one, broke off a piece, and put it in my mouth. For the first time in memory, I experienced the silky, bittersweet richness of milk chocolate.

My war had ended.

Les Oeufs Jeannette

(EGGS JEANNETTE)

WHEN WE WERE KIDS, eggs were a staple on our table. Meat or poultry showed up there once a week at the most, and more often than not, our "meat" dinners consisted of a delicious ragout of potatoes or cabbage containing bits of salt pork or leftover roast. Eggs were always a welcome main dish, especially in a gratin with béchamel sauce and cheese, and we loved them in omelets with herbs and potatoes that Maman would serve hot or cold with a garlicky salad.

Our favorite egg recipe, however, was my mother's creation of stuffed eggs, which I baptized "eggs Jeannette." To this day, I have never seen a recipe similar to hers, and we still enjoy it often at our house. Serve with crusty bread as a first course or as a main course for lunch.

6 jumbo eggs (preferably organic)
1 teaspoon chopped garlic
2 tablespoons chopped fresh parsley
2 to 3 tablespoons whole milk
¼ teaspoon salt
¼ teaspoon freshly ground black pepper
2 tablespoons vegetable oil (preferably peanut oil)

DRESSING

2 to 3 tablespoons leftover egg stuffing (from above)
4 tablespoons extra-virgin olive oil
1 tablespoon Dijon-style mustard
1 tablespoon water
Dash of salt and freshly ground black pepper

FOR THE HARD-COOKED EGGS: Put the eggs in a small saucepan, and cover with boiling water. Bring to a very gentle boil, and let boil for 9 to 10 minutes. Drain off the water, and shake the eggs in the saucepan to crack the shells. (This will help in their removal later on.) Fill the saucepan with cold water and ice, and let the eggs cool for 15 minutes.

Shell the eggs under cold running water, and split them lengthwise. Remove the yolks carefully, put them in a bowl, and add the garlic, parsley, milk, salt, and pepper. Crush with a fork to create a coarse paste. Spoon the mixture back into the hollows of the egg whites, reserving 2 to 3 tablespoons of the filling to use in the dressing.

Heat the vegetable oil in a nonstick skillet, and place the eggs, stuffed side down, in the skillet. Cook over medium heat for 2 to 3 minutes, until the eggs are beautifully browned on the stuffed side. Remove and arrange, stuffed side up, on a platter.

FOR THE DRESSING: Mix all of the dressing ingredients in a small bowl with a whisk or a spoon until well combined.

Coat the warm eggs with the dressing, and serve lukewarm.

2

The Call
of the Stove

MAMAN DECIDED to open a restaurant.

She was not one to let practical considerations stand in the way of her plans. Never mind that food was still rationed — especially meat, sugar, and chocolate — and we had to walk miles to the village of Crêpieux to get bread. Maman fully intended to run the restaurant, front and back, even though her only claim to professional cooking experience was the snippets of knowledge she had picked up by looking over the shoulder of the chef at L'Hôtel de Bourgogne during lulls between waiting on customers. We couldn't afford to buy a thriving, successful restaurant. Instead, we had to hope that we could somehow revive one in the last gasps of failure.

On the advice of a real-estate agent named M. Menu, Maman settled on an establishment ten miles from Bourg along the busy main road running through the town of Neyron. A two-story structure wedged between someone's house and an alley running down to the Rhône River, the eatery that carried the hopes and dreams of the Pépin family bore the dubious name of Hôtel L'Amour, although it had been many years since the four upstairs rooms had provided lodging for anything other than mice and dust motes.

But Maman's mind was made up, and on the appointed morning an ancient truck shuddered to a stop in front of our apartment. All of our belongings were loaded aboard, and, by evening, we had become restaurateurs. Maman had worked out a deal with the owner of the building to pay a fourth of the asking price, with the remainder to be paid in monthly allotments.

Ours would be a family enterprise from the outset. While Maman hung fresh curtains and painted interior walls, she dispatched Papa outside to give the dingy roughcast stucco façade a fresh coat of pastel pink. Maman spent days on her knees with a pail and scrub brush until the once-dingy black-and-white tile floors gleamed. By then Papa was heard pounding and sawing in the cellar, a junk-filled pit that would have offended the sensibilities of a sewer rat. In a few days it became a clean cellar for the restaurant's wines.

Maman drafted Roland, Bichon, and me into service in the hours before and after school, which, much to my relief, was run by a far less rigid administration than that of Lycée St. Louis. We came home, tossed our books on a kitchen counter, and immediately began peeling onions and potatoes or stringing beans and Swiss chard.

We were also put in charge of the two dozen hens that pecked about the back courtyard. They were fattened on vegetable peels and trimmings as well as on leftover soup. In return, the flock kept Hôtel L'Amour supplied with fresh eggs and, when the moment arrived, they became the primary ingredient in steaming plates of *poulet à la crème*. Our assistant was Bibi, a little black puppy who more than made up in feigned ferocity what she lacked in stature. Bibi was the terror of the henhouse. She strutted in each morning, head held high, her tail curled proudly over her back. To her delight, the chickens shrieked and scattered around the courtyard.

At an early age, I learned what it means for a cook to have respect for his ingredients. One morning, Bibi and I encountered a hen that had been sitting on a nest of eggs the day before. Now it lurked in the far corner of the henhouse, wings spread on the floor and a glint in the eye that followed our every move. Periodically, a small yellowish head would poke out from the feathers. With the usual bravado, Bibi began to bark, scattering the rest of the flock but not the hen in the corner. Bibi took this as an affront. She approached the bird and intensified her barking. The hen puffed her feathers, raised her head, emitted a fearsome squawk, and charged, all flying feathers and flailing claws. Bibi and I flew. From that day on, Bibi slunk across the courtyard only when necessary with head down, eyes averted, and tail firmly between her legs, and all broody hens remained firmly on their nests.

The large courtyard was shaded by a linden tree, and we gathered and dried its leaves and flowers to make *tilleul*, an infusion commonly consumed after dinner in those parts of France. The back wall was covered with grapes, mostly *noah*, or Concord grapes, and *baco*, thick-skinned black grapes with inky juice not suitable for wine but good enough for eating or for Maman's jam.

Slowly, business started picking up. Despite her lack of experience, Maman was a natural behind the stove, and the improved fare drew more customers, mostly working-class people from the neighborhood who expected simple but well-prepared food at affordable prices. In keeping with his natural inclinations, Papa arranged that Hôtel L'Amour become headquarters for Neyron's *belote* tournaments, lively card games that drew more patrons and also allowed Papa to participate in a favorite pastime while still officially "at work." His size and strength came in handy whenever a customer partook of too much wine and became rowdy. At such times, Papa calmly put his cigarette in an ashtray, laid down his cards, got up from the *belote* table, enveloped the miscreant in a bear hug, and jettisoned him before rejoining the game, literally without missing a trick.

Ever the entrepreneur, Maman made a deal with a man who

came once a week with an old motion-picture projector to show black-and-white movies in a room adjacent to the café dining room. That same room became Neyron's dancehall on Saturday nights. She also cajoled officials at the telephone company into installing a phone booth in the restaurant, a rarity, and for a time, Hôtel L'Amour became a telecommunications hub. People who came to make calls frequently stayed for a glass of wine or a bite of something from the kitchen. In exchange for a free telephone, however, we had to deliver messages to the homes in the area. It became a professional sideline for Roland and me. Maman received all manner of calls, which she wrote down, dispatching us around the county as delivery boys. Sometimes this meant jaunts of several miles, and if we were lucky, a tip of a few francs at the door of a distant farmhouse. Barring that, a farm wife occasionally favored us with a *tartine de confiture,* a slice of homemade bread slathered with quince or apricot jam.

It was during one of these deliveries to the nearby agricultural village of Neyron-le-Haut that Roland and I embarked on our brief, ill-fated career as petty thieves.

A shortcut to Neyron-le-Haut took us across vineyards planted with Gamay grapes intended for winemaking, tempting treats for two perpetually hungry boys. One glorious autumn day, Roland succumbed. Looking around and seeing no farmer, he plucked a single purple grape.

"It's good, Tati," he said, issuing a "mmmmm" to reinforce his point.

"If the farmer sees us, he'll beat us," I said. "Maybe shoot us."

Neither assertion was an exaggeration. Many farmers in the area owned shotguns and were not averse to discharging harmless but excruciatingly painful loads of rock salt in defense of their crops.

"He won't be able to see us," said Roland, pulling off an entire bunch of grapes and sitting beneath the vines to demonstrate that we would be out of sight.

I grabbed a bunch and joined him in the shade. The grapes

were sweet, juicy, and sun-warm. We stuffed ourselves. Only after we couldn't face the prospect of eating another grape did we realize that we had stained our hands, lips, tongues, and shirtfronts with telltale black juice.

During subsequent trips to Neyron-le-Haut, we grew more daring and more adept. Our targets expanded to include the farmer's *pêches de vigne,* or vineyard peaches, planted there because the short trees helped shade the vines. Short trees also meant easy pickings for young boys. The peaches had red flesh, fuzzy red skin, and a small freestone center. They were very sweet, with a slight taste of the grapes that they were protecting. They sold well at the market. If we got caught pilfering them, we would be in a lot of trouble.

In June, Roland spotted a cherry tree that was loaded with large, black *bigarreaux,* or Bing cherries. These rare treats posed a problem we hadn't faced with the low-growing *pêches de vigne.* The cherries dangled well out of reach. Furthermore, the trunk of the tree was as smooth and straight as a flagpole, making climbing impossible. We contemplated our predicament.

"Crouch down," I finally said to Roland.

"Are you crazy?"

"Crouch down. I'll get on your shoulders."

"You *are* crazy."

"No, if I stand on your shoulders, I'll be able to reach that limb." I pointed to the first branch, a good six or seven feet above and bending under the weight of tantalizing fruit.

Roland shrugged and said, "Don't blame me if you break your neck."

"Then don't ask me for any of the cherries."

He looked longingly at the branch. "Get on," he said, squatting.

I stood behind him and placed a foot on one of his shoulders.

"Put your hands up, so I can hold on to something," I said.

I counted off a mental one, two, three, and hopped with my other foot on his shoulders.

Roland's shoulders provided a shaky platform, but I lunged for the branch, grabbed it with one hand, and wildly flung my other hand around it. I hung there, summoning my strength. When my breathing slowed, I swung sideways, wrapping one leg and then the other around the limb.

Which left me with two problems. One, I was hanging upside-down. Two, the cherries were out toward the end of the limb, well beyond my reach. I began to inch outward. The branch bent. I extended my fingers. Suddenly, I heard a crack, and the entire branch broke from the trunk. I fell to the grass on my back with the loaded branch on top of me.

It wasn't the most graceful of landings, but our mission had been accomplished. We picked and ate as many cherries from that branch as we could. Then, while Roland pulled the downed branch into the bushes to hide our wrongdoing from the farmer, I rubbed some of the remaining cherries on the tree trunk to hide the white wood where the branch had been.

Now that we had perfected our cherry-picking technique, more or less, there was no question that we would launch a return raid. Cherry season in France is short. We came back a few days later.

"Up you go," said Roland.

"No," I said. "I did all dirty work last time. It's your turn."

Roland smirked. "Nothing to it," he said.

He was still in the tree when a nearby bush rustled. Before I could turn to see what caused the noise, a gun roared. Roland screamed, dropped from the tree, and began running, holding a hand over the fleshy part of his behind, the recipient of a couple of salt pellets. We ran off to a small stream, where he sat in the cool, running water to melt the salt and soothe his burning derrière.

PAPA'S CAREER as a sous-chef wasn't much more illustrious than Roland's and mine as petty thieves. There is no doubt that his oversized heart was in the right place. But the careful, deliberate temperament of a woodworker was testing Maman's patience in a busy kitchen. Maman assigned him easy tasks, such as preparing the simple first course of sliced tomato salad or anchovy fillets in oil.

Oblivious to the hectic pace around him, Papa took his time and went about his assignment with the age-old meticulousness of a skilled *ébéniste,* arranging each anchovy fillet in a forty-five-degree grid on a plate and stacking perfectly sculpted slices of tomato like a deck of cards.

"Give me those," Maman said, butting him aside, spreading tomato slices onto the plate, and coating them with her mustard vinaigrette. "Customers are waiting. We have to get these out there. *Vite! Vite!"*

Papa stood there wearing the face of an overgrown dog that knows he has disappointed his master terribly, but who, for the life of him, cannot fathom how.

But Victor Pépin came into his own in the quiet, shadowy realm below the kitchen. Papa's hobby — his love — was bottling his own wine, serious business at Hôtel L'Amour. I never thought of wine as something apart from food. When my brothers and I reached the age of six or so, Papa began adding a little red wine — about a teaspoon — to our water glasses, until the water was slightly pink. That made us more a part of the family, since we "drank" like everyone else.

Papa had an extensive but circumscribed knowledge of wine, knowing in depth only the Beaujolais. Bourg-en-Bresse, Neyron, and Lyon are at the end of Burgundy and the beginning of the Côtes du Rhône. This is the country of the Beaujolais; Lyon, crossed by two large rivers, the Rhône and the Saône, is known to the locals as having three rivers, the Rhône, the Saône, and the Beaujolais. Papa could differentiate in one whiff between a Morgon, a Juliénas, or a Brouilly, all growths of Beaujolais, all made from Gamay grapes. At the restaurant, we served generic wines from specific areas, young wines of good quality. These were our *vins de comptoir,* the wine served by the glass at the counter when the regulars came in for their morning *p'tit blanc* or their afternoon *p'tit rouge,* a little white or a little red. To this day, my preferences still run toward young wines, ten years old at the most, rather than old, pricey wines.

Papa bought wine in barrels from the small farmers. He went to the farms himself to taste the wines and buy, provided he found the right price for the quality he was after. For whites or rosés, he usually bought a *quartaut,* which holds about 50 liters. For reds, he often bought a *feuillette,* holding 100 to 110 liters, or, if he found a really good deal, a *pièce,* which is about the size of a U.S. barrel and holds 210 to 220 liters. Back in his cellar, he lovingly transferred the wine to bottles, an operation that seemed mysterious and sacred. Papa drew some of the wine through a glass syringe, poured it into a stemmed glass, examined it for clarity, sniffed it, and, finally, tasted. Although a conventional wine taster would spit the wine on the floor before proceeding to sample another wine, I never saw Papa waste even a sip.

To draw the wine out of the barrels, he used a piece of rubber tube attached to a stick of wood and inserted the apparatus into the barrel through the bunghole. The tube extended to just above the level of the sediment in the bottom, so only the clear wine would be drawn. Papa never discarded that sediment. Maman used it in the red wine sauces she served with beef or chicken dishes, much as she had done when preparing *mou* during the war.

On my first solo outing to draw wine from the cask, I followed Papa's example by positioning my head below the level of the wine. In this awkward posture, I placed the rubber tube in my mouth and breathed in some air. Nothing happened.

"You have to suck harder, Tati," said Papa. He smiled and gave Roland a nudge.

I tried again. Once more nothing happened.

"It's not working," I said.

"You're not trying hard enough. Roland can do it."

The gauntlet had been dropped. I inhaled mightily.

A gush of wine shot from the end of the hose directly into my eyes and mouth. Sputtering and blinking, I spat out the wine and jammed the hose into a bottle.

The cellar echoed with Papa's belly laugh.

But his laughter soon stopped.

"No, no, Tati, like this," Papa said, taking my hands in his thick fingers and tilting the bottle so that the wine ran down the inclined neck in a gentle flow. "You must never let the wine fall on itself in the bottle and create foam. That will disturb the clarity."

After we filled them, we stopped the bottles with corks that had soaked in an almost boiling mixture of water and wine for fifteen or twenty minutes. Then we waxed the bottles. Papa showed us how to dip about an inch and a half of the tip of each corked bottle into the melted wax; red wax for red wine, yellow or green for white. With a swift movement of his wrist, he created perfectly formed caps on the top of the bottles.

When it came time to uncork his wines, Papa held the bottle flat, parallel to the floor, with the waxed tip above a saucer. Using the rounded side of a teaspoon, he tapped gently as he rotated the bottle, until the wax cap crumbled and fell into the saucer. He then opened the wine with his corkscrew, smelled it in the bottle, and poured it gently into glasses. The corks were precious and never discarded.

Instead of being sealed into standard bottles, the wines were put in pint-size *pots,* slender green bottles with thick glass bottoms that are particular to the Lyon area. Roland and I placed the *pots* in metal baskets and topped them with the corks.

When we had finished drawing the daily quota — about ten baskets — we sulfurized the barrel so the wine wouldn't spoil. Igniting the end of a little greenish yellow stick of sulfur attached to a piece of metal wire, we lowered the stick into the bunghole and sealed the hole. The fire "ate" the oxygen left above the wine, and after the fire died, the wine was perfectly preserved until the next day, when the barrel was opened again.

From his outings to the farms to the final pouring, Papa savored all the rituals of wine. It was a pleasure he wanted to pass along to his sons. Pouring us each a glass, he held his up. I did likewise, imitating his posture.

"Take a little wine in your mouth and let it spread over your tongue. Just taste it."

I did as instructed.

"Now," he said, "chew it, just like a piece of bread."

There seemed to be a breach in logic here. But I did as instructed. Nothing bad happened.

"This is the hard part," he said. "Open your mouth a little bit and form your lips into an 'O' like you are going to whistle."

I shaped my mouth as instructed.

"Good. Now suck some air through the wine to allow it to breathe. This will let you taste it and feel its bouquet."

What it did was force a great deal of the wine up into my nose. I sneezed and sputtered, spraying a fine mist of wine.

Papa shrugged. "Not bad for a start. Perhaps you shouldn't breathe in so hard the next time."

I was hoping there wasn't going to be a next time.

On my second attempt, I inhaled the mouthful of wine deep into my lungs. For a few instants, I was unable to breathe. Several minutes of coughing followed.

Eventually, though, I got the knack and was ready to show off my newly mastered skills to my peers.

"YOU'RE LYING, Pépin." A friend leveled the accusation. We were eight years old and walking home together from school. I had been bragging a little about my vast knowledge of wine and of cellar management.

"It's true," I said. "My father lets me drink all the wine I want."

"Maybe mixed with water."

"No, right from the *pot*. I can go down to the cellar and draw it out of the barrel anytime."

Hôtel L'Amour was a few doors away. "Fine," he said. "Prove it."

We crept in through the back door, keeping out of sight. As usual, Maman was flying around the kitchen in preparation for the evening rush. Papa was off at his job in Lyon.

"Come on," I said, leading my friend down into the cellar.

With nonchalance, I drew a *pot* of Gigondas and drank from it.

"C'est bon," I pronounced, with a serious dip of my chin, and passed the bottle.

We drank alternately — just like grownups. After three or four mouthfuls, my stomach started to ache and the cellar floor began to move. My friend looked a little fuzzy. I would have been happy to stop, but the bottle was still half full, and I certainly didn't want to seem incapable of holding my wine.

It did cross my mind that I could have emptied the remainder in a corner of the earth-floored cellar. However, my well-schooled respect for wine forbade me to waste it. We finished the bottle, and my friend, a bit tipsy, went home. Fifteen minutes later, the sun and the warm air finished the mischief started by the wine, and I collapsed, all pale. Maman found me sitting on the floor. She diagnosed my sickness as an excess of schoolwork and let me go to bed early.

~~~~~

ALONG THE SIDES of the country roads between Neyron and Bourg, Papa introduced me to another one of his passions, foraging for wild mushrooms. We mostly picked what we called *rosés,* the prized white mushrooms with rosy gills that grew overnight in fields, particularly in rich pastures with grazing cows and, sometimes, bulls. We set out just after dawn, hoping to arrive before other avid pickers. We knew our sites. Signs were often posted on the fences, warning of the presence of bulls. Sometimes the threat was real, but often it was a farmer's scare tactic to prevent others from gathering the mushrooms before he could get to them.

With such tasty morsels just over the fence, my father and I ignored the newly posted warning signs one day when we came to a field known to produce bountiful mushroom crops. Who was that farmer trying to kid? A few cows grazed contentedly in the morning mist. There was no sign of any bull. We slid through the barbed wire and started walking across the field. I bent to pick a choice-looking mushroom, and when I straightened up, Papa was racing toward me. Behind him a bull scraped the ground with one of his front hooves. I climbed to the safety of the far side of the fence and watched. The bull moved forward slowly at first, then accelerated. Papa ran toward the fence. He got there just ahead of the bull, threw his basket over ahead of him — there was no question of abandoning the mushrooms — and, without slowing, dove over the fence, following the trajectory of the mushrooms, barely clearing the barbed wire. The bull stopped at the fence and stared at us with his small, malicious eyes. My father burst out laughing, still excited and red from his run, while we picked up the mushrooms from the grass. My father retold the tale of his mushrooming adventure over many a glass of red. With each retelling, the bull got closer and closer to him.

A YEAR AND A HALF passed, and Hôtel L'Amour flourished. We weren't getting rich, but we had paid off most of our debt. The restaurant had entered that phase at which Maman might have been able to hire a little extra kitchen help, maybe even scale back her schedule of fifteen hours a day, seven days a week. But that was not the way of Jeannette Pépin. M. Menu reappeared at the big kitchen table. He and Maman talked. After he left, Maman announced that Hôtel L'Amour had been sold. We were going to move. The old truck returned to our doorstep. Our belongings were loaded aboard. This time, we alighted in L'Arbresle, a little town about twenty miles from Lyon. There, Le Restaurant de la Gare awaited directly across the street from the railroad station, in much the same state of decline as Hôtel L'Amour had been. Only this time, we had a modicum of experience in the business, and thanks to the tidy profit that M. Menu had been able to negotiate for the revitalized Hôtel L'Amour, the beginnings of a nest egg. But that didn't prevent Maman from betting everything we had on another shaky venture.

The village of L'Arbresle held many attractions for boys, one of which was la Brevenne, a brook virtually in our backyard that in our imaginations took on the proportions of a mighty river. It was early spring, and la Brevenne flowed fast and cold. Papa warned us sternly not to venture near it. But Roland, Bichon (who was just getting old enough to tag along on our adventures), and I constructed a raft from some planks we had salvaged from old wooden wine racks. Ignoring Papa's warnings, we cast off to explore our new world.

Our vessel promptly sank. Fortunately, la Brevenne was only a couple of feet deep at that point, and we waded back to shore, safe but soaked.

"Papa's going to kill us," said Roland.

He had a point. Showing up at home with wet clothes would have guaranteed a severe spanking, plus extra chores. But the alternative was to freeze to death in the stiff breeze. Already, Bichon was shivering and going blue in the lips. Finally we settled on a compromise and hid in a small storage shack until we were dry enough to pass inspection.

As the weather warmed, la Brevenne slowed to a trickle, and our explorations took us farther along its length. To our delight, we found that a couple of miles from home, la Brevenne flowed into a slightly larger river, la Turdine.

Staring into the water of la Turdine, I saw a shadow move. Then a flicker of silver.

"Roland, Bichon, come here," I said. "Do you see that?"

They looked over my shoulders. There was another glint near the bottom.

Roland, Bichon, and I said it at the same time: "Fish!"

We owned no fishing equipment, but we did have imaginations. Acquiring rods posed no problem: we fashioned them from branches growing along the bank. Three spools of thread and a handful of straight pins purloined from Maman's sewing box became lines and hooks. We caught worms and grasshoppers for bait.

The great day dawned, and *les frères* Pépin set out on their first unsupervised fishing expedition. We hiked farther than we had ever ventured before, looking for that perfect hole where prize specimens were sure to lurk.

After an hour, Bichon started to lag.

"Wait up!" he called.

"We're going to where the fish are," I said.

Our little brother dragged himself along, sweating and puffing, but still following.

Finally we arrived at the spot. We sat on the bank, baited our bent pins, flung our lines into the water, and waited.

Eventually, the tip of my stick wiggled ever so slightly.

"You've got one!" shouted Roland.

I heaved back mightily, and a shiny minnow about two inches long flew out of the water and into the bushes behind me. I put down my rod and parted the leaves. There it was. I picked it up with my thumb and index finger and showed it to Roland.

"It's a *vairon*," said Roland.

It was too good to be true. Despite their size, *vairons* were considered delicacies, eaten battered and fried, like whitebait.

"Like the ones Papa catches?" I said.

"Exactly," said Roland.

Bichon yelped and yanked another *vairon* out of the river.

"Help me find it," said Bichon. But Roland and I were busy with two more fish. It didn't take long for us to amass enough for a feast.

"Let's cook them and eat them here," I suggested.

Roland thought for a moment. "We don't have anything to cook them in."

Both of us glanced at Bichon. His eyes widened. "No," he said. "Not me."

"We let you come with us, didn't we?" I said.

"If I go, will you let me have some *vairons?*"

"We'll divide them fair and square."

"You bet," said Roland. "And while you're gone, Tati and I will gather enough wood for the fire."

"Okay, I guess," said Bichon.

"We'll need oil, flour, and a skillet," I said. "And matches."

"Bread, too," said Roland.

"I'll get it. Don't worry," said Bichon. As he turned to go, the little guy was smiling, as if we'd just done him an extraordinary favor.

Even then, it was apparent that Bichon was following in the happy-go-lucky, take-things-as-they-come footsteps of Papa. He had Papa's sweet, sunny disposition. He never lost his temper. And he seemed to have fun in any situation. Bichon could encounter a group of total strangers and within five minutes he would be first-naming everybody, and they him.

We kept fishing until we became hot and bored. Then we stripped and swam, drying off on the bank in the sunshine. After that, we made an adventure of gathering a massive heap of driftwood for our cooking fire.

Bichon eventually returned, laboring with a straw bag that was so big it bumped the ground. He dropped it and beamed, as proud as I'd ever seen him. "Got everything we need."

It wasn't long before we had a fire going on the bank. But there was a problem. I had only a vague idea of how to cook the little fish, so I would have to wing it. I knew that the first step was to clean the *vairons* because I'd seen Papa do it, though I'd never done it myself. I held a fish between my fingers and ran my thumb along its belly. To my delight, its guts squirted out, just as they were supposed to. I repeated the process with our entire catch.

"Your undershirt," I said to Roland.

"What?"

"I need something to put the flour in," I said.

Roland sacrificed his undergarment. I dumped the flour into it and rubbed each minnow until it was coated. By that time the oil was beginning to smoke, and I tossed the fish into the pan. There was a great hissing and foaming, but when the steam cleared, the pan was filled with crisp, golden *vairons*. I used a forked twig to remove them from the oil and laid them on hunks of bread. We did not even wait for them to cool, but dug in.

The *vairons* were good, as good as any I'd tasted. And, best of all, I had cooked them myself.

~

THAT SUMMER, under Maman's supervision, we mastered the art of sandwich making and became somewhat efficient as junior sommeliers. We owed both skills to the restaurant's *jeu de boules*, a series of outdoor, sand-packed courts where local men gathered to play *la Lyonnaise*, that area's version of lawn bowling. In addition to being in charge of keeping the courts raked to Papa's specifications, Roland, Bichon, and I served hundreds of *pots* of wine and sandwiches to the players when they gathered there on summer weekends. The ball players drank large quantities of Beaujolais while they played four against four for hours. They consumed so much wine that we sold it not by the *pot* but by the meter. At the end of a session, Papa lined up a customer's empty *pots* and measured the row. There were thirteen *pots* in one meter, but he charged for only twelve. To accompany the wine, we split thin, crispy, foot-long baguettes and slathered them liberally with *beurre de baratte*, fresh farm butter. I filled the sandwiches with hard, fragrant *saucisson de Lyon, jambon à l'os* (ham cooked on the bone), or creamy Camembert cheese. Other fillers for the sandwiches included cured country ham, blue Roquefort cheese, and a hard, jelly-like headcheese my mother made by adding leeks, carrots, cornichons, and mustard to the boiled scraps from a pig's head — not just the meat, but the tongue, snout, and ears as well.

Summer in L'Arbresle passed as one sweet Huck Finn day after the other: hiking, fishing, swimming, tending the *jeu de boules*. One day, we came home and a red bicycle stood in the courtyard. It was a gift to Roland for having graduated from primary school, the first bicycle any of us children had owned. Always a good brother, Roland let Bichon and me ride whenever we wanted.

I was too young to understand, but Maman had a special style of restaurant management. Her approach was to acquire an old, rundown place at a low price, then fix it up, increasing its business, and sell it at a profit before moving on to another similar venture. Far from being a source of security, the success of Le Restaurant de la Gare meant that our time in the little town by the river was running out. And sure enough, before the leaves of that first glorious summer had begun to yellow, M. Menu returned. Our days as village boys were over. He had found Maman a restaurant in the city of Lyon.

In 1947 Maman proudly opened Chez Pépin on 4, rue Chalopin in a blue-collar area of Lyon called La Guillotière. The clientele of this casual, humble, and inexpensive restaurant consisted mostly of factory workers, students, retirees, and a half-dozen local prostitutes who sat around the kitchen table, chatting with Maman and Papa and even pitching in with chores during their off-duty hours. They took many of their meals in the dining room. Paulette, our waitress, viewed them as good patrons, always generous with tips. It was commonplace for the regular customers, all on a first-name basis with us, to pop into the kitchen, lift the lid off a cooking pot, and choose their menu based on the look or smell of a dish.

I managed to stay at the top of my class at the neighborhood elementary school, despite my extracurricular duties at the restaurant. But as the afternoon approached, I found myself getting anxious to be out of the classroom and in the kitchen of Chez Pépin. I felt a liberating tingle of excitement when I dumped my books on the counter, tied on an apron, picked up a gleaming chef's knife, and tackled the pile of vegetables waiting to be peeled, sliced, diced, and julienned — always trying to beat a deadline.

At each successive restaurant, my mother had refined her culinary skills and her repertoire of dishes had expanded. Her talents demanded a wider venue than our little neighborhood joint. She sold Chez Pépin and bought a nice medium-size restaurant called Le Pélican, on rue Thomassin, in the fancy part of Lyon.

We might have climbed one tiny rung above our humble beginnings, but even at Le Pélican, profit margins were slim. Solvency hung not only on Maman's skills behind the stove but also on her shrewdness during early morning forays into the crowded stalls of Lyon's Marché St. Antoine. Half of our sparse profits resulted from my mother's saving a franc here and a franc there in the market. Maman was not a well-educated woman in the formal sense, but judging from the way she worked that market, I'd venture that few M.B.A. grads possess her negotiating skills and understanding of the laws of supply and demand.

Like all boys approaching the teenage years, my brothers and I had become formidable sleepers by the time we bought Le Pélican. But not being particularly big on sleep herself, Maman saw no reason why her sons should be. Each day, we came home from school and worked in the kitchen through the dinner service, squeezing in bits of homework when things slowed. When we finally got to bed, it seemed as if our eyes barely closed before we heard Maman's insistent voice telling us it was time to get up and go to market. Still half asleep, we gulped our café au lait and swallowed a piece of jam-smeared bread before stumbling out the door behind her to "walk the market." And walk we did. We had no car, there was no bus, and a taxi was out of the question. Roland, Bichon, and I were along strictly because of our ability to lug enormous straw bags of groceries and vegetables back to the restaurant.

Marché St. Antoine was (and still is) an outdoor market shaded by the overhanging branches of massive plane trees. Two rows of stalls extended for about three quarters of a mile along the banks of the Saône River. It was a colorful, crowded place. Vendors of every known fruit or vegetable from the region hawked their wares. Butchers wearing leather aprons, with a single strap running over one shoulder, sawed and chopped cuts of meat. Each had his own specialty: beef, lamb, pork, or horsemeat. Fishmongers sold all manner of freshwater fish: carp, trout, perch, pike. Poultry sellers offered chickens, always with head and feet attached. In some stalls, game birds hung by their necks, still in their feathers.

Maman made two passes through Marché St. Antoine. The first was a scouting expedition only, not to buy but to compare prices and quality before buying, which would occur during our second pass. She had a keen sense of which fruits or vegetables, while perfectly usable if prepared that day, would spoil if held any longer. She zeroed in on baskets of mushrooms that were just starting to blacken at the edges or tomatoes that were softening. The occasional spot could be trimmed from a cauliflower, and no customer would taste the difference. Ditto for a bruise on a peach. She knew that the merchants would have to dispose of such produce before the end of the morning. And she knew how to barter for the best possible price.

But at Marché St. Antoine, gossip inevitably preceded business.

Spying a basket of overripe summer squash, Maman would approach the vendor. "*Bonjour,* Mme. Dubois," she would say. "How is your son doing? The one who moved to Paris." Only after the status of the Parisian son, his wife and children, and sundry other relatives had been discussed, analyzed, and commented on at length, did my mother glance at the produce laid before her.

"So, what have you for me today?"

"Beautiful zucchini, Mme. Pépin."

Maman hefted one. "Yes, but don't you think they are a little past their prime?"

"Perhaps. Which is why I can offer you a good price — for the whole basket of them. I'll let you have the lot for fifteen francs."

"Madame, you know I cannot afford to pay that."

"If I sold them for less, I would be losing money myself."

"I can give you only ten francs."

"How about eleven?"

And the zucchinis were poured into my increasingly heavy bag.

At Le Pélican, a complete meal had one price, five francs — less than one of today's American dollars. This included four dishes, bread, a quart of wine, and the tip. Maman's menu was set up à la carte, with a choice of about twenty dishes, divided into first courses, main courses, vegetables, and desserts. For the first course, we offered artichokes vinaigrette, *jambon* (ham), *oeuf dur mayonnaise* (hard-cooked eggs and mayonnaise), a tomato salad, or *fromage de tête* (headcheese). Main courses included *bifteck* (a five-ounce beefsteak, usually from the top round), rabbit stew, sautéed beef liver with onions, roasted veal, or stewed chicken in cream or in a tomato, mushroom, and white wine sauce. Then came vegetables, always served separately: a gratin of spinach, ratatouille, *quenelles sauce tomate* (large choux paste dumplings served with tomato sauce), tomatoes Provençal, or sautéed Swiss chard. The desserts were standards: a piece of cheese, a raw fruit, an apple tart, a caramel custard, or *fromage blanc à la crème* (fresh white cheese served with heavy cream), eaten with garlic, chives, salt, and pepper. It was a comfortable menu, with choices that reflected the season and, of course, the best deals at that day's market.

One night, after we had collapsed into bed after scrubbing the last pot, Roland confided, "I don't want to live this life when I grow up, Tati. I don't want to work anywhere near a kitchen."

Lying beside him in the dark, I thought about what he had said. It had never dawned on me that there was another life — certainly not for a Pépin. I loved the very things Roland dreamed of escaping. The hurly-burly noise of the kitchen. The heat. The sweat. The bumping of bodies. The raised voices. The constant rush of adrenaline. I loved going to the market in the morning, hurrying back, and, if it wasn't a school day, frantically preparing the food we had purchased, finishing just as the first customers came in for lunch. I loved sitting around the big table in the restaurant after the service, eating with my mother, my father, my brothers, the two waitresses, and the dishwasher. I belonged.

I was thirteen and a half years old when I quit school. I asked for a dispensation to be allowed to take the primary school final exam, which was not usually given until age fourteen. My parents somewhat reluctantly — but wisely — went along with my decision. To be sure, I was an "old" thirteen, hardened by the war, with its restrictions and bombings, with stints away from home and the long absences of Papa. At an age when most kids don't know how to cook their own breakfast, I had already worked in four busy restaurant kitchens. I was at home in each one, and they were all the home I knew.

More than anything in the world, I wanted to be a chef.

Maman's Cheese Soufflé

YIELD: 4 SERVINGS

*W*HEN MY MOTHER got married, she was seventeen and my father was twenty-two. She did not know how to cook, except for a few simple dishes that she had learned from her mother. Yet she was willing and fearless.

My father liked cheese soufflé, so my mother graciously obliged. She had never made a soufflé before, but a friend told her that it consisted of a white sauce (béchamel), grated cheese, and eggs — a cinch! To the béchamel, that staple of the French home cook, she added her grated Swiss cheese and then cracked and added one egg after another to the mixture, stirred it well, poured it into a gratin dish, and baked it in the oven. *Voilà!* No one had told her that the eggs should be separated, with the yolks added to the base sauce and the whites whipped to a firm consistency and then gently folded into the mixture. Ignorance is bliss, and in this case it was indeed: the soufflé rose to a golden height and became a family favorite.

This is a great recipe; it can be assembled hours or even a day ahead, and although it is slightly less airy than a standard soufflé, it is delicious.

6   tablespoons (³/₄ stick) unsalted butter, plus more
    to butter a 6-cup gratin dish
6   tablespoons all-purpose flour
2   cups cold whole milk
¹/₂ teaspoon salt
¹/₂ teaspoon freshly ground black pepper

5 extra-large eggs

2½ cups grated Swiss cheese, preferably Gruyère
(about 6 ounces)

3 tablespoons minced fresh chives

Preheat the oven to 400 degrees.

Butter a 6-cup gratin dish, and set it aside. Melt the butter in a saucepan, then add the flour, and mix it in well with a whisk. Cook for 10 seconds, add the milk in one stroke, and mix it in with a whisk. Keep stirring with the whisk until the mixture thickens and comes to a strong boil, which will take about 2 minutes. It should be thick and smooth. Remove from the heat, and stir in the salt and pepper. Allow about 10 minutes for the white sauce to cool.

Meanwhile, break the eggs into a bowl, and beat well with a fork. Add the eggs, the cheese, and the chives to the cooled sauce, and mix well to combine. Pour into the buttered gratin dish and cook immediately, or set aside until ready to cook.

Bake for 30 to 40 minutes, or until the soufflé is puffy and well browned on top. Although it will stay inflated for quite a while, it is best served immediately.

3
My
Apprenticeship

AUGUST 29, 1949, DAWNED CLOUDLESS and pleasantly warm in Lyon, an auspicious beginning to an important new phase in my life, the start of my three-year apprenticeship at Le Grand Hôtel de l'Europe. I had only one problem, but it was one of those enormous, seemingly insurmountable problems that can cast a pall over the most joyous occasions: I was wearing short pants. In 1940s France, shorts screamed the word *boy* as surely as diapers said *baby*. Having attained the age of thirteen, having survived a world war, having worked in no less than four restaurant kitchens, I felt every inch a man. A man who had more than earned the right to wear his first pair of long pants.

Maman had different ideas. At five-foot-two and weighing maybe one hundred pounds, I was still very much her little Tati. For weeks, I begged her to buy me a pair of long pants, but she refused. "You're too small. You'll look silly in them."

So, clad in shorts and knee socks, I sat humiliated beside Maman on the old Philibert bus as it bumped and swayed the thirty miles between Lyon and Bourg-en-Bresse, where Le Grand Hôtel de l'Europe was located.

Wonderment supplanted humiliation and all other emotions when we stepped off the bus and began to walk along cours de Verdun, a grand boulevard with a median of trees, flower beds, and park benches. Though this was the town of my early childhood, I'd never ventured anywhere near that neighborhood. Its fancy homes, wide streets, and stylishly clad pedestrians bore no resemblance to the working-class rue de l'École normale district of the war days. I had truly entered a new world.

Le Grand Hôtel de l'Europe was the most impressive edifice on that street of magnificent buildings. Maman and I passed through a portico fashioned from ornate wrought iron and roofed by a glass dome. We found ourselves in an entry hall whose floor was tiled in a mosaic of intricate floral patterns. A tiny marble-front fireplace was embedded in one wall, a dainty ornament, nothing like the soot-smudged hearths I'd known. On either side were armoires, their dark wood adorned with sculpted water lilies, so delicate they looked as if they could be picked and placed in a bouquet.

But I soon became transfixed by another sight. Through two glass doors directly in front of the reception desk was the kitchen, a vast, open room, tiled and shining with polished copper and topped by a domed ceiling of stained glass. Instead of being pushed against a wall like something to be ashamed of, an enormous stove, all black and gleaming, proudly occupied the center of the room. The workspace was surrounded by a second-floor balcony, from which guests looked down into the kitchen, which was sparkling clean. As were its occupants. In Maman's kitchens, all of us — school kids, prostitutes, neighbors who had just dropped in — worked in whatever clothes we happened to be wearing at the time. But the cooks in this kitchen were dressed in the uniforms of professionals. The chef and his assistant, or *commis,* wore the regulation toques, white jackets, white scarves, and blue-and-white-checked pants. The three younger-looking workers, apprentices, I assumed, were dressed in the same checked pants as the chef and *commis,* but they had blue checked jackets instead of white.

An elderly woman, every bit as regal and dignified as her surroundings, came to the entry hall and spoke a few words to Maman, who turned to me and said, "Tati, say hello to Mme. Denizot Rebières, the owner of the hotel."

I'm not sure whether I said hello or not. I recall nothing more of the conversation. I don't even remember Maman's leaving. Suddenly I was standing in an upstairs dormitory room beside the *commis,* a red-haired boy three or four years older than I was. I liked him immediately. He had one of those round, happy faces that always seem to be in search of the next bit of slightly illicit fun. He told me his name was Robert and pointed to one of four identical iron beds.

"That's yours," he said. "You'd better change. Chef wants to see you down in the kitchen." He pointed to a bundle of clothes at the foot of my bed and said. "Hurry up. You don't want to start out on Chef's bad side."

No one needed to tell me to hurry. Robert had no sooner turned his back than I ripped off my shorts and unfolded the garment on top of the bundle.

My first long pants were the blue-and-white-checked pants of a cook.

"*P'TIT,* COME HERE." There was a note of quiet urgency in Chef Jauget's voice. "*P'tit!*"

I had been at the hotel for a couple of weeks, and Chef Jauget was well aware of my first name. He had been a friend of my mother's during their school years, but family ties or not, Chef showed no favoritism. I was just *P'tit,* or "Kid," even though he referred to Robert and the older apprentices by their proper first names.

"*P'tit,* run to L'Hôtel de France immediately to get our *machine à désossé les poulets* [chicken-boning machine]," he said. "I loaned it to the chef there, and he hasn't returned it. *Vite!* I need it. And I want you back here. Immediately."

Off I went at a full run to L'Hôtel de France, which was on the other side of town. The chef there was waiting for me and, when I informed him of my mission, he shook his head and said, "Sorry, the chef at L'Escargot needed it. I sent your machine over to him."

L'Escargot was a least a mile away. Knowing that I was sure to get a scolding from Chef Jauget for taking so much time, I raced to L'Escargot, where the chef greeted my request with shock.

"Le Grand Hôtel de l'Europe?" he said. "But I thought that the boning machine belonged to L'Hôtel Terminus. I returned it to them. Sorry."

I barely heard his apology. L'Hôtel Terminus was a half-hour in the other direction. There, the chef explained that as soon as the boning machine had been delivered to him, he knew it had been sent by mistake. "I have no need for your boning machine, mine's right over there," he said, gesturing to some appliances in a corner of the kitchen. "One of my apprentices has just left with the machine to return it to L'Escargot. You probably passed him on the way."

By then the lunch hour was approaching. I knew Chef would be furious. Fortunately, back at L'Escargot, the cook handed me a large canvas bag fastened at the top. "Thought you'd be back. Here it is," he said. "Be careful with it, but hurry along. Chef Jauget called; he's none too pleased with you."

Lugging the bag, I started off toward the hotel. The machine was heavy, and I had to rest frequently. Each time I stopped, I was careful not to slam the bag on the ground. Finally, out of breath and perspiring, I turned the corner of rue Bichat, a few feet from the entrance to Le Grand Hôtel de l'Europe.

Chef, Robert, the other apprentices, and the waitresses were waiting for me. I lowered the bag to the ground with a proud but thoroughly exhausted smile. They stood there, saying nothing. Suddenly, a horrible doubt crossed my mind. I opened the bag. Inside were two cement blocks. Everyone roared with laughter.

I felt like the dumbest human being in Bourg-en-Bresse, if not all of France. But like countless thousands of apprentices before me, I had survived my first rite of passage.

~~~~~

WE CALLED the stove at Le Grand Hôtel de l'Europe *le piano*. Its position at the physical and spiritual heart of the kitchen allowed the cooks to move around it as they tended it like a timid group of supplicants. They worked from all of its sides and used all six of its *trous,* or central hearths. *Le piano* was still fueled by wood and coal, even though a few professional kitchens had shifted over to oil or gas by then. I was fascinated by that gigantic stove in the way that most thirteen-year-old boys might find an army tank or a sleek automobile alluring. I longed to play that piano. I stood in awe of those who did, but I knew that I would have to wait. As the newest apprentice, I was forbidden to go anywhere near it. That privilege was reserved for Chef, the *commis,* and older apprentices who had mastered the basics of the trade, earning the prestigious right to be "called to the stove."

I was no longer sent all over town on wild-goose chases for imaginary kitchen equipment, but my day-to-day tasks were far more mundane than what the guys at that mighty appliance got to do. The first meals I prepared at Le Grand Hôtel de l'Europe were served in the courtyard, not to paying customers but to a pack of ten resident dogs. I may not have been welcome at the stove, but the German shepherds, Afghans, boxers, and bulldog owned by the son of Mme. Denizot Rebières lapped up my food with gusto and didn't seem to object in the least that their bowls had been filled by the lowest-ranking apprentice in the hotel.

M. Denizot Rebières's love of pets was not limited to canines. He also kept a crocodile and a monkey, among others, in rooms above the hotel. Although the croc seemed agreeable enough, the monkey was a nasty little creature, with a mean-spirited sense of humor and enough manual dexterity to jimmy the lock on his cage. One day the monkey executed a getaway, jumped out a window, crossed the roof, and reentered through a bathroom vent. The escapee curled up and fell asleep on top of the water tank above the old-fashioned pull-chain toilet. There he dozed until a matronly woman seated herself directly below, whereupon he jumped onto her lap.

There was a scream, the door burst open, and the woman emerged, hopping with remarkable speed, given her age, size, and the fact that her underpants were down around her ankles.

Such incidents aside, my days as an apprentice settled into a predictable pattern. We were expected to be in the kitchen, working, by 8:30 every morning. Job One was always to get the piano going. A young apprentice might never be permitted near it during service, but God help him if he failed to light proper fires in it. Because the repercussions of failure were so severe, lighting the piano was not a choice job. Early on, the apprentice, who had been the junior member of the staff until I joined, informed me that the task was to be mine. He let me watch while he lit paper, then wood, and finally lumps of coal in one firebox. When that blaze was roaring, he shoveled glowing coals into the next firebox and repeated the process until *le piano* was ready for Chef and the *commis*.

The older apprentice had made the task look easy. But when it was my turn to take over the next day, I managed to coax only a sickly flicker in one hearth. Fortunately, another one of my colleagues passed by and saw me struggling. He dipped a ladle into a pot of rendered fat and poured it onto my feeble fire. With a *whoosh* it was roaring merrily. "Just don't let Chef see you do this," he said.

I had received my advanced training in piano lighting.

Le piano was like a testy monarch who demanded constant ministrations from her lowly subjects, and I was the lowliest of all. Some days I spent so much time fussing with the fires that I figured if I failed to make it as a chef, I'd at least be able to get a job shoveling coal into the firebox of a locomotive. The fires in all but one or two of the stove's hearths were allowed to die away after lunch.

Then, at approximately 5:00 P.M., all of them were brought back to life. On some evenings, with all the hearths ablaze and the dining room full, the temperature in the kitchen rose dramatically. Strangely enough, I enjoyed those really hot nights; there was an underlying excitement in them, and the heat gave me a high.

During the lunch and dinner periods of *le service,* which took place from 11:45 A.M. to 1:30 P.M. and from 7:00 to 10:00 P.M., special timing was required. I had to load the stove in a way that would generate a constant and intense heat throughout the whole service, so the food could be cooked to order and the customers served on time. If I stoked the hearths too early, the stove rapidly cooled to lukewarm during the last thirty minutes of *le service.* If I stoked the stove too late, the first thirty minutes of *le service* became a nightmare for the cooks. The meat did not sear, the soufflés did not rise, the omelets did not come out of pans, and the sauces did not emulsify. The chef saw orders pile up and the pickup of finished dishes diminish. The responsibility for avoiding these disasters rested solely with me.

Le piano's two ovens were tunnels that extended the whole width of the stove and had an opening on each side. There was no thermostat, and when the hearths were red hot, so were the ovens, with the temperature exceeding six hundred degrees. Yet Chef, the *commis,* and those apprentices accomplished enough to have been called to the stove cooked everything — from génoise to soufflé to roast chicken — in those ovens. To control the heat, the cook sometimes left the oven door ajar, with a génoise pushed to the "coolest" part of the oven and set atop several cookie sheets to cut down on the heat. Testing the temperature by placing his hands in the oven for a few seconds, Chef moved the food, covered it, or placed another sheet underneath as a means of adjusting the temperature. He knew when the food was done based on how a dish looked, smelled, or felt.

The peak of *le service* usually found me well away from the action at the stove. If I wasn't laying the fires during my early apprenticeship, it seemed that I was cleaning something. Often, I'd be bent over a huge sink filled with cold water, carefully dunking and redunking individual spinach leaves in mortal fear that I would leave a grain of grit on any of Chef's precious greens. After *le service,* my presence was required at the butcher-block in the kitchen, not for the task of preparing meat, which was still scarce and expensive and therefore handled by Chef himself, but to cover the block in sawdust and vinegar and scrape it clean with a metal blade.

I shared my early apprenticeship with a large, old green-and-blue parrot (another of M. Denizot Rebières's pets). The bird was a vociferous witness to my every success and failure. Even though I spent hours trying to teach him to say uncouth words, my efforts were fruitless. Coco knew only one word, and he repeated it endlessly, either as a way of ratting on me or reminding me of what I was not, but dearly wanted to be: "Chef! Chef! Chef!"

IN GENERAL, I worked hard and performed well, so within a few months I received a promotion. I wasn't called to the stove, not by a long shot, but Chef let it be known that I was ready to advance from cleaning to general preparation, or *mise-en-place,* where my tasks included chopping parsley, cutting and shaping vegetables, picking bits of meat and fat off trimmed bones for use in stock or for the clarification of consommé, plucking and eviscerating poultry, gutting and scaling fish, as well as skinning and cleaning rabbits and hares. No one actually taught me how to do these things or anything else. Not formally. The chef and *commis* had me stand and watch as they worked, making me fetch a tray as needed, or clean a knife, or wipe a table. My education as an apprentice was strictly a process of observation and imitation.

One of the worst tasks was peeling pearl onions, which arrived in our kitchen in hundred-pound sacks to be pickled, either on their own or with cornichons, or gherkins. A much more pleasant job was peeling and cutting the fruits for the fruit salad because it provided the opportunity for a little pilfering. Oranges, bananas, and pineapples were scarce and exotic. Except at Christmas, most French boys never got them. Chef knew this and kept his eye on apprentices assigned to prepare the fruit to make sure that none of us ate any of our handiwork. When he left the room for a few minutes, we were instructed to whistle loudly so that he could be certain we were not swallowing anything while he was gone. Of course, two of us whistled while the third apprentice stuffed his mouth with fruit as quickly as he could. In a good democratic manner, we took turns whistling and eating the forbidden fruits, even though we knew that we would endure Chef's wrath if caught.

Chef Jauget was tall, black-haired, and skinny, except for the little round belly that looked as if it had been fastened to his midriff as an afterthought. He was impeccably clean, his jacket and scarf flawlessly white and devoid of stains, even at the height of *le service*. No matter what he was doing — trimming a veal roast, nursing a soufflé on the piano — his hands and fingernails were as clean as a surgeon's. While some chefs are yellers, Chef was quiet, controlled, and intense, which made his infrequent flare-ups all the more terrifying. There was no hint of democracy in the kitchen, and none was expected. Chef's word was final. But he was also our father figure, teacher, and mentor. We had no books, no written recipes. All our knowledge came from watching his hands, imitating him, and trying to recognize and duplicate his tastes. To us, he had but one name: Chef.

I worked hard to impress Chef. All those years in Maman's kitchens were paying off. There was, however, one impediment to my progress. Even more than most thirteen-year-old boys, I was a free spirit, always ready to ham around, do anything to make other people laugh — provided Chef's back was turned. One time I discreetly slipped the insides of a fish into the back pocket of an unaware colleague. I developed an ability not only to slice a carrot finely and uniformly but also to finish the job with a deft flick that sent the stub flying at the bent-over head of another apprentice. If a fellow apprentice was making crêpes for the employees, I'd do my best to ensure that a length of kitchen twine was added to the batter if he turned his back. Such antics were common and always reciprocated, but I seemed to get caught more often than my peers.

Chef was passing behind me one morning and heard me burst out laughing as the boy across the table cracked an uncooked egg into a bowl of hard-boiled eggs he was preparing for *le service*.

"That's not funny, *P'tit*," Chef all but bellowed. "We're in a hurry here."

I felt a sharp pain where Chef's shoe hit my butt and knew from the loudness of his voice that I was going to receive the most common punishment of all. I was going to be put "on guard," meaning that I would be the sole employee required to remain in the kitchen during *la coupure*, the break between lunch and dinner. During this daily lull, everyone else was free to go to the dorm, visit town, or walk by the river. Having to stay on guard meant that I alone would work without a break for fourteen hours, from 8:30 A.M. until 10:30 P.M.

Chef issued some quick orders and then left me alone. I only half-listened. I already had the on-guard regimen more or less memorized. Facing two and a half hours of solitude, I set about cleaning the floors, the walls, and the stove, and then spent an hour making designs with sandpaper on the stove's iron guard rails. This last chore was a favorite with Chef Jauget. The stove rusted constantly. It had to be sanded and oiled everywhere and every day, from its flat surface to the oven doors to the infamous handrail, where an apprentice, using elbow grease and a strip of sandpaper, had to create a lattice design — purely for decoration. Chef assigned this useless task with great enthusiasm. A total waste of energy, it was intended as a way for him to maintain discipline by demanding blind obedience.

While I was putting the finishing touches on *le piano*, I noticed a ten-gallon pot of consommé barely simmering in a back corner. What had Chef wanted me to do with that? Something, no doubt. But what had he said? Damn, I wished I'd paid attention.

The surface of the clarification (a mixture of very lean chopped beef, vegetables, and an egg white) had solidified into a thick, grayish crust, or raft, and the stock, simmering and filtering through a hole in its center, was becoming golden and crystal clear, as a consommé should be.

For no reason, except maybe to try my hand with a whisk, I seized the largest one in the kitchen and stirred the consommé vigorously in an effort to combine the ugly crust with the clear liquid beneath it. I felt like a real chef. I whisked with all the speed and strength I could muster. What I didn't know was that the crust shouldn't have been disturbed at all, and the liquid beneath it should have been ladled out gently and strained through a wet towel. By the time Chef arrived to start dinner, the liquid in the pot had the texture and viscosity of pan gravy. He took one look at the consommé, then at me, then at the consommé, and his face got redder and redder. Without a word, he grabbed the nearest weapon to hand, a ladle, and advanced toward me.

~

As APPRENTICES, we received no pay. We didn't consider this treatment harsh. After all, previous generations of apprentices had to pay the owner of the hotel to be allowed to learn. None of us got money from our parents, but we generated a little cash in a number of ways. When not on guard, I rarely spent afternoon breaks idly. I discovered a spot where the river and its banks yielded beautiful watercress, frogs, and crawfish. There was always a ready market at the hotel for such delicacies. I also sold wild lilies of the valley on the first of May and, in the fall, mushrooms from nearby forests. M. Denizot Rebières occasionally slipped me a little change for taking care of his dogs. The money I earned didn't amount to much, but it enabled me to see an occasional movie or to buy books. Having left school so early, I had little taste for classic literature, but I became addicted to *Three Musketeers* adventure stories and bought one whenever I had some spare change.

Staff in restaurants today usually partake of the same fare as customers. Except on holidays and special occasions, we got dishes concocted from leftovers. One of the most prominent of these was a type of shepherd's pie, *gratin Parmentier,* a catch-all made with whatever meat we managed to scrape from bones, which was covered with mashed potatoes or turnips, browned in the oven, and served to us along with soup. It might not have been up to the standards of what the folks out front were getting, but the food was plentiful, and most of us hadn't eaten nearly as well earlier in our lives.

I worked seven days a week straight through the month. At the end of each month, I had four days off, and I took the bus back home. I brought my dirty bed sheets, aprons, jackets, pants, toques, and towels with me, and Maman washed and ironed them. In return, I put in full days in her restaurant kitchen, just as I had before becoming an apprentice. Visits home never were exactly restful. But they were deeply appreciated. Bibi, her muzzle beginning to show hints of gray and her middle section distinctly plumper, thanks to the steady diet of the sugar cubes she loved to beg from soft-hearted customers, leapt into my arms as soon as I walked through the door, thoroughly licking my face until it was cleansed of every foreign scent. Bichon, looking more like Papa every time I visited, was showing an increasing interest in restaurant work. I don't think he would have admired me more had I been the leading scorer for the French national soccer team.

I missed Roland. At around the time I secured my apprenticeship, he entered a scholarly competition, one of tens of thousands of students from across the country vying for 150 places at Hautza, a prestigious military academy. For weeks, he moped around the place, complaining to anyone who would listen that he didn't have a chance of acceptance, that the exam had been a total waste of time. But Roland always had been a master of underestimating his abilities. To no one's surprise but his own, he got accepted. Now he was away during the school year, pursuing engineering studies.

Le Pélican showed more signs of prosperity each time I returned. Papa was able to resign from his day job in the furniture repair department of Les Galeries Lafayette to devote himself full time to the restaurant's wine cellar and lively café business. One morning when I stepped off the bus from Bourg, he was there to greet me and proudly led the way to an ancient Renault, swinging the door (the kind that opened from the front) and gesturing for me to enter. The rattletrap barely accommodated the two of us, but it was the Pépin family's first automobile.

I MAY HAVE been a superstar in the eyes of Bichon and a valued addition to the kitchen staff on my trips back to Le Pélican, but at Le Grand Hôtel de l'Europe, I was still called *P'tit,* still barred from *le piano.* I was certain my knife skills were as good as any other apprentice's. I had mastered lighting the stove, which now leapt to life with one match. I could dress poultry and scale fish with the best of them. But Chef didn't seem to notice. Maybe he still hadn't forgiven me for the consommé debacle.

One afternoon about a year after I started, I was standing at the butcher-block, scraping fragments of meat off a veal bone — raw ingredients for pâté. Chef suddenly materialized. I jumped and instinctively speeded up my scraping, certain that I had goofed or forgotten something and was about to be sentenced to another week of guard duty.

Quietly and with no inflection he said, "Jacques."

It was the first time I'd heard him utter my proper name.

"Tomorrow you start at the stove."

I should have felt elation, or at the very least a burst of pride. I'd attained the goal I'd dreamed of from the moment when I'd first glimpsed *le piano* through the kitchen's glass doors. But if I did feel those well-earned sentiments, they were overcome by another more powerful feeling, one that would become a familiar companion throughout my life: doubt. This was all a mistake. No way was I ready to hold my place at the stove. For God's sake, the thing almost came up to my chin.

But the next day I dutifully took my place at Robert's side, whispering a silent prayer that he couldn't tell what an unworthy assistant he had. In my first minutes on the job, I knew that my height, or rather lack thereof, would be an issue. Being so close to the stove's top, my face immediately became the color of a ripe tomato and stayed that way.

"I need platters," Robert ordered, not looking up from the skillet in front of him.

One problem. There was no way I could reach the platters, which were kept warming on a shelf above the stove.

"Platters!" Robert repeated. Now there was an edge to his voice.

In a flash of inspiration, I flung open the oven door and used the white-hot surface as a step.

I learned at the stove by visual osmosis. Chef did not impart much in terms of specific explanations. Instead, he allowed me to look and imitate. Recipes were immaterial and in any case nonexistent; he wanted me to learn how to cook by using my senses rather than by following written or verbal instructions. Sight, feel, hearing, and smell taught me about food.

By touching a piece of meat, I learned to determine its degree of doneness. Raw meat was spongy, well-done meat hard. I learned precisely how to determine all the stages in between by pushing a finger against the surface of the meat. Hearing was significant, too. The snap of an asparagus spear, the crunch of an apple, the pop of a grape are all indicators of freshness and quality. I learned to listen to the sizzling sound of a chicken roasting in the oven. When *le poulet chante* (the chicken sings), I knew that the layers of fat had clarified, signifying that the chicken was nearly done. Smell was of importance in recognizing quality. A fresh fish smells of the sea, seaweed, and salt. Fresh meat has a sweet smell, fresh poultry practically no smell at all. Melon, pears, tomatoes, raspberries, oranges, and the like each have their own distinctive fragrance when perfectly ripe.

Being a teenager, and regularly putting in fourteen-hour workdays, seven days a week, I was able to fall into the most profound slumber as soon as I lay down, remaining in that state dreamlessly until I instinctively bolted from bed a few minutes before starting time the next morning. One night my sleep was interrupted by a loud rapping on the door of our dorm. It was in the dead of winter, a slow time at the hotel. Robert and the oldest apprentice were taking their four days of vacation.

"Jacques, you must get up," came the voice of the night receptionist. "Some guests have arrived from Geneva. They want dinner."

It had been only a few months since my call to the stove, but as the senior apprentice on duty, the kitchen was my responsibility. The new arrivals had to be fed — something. Whether they would like it or not was another question. In the darkness, I struggled into my checks and ran down to the kitchen.

Luckily, *le piano* still retained some heat from the service, which had ended a half-hour earlier. I immediately added some coals, along with a liberal splash of Chef's precious liquid fat. He was at home in his own bed, and this was no time to stand on ceremony.

Angèle, one of the waitresses, came into the kitchen with a weary expression on her long face.

"Two couples," she muttered. "They want to start with pâté —"

I treated myself to a sigh of relief. The pâté was already made and in the refrigerator. I'd just have to slice it and plate it. No problem there.

"— and," Angèle continued, drawing out the word with a teasing smile, *"poulet à l'estragon."* Chicken stewed in white wine with tarragon and served with a cream and egg yolk sauce. That was clearly more of a challenge than the pâté. Not an insurmountable one, but one I'd never faced, certainly not alone in the kitchen.

I went to work, hesitant and uncertain at first, but more confident as the ingredients began to react to my techniques and feel. Working from memories of what I had seen Chef and the *commis* do when they made *poulet à l'estragon,* I cut a chicken into four pieces, two legs and two breasts. I then cooked the pieces *à blanc,* so they did not take any color, slowly in butter. I added white wine, along with a little chicken stock. Next in were a small onion and a bouquet garni, consisting of a few sprigs of thyme, parsley stems, and a bay leaf, tied together. I seasoned my dish with salt and pepper, covered it, and cooked it over medium heat for about thirty-five minutes. I then removed the chicken from the broth, keeping it warm on a serving dish, and created a sauce by whisking a *beurre manié,* a mixture of butter and flour in equal proportions, into the broth with rich, thick farm cream and fresh tarragon.

Finished forty minutes later, the dishes looked right, felt right, and smelled right, but one thing I had learned in my months at the stove was that Chef had at least fifty ways to point out what I had done wrong with any given dish, even one that to me seemed flawless. And then there was always the possibility that grumpy, road-weary travelers would complain about dinner no matter how perfectly I prepared it.

With trepidation, I inspected the finished platter one final time, and then told Angèle to take it out.

I'd like to report that I acted like a seasoned professional in the minutes that followed. But it would be a lie. Angèle was gone for what seemed like an hour. Were they complaining? Were they about to send their meals back to the kitchen? I sneaked over to the doors and, trying to conceal myself as best I could, peered into the dining room. Two well-dressed, middle-aged couples sat together at the only occupied table. Angèle was pouring wine. They were eating. Eating my food.

I was cleaning up when Angèle came back, wearing the sort

of smile normally found only on the faces of devoted mothers. "Jacques," she said, "they want to see the chef. Come, they liked your cooking. They want to say hello and thank you."

It was impossible to tell whether the warmth of my face had resulted from overtime at *le piano* or from extreme shyness. I was sweaty, dressed in clothes that were spotted and stained after fifteen hours of work. The dining room was for graceful, well-dressed people, people whom I would address with *vous* out of respect and recognition that they belonged to a higher social order than I did. But I couldn't refuse.

I don't know what my customers expected to see emerge from that legendary kitchen, but from the looks on those four well-fed faces, I guarantee it wasn't a five-foot-two-inch kid who had yet to fill out his apprentice's uniform.

~~~~~

GRADUALLY, Chef's attitude toward me began to change.

"Hey, Jacques," he said one day, "what are you doing during break?"

"Nothing in particular."

"Want to come with me?"

Chef owned a small, beat-up motorcycle. I perched on the back, and we roared out of town, eventually arriving at Pont d'Ain, a hamlet about twelve miles from Bourg. We swam for a couple of hours in the clear, cold Ain River. Afterward, we restored ourselves at the corner café with crusty bread, sparkling local wine, and white cheese strongly seasoned with garlic and herbs.

Other members of the staff began to view me not as a kid but as a colleague. One afternoon Robert and I went to a café in town during break. He confided in me that he would soon be leaving Le Grand Hôtel de l'Europe. I considered this an unthinkable career move. Robert was second in command of what seemed to me a bastion of haute cuisine.

"In a few months, I'm off to Paris," said Robert, and he began to describe wonders I could barely imagine. Boulevards, bistros, opera. Girls, for heaven's sake. And jobs. The finest restaurants, not just in France, but in the entire world, always looking for competent young cooks. Yes, Robert was going to get out of Bourg. He was going to make it big. "You should go to Paris, too, Jacques," he said.

We paid for our coffees and tramped along cours de Verdun to the hotel, two kids from the country who had to prepare for dinner service.

"HEY, *P'TIT*," Chef called, a note of urgency in his voice.

The new apprentice all but snapped to attention.

"I've lent my soufflé weights to the chef at L'Hôtel de France. He was supposed to have returned them yesterday. I need them for lunch. Go get them. *Vite! Vite!*"

P'tit took off at a full run.

Chef, Robert, Angèle, and I sat down outside Le Grand Hôtel de l'Europe in the warm sunshine and waited. An hour later the boy appeared, laboring under a familiar canvas bag. This time, it contained beef shoulder blade bones. We all ruffled the kid's hair and slapped him on the back, laughing until tears came to our eyes.

On May 15, 1952, Mme. Denizot Rebières summoned me to her office.

"Hello, *Petit* Jacques," she said, smiling faintly.

As always in her presence, I felt overwhelmed. I couldn't have spoken if I wanted to.

"Here it is," she said, handing me a typewritten document on a piece of Le Grand Hôtel de l'Europe's letterhead.

I stood and read it: "During his stay at this establishment, Jacques Pépin always gave complete satisfaction in his work and in his conduct. He leaves without entanglements."

I was no longer an apprentice.

Poulet à la Crème

(CHICKEN WITH CREAM SAUCE)

YIELD: 4 SERVINGS

*I*T WAS NATURAL that the first real dish I prepared on my own at Le Grand Hôtel de l'Europe would be chicken. Fertile, with gentle hills, scattered groves, and small rivers and lakes, the Bresse region is known for producing the best chickens in France. Its soil, low in phosphoric acid and calcium, yields a great variety of worms and insects, choice food for these free-range birds, which are distinguished by their blue feet, white plumage, and red cockscomb, the colors of the French flag. At the hotel we prepared chicken daily in a variety of ways, including roasted, stewed, sautéed, poached, in cream sauce, in red wine, and braised with vegetables. The undisputed specialty of the house was *poulet à la crème*. The thick, acidulated cream sauce, slightly pink in color, velvety, and wonderfully rich, was served not only with chicken, but with pike quenelles and frogs (with tarragon added), as well as poured liberally on fresh farmer cheese and raspberries. *Poulet à la crème* was usually served with rice seasoned with onions and thyme. With the addition of 1 tablespoon of chopped fresh tarragon, the dish becomes *poulet à l'estragon*.

The chicken is conventionally cut into four pieces and cooled with the bones in, which keeps the meat from drying out. It is served with the bones left in or removed, depending on the whim of the chef or the class of the restaurant.

1 tablespoon unsalted butter
1 chicken (about 3 pounds), cut into 4 pieces
    (2 legs and 2 breasts, with bones)
½ teaspoon salt, plus more to taste
¼ teaspoon freshly ground black pepper, plus more to taste

½ cup fruity white wine (I used Mâcon white, a Chardonnay)
½ cup good chicken stock
1 small onion (about 3 ounces), peeled and left whole
1 bouquet garni, made of a dozen sprigs of parsley, 2 bay
  leaves, 2 sprigs thyme, all tied together with string

1 tablespoon unsalted butter, at room temperature
1 tablespoon all-purpose flour
1 cup heavy cream

Melt the tablespoon of butter in a sturdy saucepan, and add the 4 pieces of chicken, skin side down. Sprinkle the chicken with the salt and pepper, and brown over medium heat, turning, for about 10 minutes. The chicken should be lightly browned, with the skin a blond rather than a dark brown color. Remove and discard some of the rendered fat, leaving only 1 to 2 tablespoons in the pan.

Add the wine, chicken stock, onion, and bouquet garni. Bring to a boil, and boil gently, covered, for 20 to 25 minutes, or until the chicken is tender. Transfer the chicken to a platter, and discard the onion and bouquet garni. Boil the liquid in the pan until it is reduced to about ¾ cup.

Meanwhile, make a *beurre manié*, or kneaded butter, by whisking together the tablespoon of soft butter and the flour in a small bowl. Pick up this mixture on the looped wires of a whisk, and whisk it into the reduced liquid in the pan until the mixture is smooth. Bring to a boil to thicken the liquid, then add the cream, return to a boil, and boil gently for 5 minutes. While the sauce is boiling, you may want to remove the bones from the breast and leg pieces of the chicken, leaving the thigh, drumstick, and wing bones in place. Arrange the chicken on a serving platter.

Taste the sauce, and add salt and pepper if needed. Strain the sauce through a fine sieve held over the chicken, and serve immediately.

4

Seasons

MY FIRST JOB after apprenticeship was a summer position, called a "season," at L'Hôtel d'Albion in the hills just above Aix-les-Bains, a lakeside spa on the road from Italy to France. Technically, I was a third *commis,* a trainee, one tiny step above apprentice. As such, I was housed in a room in the hotel near the kitchen with four other trainees. Workdays began at 8:00 in the morning and, with a couple of hours off during the afternoon break, extended until 9:30 or 10:00 at night. The Albion employed a dozen cooks in all. This small brigade fed two hundred guests twice a day, seven days a week, a pace far more intense than anything I had known in Bourg-en-Bresse.

Chef Cullet was a squat, somber autocrat. Above all, he demanded absolute punctuality. He expected all *commis* to be in the kitchen by 7:30 A.M. sharp so that all would be ready when he made his grand entrance and inspection tour at 8:00. Most nights, the allures of Aix-les-Bains and the hormonal energy of youth kept us out on the streets or down by the lake until midnight or later. At 7:30, we were inevitably still sound asleep. Fortunately, Chef traveled aboard a small Alcyon motorcycle. Despite its size, that Alcyon must have been the noisiest vehicle ever to ply the roads of postwar France. When Chef downshifted at the foot of the hill, the little bike backfired with a crack. We leapt from our beds, knowing that we had exactly six minutes — the precise time required for the Alcyon to bear its portly burden up the hill — to dress, wash (or at least moisten our faces), don our toques, and dash to our stations.

Once again my height, or lack of it, put me at a disadvantage. I spent much of the workday in front of two open grills, one for fish, one for meat. The grills were fueled by high-grade hardwood charcoal and burned with the intensity of blast furnaces. In the cramped space, there was no room to back away or move to the side. Like the food I prepared, I sizzled over those fires for five or six hours each day with no chance for escape. The most difficult dish to prepare was the mixed grill, which consisted of tiny lamb chops, slices of calf's liver, strips of bacon, broiled tomatoes, and large mushroom caps. Each item had to be grilled individually, which made sense, given their different cooking times. But because of a wrong-headed notion lodged in Chef's one-track brain, I had to set each item on the grill, turn it, and then remove it with my fingers. According to Chef, a fork punctured foods and made their juices run, and a metal spatula imparted unpleasant tastes. I kept dipping my fingers in a bowl of ice water to protect them from the heat, but by the end of the first month, their tips were burned white.

But I also learned some important lessons under Chef Cullet. Within days of reporting to L'Hôtel d'Albion, I understood that, as an apprentice, I had been exposed to the foods of one small region of France prepared in the manner of one kitchen. Far from providing a complete training course, Le Grand Hôtel de l'Europe and the tastes of Chef Jauget had imparted only a small part of what I would have to learn. Chef Cullet demanded different techniques, had different tastes, and made different dishes from those with which I was familiar. *Féra* and *lavaret,* two kinds of whitefish from the lake, sautéed with butter, almond slivers, and lemon juice or poached in white wine with cream, replaced the chicken of Le Grand Hôtel de l'Europe. Patrons favored the lamb mixed grill over the coq au vin of my apprenticeship. In addition to mastering new dishes, I also learned how to move quickly and work fast as part of a twelve-person brigade that had to produce some four hundred meals a day.

During the afternoon break, we six trainees tramped down the hill en masse to the public beach. There, in addition to cooling off in the lake, we did our best to attract the attention of the waitresses, chambermaids, and shop girls summering in Aix-les-Bains. Our attempts were not a pretty sight. At sixteen, I was surprisingly mature in a professional and economical sense. It had been three years since I'd accepted a sou from my parents or slept under their roof as anything but a visitor. I was earning a living. I had a profession. But my only prior brush with the world of sexuality had been the prostitutes who had frequented Le Pélican. Although they were fixtures in that working-class neighborhood, as much a part of the scene as the dusty-booted workmen and tired young mothers pushing perambulators, I was vaguely aware that there was something naughty about their trade. I was fascinated by them in the same way I was fascinated by anything adult or off-limits. But I was ignorant about the specifics of their worklife and equally uninformed about how I should go about getting a girl of my own age to like me. Why were they not impressed by my repertoire of flips, jackknifes, and swan dives? My tactic of dousing an intended girlfriend with glacial lake water while she sunbathed drew a withering look.

I have no idea why a girl actually agreed to go to the movies with me toward the end of the summer. It was my first date. Hers too, I suspect. Aside from sitting together stiffly in the dark, neither one of us knew what was expected. Unfortunately, we never found out that summer. The season burns bright but fast, and mine was soon over.

~

WHEN L'Hôtel d'Albion closed for the season, I found work in Bellegarde, twenty miles west of Geneva at the foot of the Jura Mountains. Except for the dishwasher, I was alone in the kitchen, L'Hôtel Restaurant de la Paix's brigade of one.

My kitchen had two doors that opened upon vastly different worlds, both of which I had to keep supplied with food. One door led to the dining room, where, on a busy day, I'd prepare meals for two or three dozen businessmen. Door Number Two led to the café, where I had to supply local *belote* players with a never-ending stream of cheese fondue to be washed down by barrel after barrel of *vin ordinaire.*

The few lonely traveling businesspeople who made up our clientele never came close to filling those rooms to capacity. Things were so quiet at L'Hôtel Restaurant de la Paix that the "real" chef, the son-in-law of the owner, decamped from sleepy Bellegarde every winter in favor of the glittering ski resort of Chamonix and its high-paying kitchen jobs. This left me, approaching my seventeenth birthday and barely six months out of apprenticeship, in charge of my own kitchen, with some gentle guidance from Mme. Saint-Oyant, the owner of the hotel.

Luckily, the bill of fare at L'Hôtel Restaurant de la Paix was as straightforward and simple as the hotel itself. Lunch and dinner menus were identical. Diners could start with a soup du jour. Fish — whiting, pike, or trout — was inevitably sautéed in butter. For main courses I served black sausage, *bifteck* (beefsteak), calf's head, veal *escalopes* in cream sauce, and hare and red wine stew. I made do with a couple of classic desserts, such as caramel custard with *coupe Mont Blanc* (a meringue with a purée of chestnut and whipped cream) and pineapple with kirschwasser.

L'Hôtel Restaurant de la Paix may not have added a great deal of new dishes or techniques to my repertoire, but during that winter in Bellegarde, I picked up something that every chef needs as surely as he needs a set of good knives: confidence. In Bellegarde, for the first time I realized that I could make food move in a direction that was mine. I could assert myself in the seasonings, in the

color of a sauce, or in its amount of reduction. I and I alone decided on the ratio of potatoes to leeks in the soup, whether or not
to strain it, whether or not to finish it with butter and cream. I
could add chopped herbs to the mayonnaise for the fish if I chose
to, or not. In short, I ran the show. It was somewhat unsettling, but
there was also something exciting and electric about it.

I slipped into a comfortable pattern until Mme. Saint-Oyant
came into the kitchen and announced that in two weeks the hotel,
and by extension its young chef, would be hosting Bellegarde's
Banquet des pompiers, the Firemen's Ball. Madame made it
known that the prestigious assemblage ranked at or near the pin-
nacle of social events in that small town, and the sixty attendees
would include a veritable Who's Who of local dignitaries: the fire
chief, the police chief, the mayor, the school principal. Even the
priest.

"Can you handle it?" she asked.

"Certainly," I said, even though it would be by far the single
biggest culinary production of my short career.

The pressure was on. I began planning my banquet immediately. My guests would begin with leek and potato soup that was finished with cream, butter, and chervil. The fish course would be
colin, or hake, poached in a vegetable stock and served with an
herb mayonnaise. Roast chicken would stand as the main dish, accompanied by potatoes and buttered peas. That would be followed
by a salad, then a cheese course, and finally caramel custard with
Chantilly cream.

Two days before the event, I began my preparations. I peeled
and diced the leeks and potatoes, stewed them in butter, finished
them with chicken stock, and placed them in the refrigerator until
the big day. The fishmonger delivered five large hake, which I
cleaned, washed, and refrigerated. I spent hours carving beets,
leek greens, tomatoes, and hard-boiled egg slices into delicate
floral shapes that would garnish my fish. All the vegetable scraps
went into a pot of water to become stock.

Despite my timely preparations, the banquet day arrived all too soon. In the morning I poached the hake so that they could be decorated and then served at room temperature. I put the final touches on the soup so that it was ready to be warmed and finished. I roasted fifteen large chickens. As I checked the seasonings of the soup, the dining room began to fill with the hubbub of people greeting one another. It settled down to a quiet buzz of conversation and the occasional clank of silverware as the courses left the kitchen one by one. By the time dessert was served, the room was loud with the merriment of happy, well-fed people. I was a success — though Mme. Saint-Oyant had had the good sense to take out a little insurance policy: she'd allotted each attendee one bottle of white wine and one bottle of red.

History did not take note of the respective roles of the food or the wine in the evening's success. It did, however, record the image of the triumphant young chef. A photographer from Bellegarde's weekly paper was on the scene. He took a picture of me — magnificent in toque, jacket, and scarf — standing proudly behind platters of my artistically presented hake.

I was famous.

BARELY SEVENTEEN years old, I had reached a critical juncture in the career of any serious young chef, even today. One road led to a future of high-ranking (and high-paying) positions in a series of small, local kitchens. Chefs Jauget and Cullet had followed this route. In their own worlds they were respected and financially comfortable, but confined. The other road led to constantly reinventing myself in entry-level positions under a multitude of chefs. In Bellegarde, I realized that my future lay down the second road. I had no neatly laid out scheme or career path. It was more of a restlessness, like a stiff breeze always blowing in the direction of a better restaurant, a more prestigious chef, a bigger town.

In France, particularly in the early 1950s, that meant one

thing: Paris. I had never been to Paris. No one in my family had. It's difficult today to comprehend how circumscribed my life had been: a slightly lopsided sixty-mile-wide circle with Lyon at its western side and Geneva on the northeast encompasses Bellegarde, Aix-les-Bains, Bourg, Neyron, L'Abresle, Chambéry, St.-Jean-de-Maurienne, Pont d'Ain — all the towns and villages I had ever spent time in, the entire world as I knew it. Now my heart was set on a city three hundred miles away.

After Bellegarde, I returned to Lyon and took up a position at a local landmark restaurant, called La Coupole. When I wasn't on duty at La Coupole, I was back in the old kitchen at Le Pélican with Maman and Bichon. Although she was clearly in charge of her kitchen, the boss, Maman now occasionally asked my professional view about a dish. Bichon was coming to the end of his formal schooling and would soon begin his apprenticeship at La Brasserie du Nord in Lyon. He watched me and aped my every move in the kitchen.

One of the tricks I had learned from Chef Jauget was how to determine when caramel is ready by swirling my index finger through it. After Bichon saw me dipping my finger first into a bowl of cold water, then nonchalantly into the hot syrup, then back into the cold water, he was highly impressed and couldn't wait to give my "digital thermometer" technique a try.

"Go ahead," I said.

He duplicated my moves, but not exactly. The resulting howl could be heard throughout the restaurant.

But I knew that my stay in Lyon would be brief. I had been there less than a month when I informed Maman that I intended to pursue my career in Paris.

"Do you remember that guy I used to work with in Bourg? The *commis*, Robert?"

Maman nodded, making no attempt to hide her concern that her son was going to be exposed to all the evils and temptations of a distant metropolis.

"He wrote to me. He's got a job there. And he's offered me a place to stay."

Maman's expression did not change.

"And he's got work lined up for me."

I wasn't lying to her, not technically. Shortly after arriving in Bellegarde I had gotten a letter from Robert, telling me that he had realized his dream of leaving Bourg and Le Grand Hôtel de l'Europe and was living and working in Paris. I had written back to him immediately. For some reason, he hadn't answered my letter, but I was quite sure he would let me stay at his place temporarily. And if Robert had had no trouble securing a job in Paris, surely I'd be able to find work, especially with the guidance of an insider. Despite her hesitancy about my leaving home for the city, I knew Maman wanted me to have a shot at the big Parisian restaurants. No sense causing her undue worry.

Ramequins au Fromage

(SWISS CHEESE FONDUE)

YIELD: 4 SERVINGS

*T*HIS IS an interpretation of the famous Swiss cheese fondue (French for "melted") as we made it in the Lyon–Bourg-en-Bresse area. Traditional Swiss fondue is a combination of melted Gruyère and Emmenthaler cheeses, white wine, and nutmeg, boiled together and lightly thickened with cornstarch, then finished with kirschwasser. My version uses a lot of garlic, no thickening agent, and no kirsch. The cheese tends to thicken in the bottom of the pot (an enameled cast-iron pot is best), and the flavored white wine comes to the top. As diners drag their bread cubes gently through the fondue, the liquid on the surface and the thicker mixture underneath combine. Only crusty, country-type French bread should be used. If it falls off your fork into the cheese, custom requires that you buy a round of drinks for everyone at the table.

Fondue is usually made in the kitchen at the last moment, then brought to the dining room and kept hot over a Sterno or gas burner set in the center of the table. My father always warned against drinking cold white wine with the fondue, claiming it would cause the stomach to swell, but I have drunk my wine throughout without any ill effects. Fondue is a meal in itself at our house and is usually followed by a salad and fruit for dessert.

    2   tablespoons unsalted butter
    1   teaspoon finely chopped garlic
1 ½   cups (½ bottle) fruity white wine, such as
          a Sauvignon Blanc
        About ¾ teaspoon salt, or to taste

$^1/_2$ teaspoon freshly ground black pepper

3 packed cups grated Swiss cheese, preferably Emmenthaler or Gruyère (about 12 ounces)

About 36 cubes (each 2 inches square) crusty French-style bread

Melt the butter in a sturdy saucepan (preferably enameled cast iron), and add the garlic. Cook for 10 seconds over high heat, then add the wine, salt, and pepper. Bring to a boil to evaporate the alcohol in the wine. (You may flambé it, if you like, at this point, but one way or the other the alcohol will rise in the form of vapor.)

Add the cheese, and stir gently with a wooden spatula or spoon until it is totally melted and the mixture is just reaching a boil. Do not let it come to a strong boil. Taste for seasoning, trying the fondue on a piece of the bread, and then correct the seasonings, if necessary. Bring the pan to the table, and set over a burner to keep hot.

Instruct guests to use this technique: Impale one piece of bread, soft side first, on a dinner fork, and stir it gently into the mixture until coated with the cheese. With a twist of the wrist, lift the bread from the cheese, and set it on a plate for a few seconds to cool slightly before eating.

When only about 1 cup of the mixture is left in the bottom of the pan, make the "soup" by adding a dozen or so pieces of the bread to the pot and mixing well to coat them with the leftover liquid and cheese. Don't forget to eat the crusty bits of cheese sticking to the bottom of the pan.

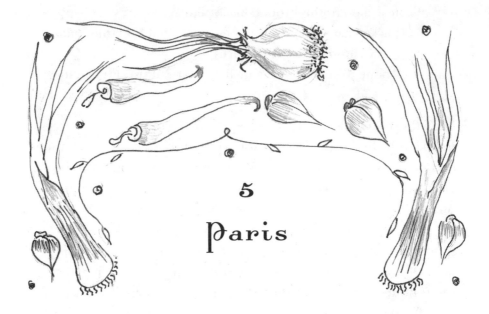

5

Paris

I STEPPED OUT of the Gare de Lyon into a scorching May afternoon — me and all my possessions, which amounted to three changes of clothes in one of Maman's old suitcases and a set of carbon steel chef's knives in a wooden chest Papa had made for me. Putting my luggage down, I sat on the curb to assess my situation.

Things did not look too promising from where I sat. I was lonely and afraid. If at that moment I had disappeared from the face of the world, no one would have known. I was also completely lost. True, in my pocket I had the letter that Robert had sent months earlier, but a creased and smudged envelope was one thing and finding my way through the rat's nest that Paris calls a network of streets was quite another.

Relying on youth, the wide-eyed innocence of a boy just in from the provinces, and the kindheartedness of Parisian pedestrians, I stopped every few blocks, pointed to Robert's envelope, and asked directions. In that manner, over the course of the afternoon, I tramped the unfamiliar streets, sweating under my load, until I ended up in the neighborhood of La Bastille. It was there that a passerby pointed to an actual building — a doorway — when I asked for directions.

The moment of truth had arrived. Did Robert still live there? If so, would he be at home? And would he welcome me, or was that invitation he had extended in Bourg over a year earlier one of those insincere offers people come up with: "Oh, you must come and visit sometime . . ."?

I knocked and waited. Knocked again, louder. After a few minutes I heard rustling inside and then the rattle of the lock. The door swung open and I found myself nose-to-nose, not with Robert, but with an attractive if somewhat sleepy-looking young woman. I was still fumbling for words when she stepped aside, and suddenly I was shaking hands with Robert and being subjected to a barrage of words, which included introductions to Robert's live-in girlfriend, an invitation to spread a bedroll in a quiet corner of the apartment for as long as needed, and an insistence that we all go out to a neighborhood bistro to celebrate.

"Tomorrow," Robert said, "you and I will go to the Société. You'll be cooking by nightfall."

I'LL NEVER understand why New York, or for that matter all other cities with thriving, sophisticated restaurant scenes, don't have chefs' associations similar to la Société des cuisiniers de Paris, an organization that exists primarily to match chefs to available jobs and vice versa. The morning after I turned up at his door, Robert told me to grab my knife chest and follow him.

"Here it is," he said, outside a nondescript commercial building on rue de la Sourdière. "Good luck."

He set off toward the restaurant where he worked.

Inside, the place looked like a small, financially troubled bank, one that had not been able to afford new furniture and fixtures for several decades. A couple of bored-looking functionaries stared out from behind teller-style grilles. I approached one and informed him that I was a chef in search of work.

This failed to excite him.

"Membership card," he said.

"I'm not a member."

He handed me a form. "Fill this out. Be sure to include where you apprenticed and list any work experience. You have your certificates with you, I hope?"

I nodded yes.

"I'll need to see those as well." He pointed to a counter where there were some pens and inkstands.

I dutifully completed the form and then handed it back to the clerk, along with the membership fee, which amounted to only a few francs.

"Wait in there," he said, pointing to a door.

My first thought when I entered the room was that Robert had made a mistake. Either that, or I was again the butt of one of the practical jokes young chefs delight to play on their peers. A half-dozen other men were seated in a space that embodied the shabby neglect of waiting rooms everywhere: cast-off, mismatched chairs, ashtrays full of stubbed and bent cigarettes, and a library of magazines so well thumbed that their pages had the texture of fine chamois. But the most distressing thing was the age of the other men. I was the youngest by a good half-century. In a horrific mental image, I saw the assembled codgers sitting there day after day, year after year, decade after decade, growing older and older while they waited for chef's jobs that would never materialize. If they were even chefs at all. Their red noses and the burst capillaries on their cheekbones suggested that my new associates' experience with wine was by no means limited to its culinary uses.

But to my surprise, after a few minutes the fellow from behind the counter appeared at the door and called out, "Henri."

One of the old guys smushed his cigarette, bid good day to his colleagues, took a piece of paper from the functionary, and left the room.

The geezer seated next to me seized the opportunity to initiate a conversation, the usual small talk about where I was from and what I had done. Whether I wanted to or not, I learned that he was a retired chef, but that whenever he felt the need for extra pocket money or began to go stir-crazy listening to his nagging wife, he'd come down to the Société and pick up a little work. A day or two here, a day or two there. "Of course, an old guy like me, that's all I want," he said. "A young fellow like you, don't worry. They'll find you a full-time position."

As if on cue, the door opened and the man to whom I had given my forms said, "Pépin."

He handed me a document. It informed me that M. Jacques Pépin was officially second *commis* at La Maxéville. I was to start work that day.

~~~~

NOTHING IN MY experience could have prepared me for La Maxéville. A brasserie on boulevard Montmartre, it was scary, considering my provincial training. In addition to serving lunch and dinner, La Maxéville was successful off hours with the tourists and boulevardiers, thanks in no small part to its full-string orchestra, whose members were women in long dresses.

La Maxéville was archaic in every way, nowhere more so than in its kitchen — designed, I assumed, by the architectural team responsible for Paris's network of catacombs. Located in the third sub-basement, the space was as dark and dank as a cave. Reaching up to a shelf, I half-expected to pull down the tibia of some unfortunate plague victim. Thirty chefs toiled in that vault, milling out meals as uninspired as our confines were unappealing. From onion soup to sauerkraut, La Maxéville featured ordinary brasserie food. This was not why I had left home and come to Paris. After a few weeks, I went back to the Société and asked for another job, one where I could learn from the best.

They complied. And then some.

In those days, Le Meurice, a hotel on rue Rivoli, was arguably the most aristocratic establishment in Paris, and its dining room menu offered the most sophisticated and traditional French cuisine in the city. Instead of laboring in a basement, I found myself in a kitchen so spacious and empty that I could have roller-skated from station to station. During the war, when Nazi generals requisitioned Le Meurice as their Parisian base of operations (if you're going to occupy a nation, may as well do it in style), nearly eighty chefs worked in the kitchens. By the time I came, there was a brigade of only sixteen.

My boss, Executive Chef Ripert, was a dapper little man in his sixties with a narrow, straight moustache. He came to work carrying a cane tucked under one arm and wearing a black suit with a white, starched collar, a derby perched on his head. Chef Ripert had worked under Auguste Escoffier himself, and the great chef would have been proud. His protégé had neither forgotten — nor altered — a single classical detail.

And that included his way of communicating with the staff. Chef Ripert gave orders through a megaphone, and the noise that it generated, combined with his south-of-France accent, made him nearly incomprehensible. Still, great stuff was produced in that kitchen. It was my first exposure to haute cuisine, and I committed to memory every bellowed command and every step in every dish.

I was *commis entremetier*, a job that consisted of preparing the vegetables and soups along with garnishes. I learned how to make a *bouquetière* with twelve different vegetables cooked to order. I cooked authentic petite marmite, a consommé garnished with stuffed chicken wings, cubes of beef, gizzards, baby leeks, turned carrots, and turned turnips. Instead of turning the vegetables into miniature football shapes in the conventional way, I was expected to shape them into miniature tops, flat at one end and tapered at the other. Like everything else at Le Meurice, each petite marmite was prepared individually to order and from scratch. Each one cooked slowly for a long time in its own earthenware terrine until the liquid was clear and strong enough to gel when cooled. I garnished each one with beef marrow, small molded cabbages, croutons hollowed from tiny rolls, and grated Parmesan cheese.

Cooking under Chef Ripert was more structured, complicated, and demanding than anything I had ever experienced. There was no room for mistakes. This was, after all, the venerated cuisine of master chef Marie-Antoine Carême, featuring extremely intricate preparations and passed down to us firsthand through Escoffier. The work was so detailed that, even with sixteen chefs, if we had to serve more than forty customers at one time, there was pandemonium in the kitchen.

Yet we were not always weighed down by work; we had our good times. We *commis* spent our afternoon breaks at the Tuileries Gardens across the street from the hotel, where tranquil carp swam in the basins. To amuse ourselves, we made floats from the wooden covers of Camembert or Brie boxes. We'd push a length of twine through a hole in the center, attach a makeshift hook fashioned from a twisted pin, and bait it with a hunk of bread. Occasionally, to our delight, a carp would seize the bread, and the lid would speed across the surface of the water — much to the amazement of passersby.

After a few months as *entremetier*, I wanted to broaden my skills and requested that I be moved to another job in the kitchen. Unfortunately, with minimal turnover and such a small staff, no other job was available, nor was it likely that a vacancy would open in the foreseeable future. For all its qualities, Le Meurice was no place for an ambitious young chef impatient to learn everything. When I discussed this with Chef Ripert, he was kind enough to find me a new job with new challenges.

But I hadn't counted on one major challenge of this new post: getting along with my boss. From my mother to chefs as varied as Jauget, Cullet, and Ripert, I had always managed to work well with whoever was running the kitchen. And although he or she may have grumbled about my less-than-totally-serious demeanor, every boss I'd worked for had appreciated my enthusiasm and love of cooking and, at some level, genuinely liked having me in the kitchen. Not Chef Crampette. I became his nemesis, and he mine.

Honestly, I wanted things to work out. Chef Crampette oversaw the kitchen at La Rotonde, the famous brasserie in Montparnasse. Along with La Coupole across the street, La Rotonde was a mecca for artists, writers, models, and boulevardiers. Every bohemian intellectual on the Left Bank came by at one time or another. I had been there only a few weeks when one of the waiters summoned me to the door leading out to the dining room.

"Look there," he said, pointing to a solitary man at a table.

The customer was uglier than most and made no attempt to hide it. He had wispy strands of slicked-down black hair, heavy-framed glasses, and an undertaker-style suit. He was hunched over the table, simultaneously reading and chewing.

"Jean-Paul Sartre," said the waiter. "He comes often."

A few months earlier, that name would have meant nothing to me. But since coming to Paris, I had begun to absorb some of the culture and intellectual life around me. It was hard not to. Government funding meant that I could go to the Opéra comique or to the national theater to see Offenbach's *Tales of Hoffmann,* Molière's *Tartuffe,* or a Feydeau comedy. With the likes of Albert Camus, Samuel Beckett, and Simone de Beauvoir dining at La Rotonde, curiosity prompted me to read their plays and books. Through them, I discovered a rewarding literary world beyond *The Three Musketeers.*

Our menu was extensive and first rate as well as earthy and eclectic. *Fillet de sole tout-Paris* (sole with two sauces, one made with crayfish, the other with a reduction of Champagne speckled at serving time with a glazed reduction of fish stock). Truffled capon. Herring in oil with potato salad. Simple onion soup. It was a good place to work.

That is, were it not for Chef Crampette. He was a short, fat man with an enormous, jiggling rear end and a face that would have looked more at home on an old, ill-natured bulldog. Chef

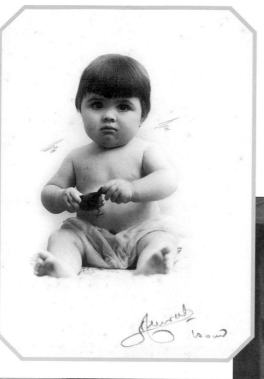

At eight months,
holding a toy chicken.

ABOVE: My mother, Jeannette,
wearing a homemade rabbit coat,
circa 1942.

LEFT: My father, Victor, just
before the Second World War.

With my brother Roland, who is holding Bichon, on the steps of our house in Bourg-en-Bresse.

ABOVE: Outside Chez Pépin, my mother's Lyon restaurant, circa 1947. *Left to right:* me, Roland, Jeannette, La Marraine (my aunt), Paulette (the waitress), Le Parrain (my godfather), Paulette's boyfriend (*kneeling*), and Bichon (*center, standing*).

RIGHT: At eleven, on the bridge over La Brevenne near the village of L'Arbresle.

ABOVE: A taste of fame: at sixteen and a half, as shown in a newspaper photograph, with the banquet I prepared for the Firemen's Ball in Bellegarde.

RIGHT: Between fellow *commis* at Le Plaza Athénée, on the Champs-Elysées in Paris, 1954.

Bichon (*center*) with me and Roland on leave during the Algerian war, 1957.

Preparing for a party organized by the *New York Times* food editor Craig Claiborne in Claiborne's East Hampton kitchen, 1965. With me are (*left to right*) Roger Fessaguet, chef at La Caravelle; Pierre Franey, chef at Le Pavillon; Réné Verdon, chef at the Kennedy White House; and Jean Vergnes, chef at Le Colony.

Carving a watermelon.

"The grandest picnic of all time," on Gardiners Island, New York. *Left to right:* Pierre Franey, me, Roger Fessaguet, Jean Vergnes, and Réné Verdon.

OPPOSITE: Gloria, early 1960s.

LEFT: With Helen McCully, editor of *House Beautiful*, late 1960s. (Courtesy of *House Beautiful*)

BELOW: With Bichon (*left*) and Roland behind the bar of Le Pélican, my mother's restaurant, 1962.

Gloria and I on our wedding day, September 1966, at Craig Claiborne's house with the justice of the peace, Jean-Claude Szurdak, and Anita Odeurs.

The wedding party: Howard D. Johnson (*seated*), Gloria and I and Craig Claiborne (*standing*), Marjorie Johnson, the justice of the peace, and his wife.

Crampette was the only remaining person in all of Paris to sport a Hitler-style moustache. He had but one mood, ugly; one facial expression, a scowl; and one posture, head down, lest he be forced to acknowledge a pleasantry — unless, of course, the owner of La Rotonde happened to be in the kitchen. Then Chef Crampette was all smiles and fawning subservience. There was nothing he wouldn't do (or make us do) to please the man who signed his paycheck. On one of those occasions I had my first serious contretemps with Chef Crampette. I swear it was a complete accident. Chef was quietly discussing food budgets with the owner. I was, as usual, slammed with lunch orders, and without paying too much attention to Chef and the owner, I reached for a heavy copper saucepan hanging about six inches directly above Chef's bald head.

Can I be blamed for underestimating the weight of the pan? Is it my fault that the thing was too heavy for me to hold with one hand? That my wrist buckled and the long cast-iron handle of the *sautoir* landed on the back of his head? Fortunately, no serious damage was done, other than to Chef's ego and my standing in the kitchen.

The next confrontation was also an accident, more or less. Chef had bent down to get something from far back under a counter on which I was working with a paring knife. A pair of beach-ball-size buttocks was all that remained visible of Chef. Too good to resist. Catching the attention of a couple of *commis*, I made fake stabbing thrusts with my knife, stopping inches away from Chef's formidable posterior. They cheered silently, which urged me to greater heights. I turned to face some other colleagues, winking and grinning broadly, still thrusting the knife. Chef chose that precise moment to step backward. I had just begun another vigorous thrust. My knife pricked his right buttock.

He jolted forward. "You idiot!" he screamed. "I'm going to fire you."

Somehow, I survived, but not for long. A few weeks passed,

and I worked diligently, keeping the lowest possible profile. I remained a model employee until one evening when Chef Crampette went into the cold department to secure a bottle of cognac, which was stored in a cabinet that was too high for him to reach. Chef solved the problem by opening a small, thick refrigerator door under a shelf. He used the door as a step onto the counter, from which he could reach the cognac. It so happened that I had gotten an order for sole. It was in the middle of the rush. As was my habit, I dashed into the cold room, grabbed a fish out of the fridge, and then, in a movement I had perfected over the course of hundreds of trips to that room, I executed a crude pirouette, fish in hand, slamming the fridge door shut with a quick kick of my heel. My back was turned when Chef descended, his foot meeting emptiness.

Nothing was broken, not even the cognac bottle. But my career at La Rotonde was over.

GIVEN THE CIRCUMSTANCES, getting out of town for a couple of weeks didn't seem like such a bad idea. A colleague suggested I go with him to the Casino of Deauville in coastal Normandy, which opened during the Easter vacation. I heard about the job on a Wednesday afternoon. Like just about every other chef in greater Paris, I was at La Grille for the midday break. Located near la Société des cuisiniers, La Grille was originally named after a bistro with a front entrance that was adorned with a thick steel gate where chefs once congregated. Eventually, the chefs' gathering overflowed that establishment, expanding to take up the whole block along rue St. Roch, but it was still known as La Grille. Cooks swarmed everywhere, seated in bistros, chatting in clusters along sidewalks, clogging the street. La Grille was a great democracy in our intensely hierarchical profession, filled with executive chefs, *chefs de partie, commis,* trainees, apprentices. It was a vast, open-air schmoozing session, an informal job market, a place to meet old friends and make new ones. Gossip and shoptalk were the local currency.

There was another reason I wanted to go to Normandy. A year had passed since I'd arrived in Paris, homeless and jobless, a rough country kid long on ambition and low on sophistication. I had worked in bistros, brasseries, and fancy dining rooms. A couple of weeks in Normandy would be the perfect break. Who knew, maybe getting away from Paris would give me some perspective. Besides, I'd never seen the sea.

Located on the coast about 120 miles from Paris, Deauville is a chic summer resort with gambling casinos, big hotels, and the romantic, misty landscapes so dear to the impressionist painters. It is also the land of Calvados, apple cider, Camembert, and crème fraîche.

And, of course, the sea. It was April and the weather was chilly. The water was gray, looking melancholy and appropriately romantic, everything a boy from Lyon could have asked. Then there was the marvelous smell, scents I had encountered only on the seaweed lining a crate of oysters or on a fish fresh from market. Kids from town were throwing nets into the water from the beach, harvesting who-knew-what. Something good, I suspected.

This was too much to resist. I found an old, discarded net, ripped but more or less serviceable. A couple of other cooks liberated a skillet and some freshly churned butter from the casino kitchen. We met on the beach the next day at 7:00 A.M. Impervious to the cold, a friend and I hauled the net through the outgoing tide, doing our best to imitate the local kids.

The tattered net came up full of tiny gray shrimp no bigger than the tip of my little finger. By then a driftwood fire was ablaze, butter sizzling. We sautéed our catch and ate the hot delicacies with our hands. I haven't encountered any shrimp since whose flavor and sweetness came close to that taste.

Onion Soup Gratinée

YIELD: 4 SERVINGS

ONE OF MY greatest treats when working in Paris was to go with my fellow chefs and *commis* to les Halles, the big market of Paris that spreads through many streets of the Châtelet neighborhood.

The excitement in the streets and cafés started a little before 3:00 A.M. and ended around 7:00 or 8:00 A.M. Our nocturnal forays would, more often than not, finish at Le Pied de Cochon (The Pig's Foot), the quintessential night brasserie of les Halles. There, large, vociferous butchers in bloody aprons would rub shoulders with tuxedoed and elegantly evening-gowned Parisians stopping by for late-night Champagne and a meal after the opera or the theater. The restaurant was famous for its onion-cheese gratinée; it was one of the best in Paris, and hundreds of bowls of it were served every night.

For this recipe, you will need four onion soup bowls, each with a capacity of about 12 ounces and, preferably, with a lip or rim around the edge that the cheese topping will stick to as it melts to form a beautiful crust on top of the soup.

> 2 tablespoons unsalted butter
> 3 onions (about 12 ounces), cut into thin slices
> About 7 cups good-quality chicken stock, or a mixture of chicken and beef stock
> About 1/2 teaspoon salt, more or less, depending on the saltiness of the stock
> 1/2 teaspoon freshly ground black pepper
> 16 slices of baguette, each cut about 3/8 inch thick
> About 3 cups grated Swiss cheese, preferably Gruyère, Comté, or Emmenthaler (about 10 ounces)

Melt the butter in a saucepan, and sauté the sliced onions in the butter over medium to high heat for about 8 minutes, or until lightly browned. Add the stock, salt, and pepper, and boil gently for 15 minutes.

Meanwhile, preheat the oven to 400 degrees. Arrange the bread slices in a single layer on a tray, and bake them for 8 to 10 minutes, or until they are nicely browned. Divide the toast among the bowls, and sprinkle ¼ cup of cheese into each bowl.

When the stock and onions have cooked for 15 minutes, pour the soup into the bowls, filling each to the top. Sprinkle on the remainder of the cheese, dividing it among the bowls and taking care not to push it down into the liquid. Press the cheese around the rim or lip of the bowls, so it adheres there as it cooks and the crust does not fall into the liquid.

Arrange the soup bowls on a baking sheet, and bake for 35 to 45 minutes, or until a glorious brown, rich crust has developed on top. Serve hot right out of the oven.

6
Le Plaza
Athénée

I HAD COME a long way. Or so I had thought until I presented my-self to Lucien Diat, the executive chef at Le Plaza Athénée. In-stantly, I reverted to that cringing boy who had come to Le Grand Hôtel de l'Europe in short pants.

"Presented myself" is not totally correct. No one presented himself to M. Diat. It would be more accurate to say that I was granted a brief audience before the Great Man (whose brother, in-cidentally, was Louis Diat, the famous chef at the Ritz-Carlton in New York). Enthroned in his glass-walled office above the kitchen, M. Diat — always Monsieur, never, ever Chef — received the docu-ments I had been given at the Société in the dismissive manner of a king accepting the credentials of yet another ambassador from a small, inconsequential principality.

"You will be second *commis,*" he proclaimed. "Get dressed and go to the *garde-manger.*"

Once again, I found myself near the bottom of a kitchen hier-archy.

But this was a kitchen unlike any I'd worked in or ever would work in again. I felt like some kid from the minors finally striding out onto the turf of Yankee Stadium. No doubt about it, I was play-ing in the Big Leagues. Le Plaza Athénée had — and, now run by Alain Ducasse, still has — one of the very finest dining rooms in the world. To serve two hundred meals a day, the hotel employed forty-eight full-time chefs, four times the number of us who had served the same number of customers in Aix-les-Bains. M. Diat or-ganized his kitchen in a rigidly structured brigade. Below M. Diat was the sous-chef, also called *l'aboyeur* (the barker), because his job was literally to bark out orders over the intercom system. Below that were ten *chefs de partie,* each in charge of a separate area such as sauces, the cold department, fish cooking, roast and grill, vege-tables, and soup. There was a night chef, a turning chef to replace people who were off and another to fill in for any *chef de partie* on vacation, a *chef de partie* for the afternoon, and a chef in charge of the pastry department. Below each *chef de partie* was a first *commis;* below each first *commis* a second *commis,* and in some departments, third *commis* trainees.

At Le Plaza, the first *commis* were between twenty and thirty years old, and the *chefs de partie* between thirty and sixty years of age. Diat's machinelike brigade worked according to very strict and well-defined laws. The *chefs de partie* had their own dining room and locker room with showers. We *commis* had our own place to change, shower, and eat, and even there, the first *commis* dined on one side of the table, we second *commis* on the other.

Each of us stayed at one job until we had mastered it. Then, once we performed to M. Diat's satisfaction, which is to say flaw-lessly in even the most minute detail, we'd get moved to another department to start all over again. When a cook had made the rounds of all stations as a second *commis,* he would move through all the stations as a first *commis.* The result was a staff that had tre-mendous depth. A *commis* in the *garde-manger* knew exactly how to trim a veal chop because he had also spent months working at the elbow of a grill chef who would discard any cuts of meat less than perfectly trimmed. But bad cuts never reached the grill chef be-cause the *commis* working the grill had also worked in the *garde-*

manger and could whip out a knife and fix any problems on the spot.

During my stay at Le Meurice, none of the sixteen cooks had ever changed jobs. Unless someone had died or retired, I would have been the *commis* in Le Meurice's vegetable department forever. By contrast, M. Diat's style of management was more representative of the traditional French *brigade de cuisine,* and it was diametrically opposite to what often happens in kitchens now in restaurants in the United States, where the emphasis is on specialization. Today the idea is to take someone, often an immigrant from Latin America, and train him or her to do one specific task. And that's it. The person may know nothing else about cooking, but nobody will be able to touch him or her at that job, be it turning a carrot or grilling a hanger steak.

One thing that we were absolutely denied at Le Plaza was any room for what today would be called self-expression, though none of us would have thought of using that New Age term. All of our efforts were directed toward performing individual tasks in the precise manner of the house. There were no recipes or written procedures. Working beside M. Raimo, the *chef poissonnier* (fish cook), I watched his every move while making sure all the ingredients and utensils were at the ready a half-second before his hand shot out for them; I anticipated his moves with the foresight of an operating room nurse. After a time, the chef let me try my hand at a garnish. Finally, on a busy day, he had me cook. I imitated everything I'd ever seen him do, producing a fillet of sole that had the look, smell, and taste that only the sole at Le Plaza Athénée had. Not better than Maxim's or Le Meurice's, but as good as theirs and distinct from any other sole anywhere. Perfection was when a diner had no idea who was "cooking tonight" or had no occasion to ask such a question. Be it Jacques Pépin or any of twenty other *commis,* the sole would taste exactly the same every time. Ours was not the flash of star chefs. It was the toil of the many.

Every day as meal service began, M. Diat emerged from his office and descended upon the kitchen. Even if I was in the walk-in fridge, I would know the moment he entered because the noise level dropped by half. He crossed the room and stationed himself at the pass, the counter where chefs put plates for pickup by waiters. Not a single dish left the kitchen without passing through M. Diat's hands and receiving his blessing.

Lord help the poor cook whose work didn't meet M. Diat's standards — something that very rarely happened.

"What is this?" M. Diat would say, his voice never rising above conversational tones. "Put this back in the oven."

Or: "Present this platter again."

Then there was his *look,* a look that will recur in my nightmares as long as I live, not so much a look of anger as one of disdain, a gaze that lasted but a fraction of a second, yet made it clear that your pathetic little error was far beneath the level of his contempt. Quaver in the glare of those pale gray eyes, and you never made the same mistake again.

And if you did, there was The List. I first encountered The List one morning when I reported to work and came across a scrum of my fellow *commis* jostling for a glance at a piece of paper thumbtacked to the wall. They were like schoolboys, and Teacher had obviously posted the results of final exams. Some of my coworkers left with their heads down, shrugging off their disappointment by saying, "It's okay. Maybe next time." Some strutted off with smiles. Most merely sighed with relief.

The List outlined our assignments for the next six months. Whether we had risen to a more prestigious station, fallen to one not so desirable, or stayed in place was the only way to tell if we were doing a good job. No one, certainly not M. Diat, would have dreamed of paying a direct compliment.

~

"BONE IT OUT."

So much for the orientation session to my new post at Le Plaza Athénée's *garde-manger.*

The *chef de partie,* Chef Berutti, pointed to a leg of veal flopped over a butcher-block table. The appendage looked as if it had been hacked off the back end of a calf only moments before and hastily skinned for my benefit. Otherwise, it was still pretty much in working order.

My new boss's instructions, while explicit, were hardly detailed. I realized that the veal leg represented his version of a test. Pass, and he would know whether he could trust me. Flunk, and . . . well . . . Le Plaza did have those third *commis* positions.

It had been a long time since I had boned a leg of veal. Working from faded memories dating back to my apprenticeship, I separated the leg into different muscles: top round, bottom round, top knuckle, top sirloin, and shank. I then trimmed each of these cuts. It was an exacting process. Affecting a false nonchalance that I was far from feeling, I concentrated on the job and finished it to his liking.

In the *garde-manger* at Le Plaza, I was exposed to esoteric, expensive, and often unusual foods: exotic fruits like papaya, mango, and cherimoya. But the strangest of all arrived one morning in a basket from Hédiard, a fancy specialty store. Chef Berutti placed the basket in the walk-in fridge and kept it under constant guard.

"What are those fruits Chef is so worked up about?" I asked another *commis*.

"*Des poires avocat,*" he replied. "Avocado pears."

I had a weak spot for pears. I adored all varieties: Comice pears, Anjou pears, Bartlett pears. To be watched over so carefully by Chef, a *poire avocat* must have been the ne plus ultra of peardom. I was dying to sink my teeth into one.

The opportunity presented itself the next time I found myself alone in the walk-in cooler. I glanced around for Chef. Not seeing him, I snatched the largest and juiciest-looking pear, polished it briefly on my jacket, and vigorously bit it. My teeth penetrated thick, leathery skin and stopped jarringly upon contact with something hard and slime-covered. I drew back, surprised and queasy. How could people eat these pears? Notwithstanding the skin and the pit, the flesh itself was oily, mushy, not at all sweet.

Avocado misadventures aside, I must have been performing satisfactorily because when M. Diat next posted The List he had promoted me to the rank of second *commis* at the grilling and roasting station, where I came under the tutelage of Chef Duclos, whose motto was a quotation from Jean-Anthelme Brillat-Savarin: *"On devient cuisinier mais on naît rotisseur"* (One can become a cook, but one has to be born a roast cook).

Chef Duclos was certainly born to his calling. Unlike most of the cooks in M. Diat's kitchen, who, contrary to stereotype, were trim and wiry, Chef Duclos was a short, almost perfectly round gent. He looked as if he had spent his life feasting on fat roasted capons and juicy racks of lamb. Despite his girth, Chef Duclos worked with the grace and artistry of a professional dancer. Dainty sliding steps, delicate twirls, deft arm motions — his every movement was orchestrated, economical, beautiful to the eye. He could put in an entire shift without moving his tiny feet outside the same two-foot circle. To accomplish this, his *mise-en-place* was arranged in a strict order with no variation whatsoever. If he had been suddenly struck blind, Chef Duclos would have been able to continue working by feel alone. The *beurre maître d'hôtel*, butter for use on steak, always rested just above his cutting board on the right corner, next to the watercress in ice water. His chopping knife lay on the right side of the board, with his spatula, fork, and paring knife on the other side. It was amazing to see him work; calm, deliberate, confident, precise, there was not one gesture lost, not one extra movement.

Chef Duclos prepared the best roast chicken I had ever tasted. He started with fine birds from my native Bresse region, chickens that had been allowed to run outside in the sunshine, flapping their wings, scratching for seeds and insects. Bresse chickens had firm-textured flesh with pronounced differences between dark and white meat and the slightly gamey taste that is true chicken flavor. The skin was crunchy, buttery, salty, and nutty. Chef let the best qualities of his chicken come through, seasoning it with nothing more than salt, pepper, and butter, cooking it to order in a very hot oven, basting every ten minutes or so. There was no magic in Chef Duclos's chicken. What made his chicken the best was the perfection of every small step. The best chicken and butter. A searingly hot oven. Just the right amount of carefully made stock. Removing the bird from the oven the second it was cooked.

To serve his chicken, Chef Duclos took the copper saucepan (there were only copper and cast-iron saucepans in Le Plaza's kitchen) from the oven, placed it on the edge of the stove, and transferred the chicken to a hot silver tray that he had grabbed from a shelf behind him, without looking. With one hand, he poured the fat out of the saucepan, added some white wine and brown chicken stock to the pan with the other hand, put it back on the stove for a few minutes to reduce the liquid, and then strained it into a sauceboat. He did this in one fluid motion in just a few seconds, without stepping to the left or right. Simultaneously, he closed the oven door with the toe of one shoe, blindly plucked a handful of watercress from behind him, and arranged it next to the chicken on the tray. Still without moving forward or backward, he took a tablespoon of butter and dropped it into a hot saucepan. When it had turned a hazelnut color, he poured it over the finished bird, then pivoted on his two feet. Holding his plated chicken in one hand, he grabbed the sauceboat in his other and placed them on the pass at the pickup station, where M. Diat awaited to render judgment.

Chef Duclos and I prepared a great deal of Dover sole and *loup de mer*, a type of striped bass, always over intense heat. We seasoned each piece with salt, pepper, and a dash of peanut oil, then marked it with an exact *quadrillage*, perfect cross-hatched grill lines. We removed the fish after a minute or two, brushed it with melted butter, and finished it in a hot oven. The result had a taste of charcoal yet was never dry or overcooked. In addition to the fish, we grilled lobster and langouste (spiny lobster) and flavored them with herb butter. However, it was the adjacent grill, where the meat was cooked, that was the busiest. *Entrecôte minute* (a thin slice of beef sirloin), filet mignon, *poussin* (a tiny, young chicken), and veal or lamb kidneys — each had to be grilled perfectly in its own time and with a specific intensity of heat.

The veal chops of Chef Duclos were nothing short of perfection. First he seared and marked them on both sides on the grill. Then he browned each one of the four edges, keeping the chop upright by leaning it against a chunk of raw potato, cut so its bottom could be wedged between the bars of the grill.

One of the most important things I learned from working with Chef Duclos was how to deal with the orders as they came in. There were no rules; each cook developed his or her own system. The orders arrived in groups, and as the sous-chef barked them out, the workers in each section had to register and remember their roles in the respective dishes. There could be no mistakes. When the waiter was ready to pick up a dish, it had to be ready or it would set back the table and, with a trickle-down effect, mess up the whole kitchen and dining room.

"Two trout, rack of lamb, chicken," the sous-chef announced. Immediately, two dozen cooks took note. In the vegetable department someone started the appropriate side dishes. A *commis* in the *garde-manger* cleaned the fish, trimmed the lamb, selected a chicken, and ran them to the appropriate stations, sliding for the last ten or fifteen feet across the sawdust-strewn floor. *Sauciers* corrected the individual sauces needed. It was organized chaos, but somehow synchronized. That table's orders, involving dozens of individual tasks, would arrive at the pass at the same instant, all perfectly prepared. I loved it. I felt invincible. Often, in the middle of lunch or dinner, the ordering, the cooking, and the plating of food became so rushed and so frantic that it gave me a high. Barked orders imprinted themselves in my brain automatically, even if I was simultaneously plating one dish while sautéing food for another. As the orders came in, I set out reminders for myself, an empty skillet on the stove, a clean plate in the middle of the cutting board, or a piece of parchment paper on the table, some memory jogger to tell me that I had a trout with almond to put in that skillet in a half hour, that a pilaf of rice and mussels was to go on that plate, and that the parchment paper was to become a papillote, or paper casing, for a veal chop that I'd have to start preparing ten minutes before the trout in order for the dishes to come out at precisely the same time.

SOMEHOW, a year passed. The List appeared, and I found opposite my name the words "first *commis*." If a second *commis* is the buck private of a kitchen brigade, a first *commis* is more like a lieutenant, someone who has survived a few battles, who remains calm under fire, and who has earned a measure of trust. Before my second year was out, I had attained what was considered the ultimate first *commis* posting: the sauce. To be considered a great *saucier* was the highest accolade a cook could receive. The subtlety, intricacy, and lightness of a sauce could make a dish.

Stock is the basic ingredient of most sauces, and stock was critically important at Le Plaza's sauce station. Back in Bourg-en-Bresse, the only stocks Chef Jauget used were brown and white chicken stocks. For the brown stock, the chicken bones were roasted to a brown color in the oven before they were tossed into the stockpot, whereas for a white stock the roasting was omitted. In addition to these, we made white veal stock, white fish stock, and white beef stock for consommé at Le Plaza. Sometimes we reduced the white fish stock, usually made from sole, to a syrup to make an essence, or *glace,* to finish sauces for fish. We made brown lamb stock and brown veal stock that we reduced by half and lightly thickened for a *demi-glace.* The *demi-glace* had no salt and was basically fatless and fairly mild, so it was perfectly adaptable to various dishes. It took on the taste of a *bordelaise* with a reduction of red wine; of a *périgueux* with truffles and Madeira; or a *chasseur* with tomatoes, white wine, and tarragon.

A slight variation in seasoning, viscosity, reduction, or cooking time could make the difference between an average and a superlative sauce. Some sauces, such as veal and chicken velouté and béchamel, had to be cooked slowly for two to three hours to stabilize them so they would not break down when used to finish specific dishes. If a reduced veal stock had achieved the right taste and color but its consistency was still a shade thin, it was pulled off the fire and thickened with arrowroot so that it did not become too potent and had the proper consistency.

These stocks and sauces played an indispensable role in every dish, either as a thickener or as a flavoring agent. For example, creamed spinach, fresh spinach sautéed in butter and seasoned with nutmeg, salt, and pepper, with cream added, was brought to the right consistency with a tablespoon of precooked béchamel. A seemingly simple dish such as fillet of sole cooked with white wine and shallots might require three sauces: a fish velouté to give it the proper texture, a fish *glace*, a dash of hollandaise, and sometimes, a bit of whipped cream, if the fish was to be glazed under the broiler. There was a strict order to follow, but within that structure the talent of the chef could come through.

After we had boiled the beef and poultry bones long enough to be strained for stock — twelve hours — we would re-wet them, a technique called *remouillage*. We then simmered them again for another five to six hours. We strained the second liquid through the finest *chinois* (strainer), then reduced it to make a *glace de viande*. The *glace* was the color of caramel and had the consistency of heavy syrup when hot but was hard as a block of rubber when cold. Like the demi-glace, it had no salt and no fat, but it was very potent. It had transcended the level of a sauce and become a flavoring agent. The *glace* was the secret weapon of the cooks, an alchemist's gold that would transform an ordinary veal chop into three-star fare.

As first *commis* in the sauce department, I had the responsibility of producing the *glace de viande*. I inevitably made too much for the needs of the house, and I sold the extra to caterers in les Halles, sharing the profit with the *chef saucier.* This was an accepted part of kitchen tradition — a special bonus for the all-important *saucier* and his lieutenant.

WITH SO MANY young chefs between the ages of eighteen and twenty-five toiling under the same roof, there were a lot of pranks played at Le Plaza. Our chief dupe was an old fellow named Félix Séoul, known to us le père Félix. Because of his long years of service, he worked outside the hierarchy of the brigade. Père Félix was a living culinary encyclopedia. He had worked with Escoffier and had an amazing memory of the hundreds of garnishes in classical cuisine. Whenever there was a discussion among *commis* as to the composition of a dish, Père Félix was called upon to arbitrate and resolve the argument. He was infallible.

Père Félix loved red wine and regularly consumed a bit too much, becoming tipsy by the end of the night, when he was responsible for writing down the inventory of the walk-in icebox. Near-sighted as well as pleasantly drunk, the old man shambled into the fridge and scrupulously counted beef tenderloins and jars of cream left for the next day. Then he wobbled out, jotted this information on a sheet of paper, and reentered the fridge to check on other items. As soon as he was out of sight, one of us erased what he had just written on his list. Eventually, he emerged from the icebox, squinted at his list, shook his head in puzzlement, and went back into the box to work on his inventory again. Whenever he left his glasses on the table, we snatched them, coated them with our beautiful, clear aspic, and returned them to the table.

When he reached the age of sixty-five, rather than retiring, Père Félix became the head chef of Le Plaza's employee kitchen, a position of high honor and respect. In his new position as our *communard,* the name given to the staff's cook, Père Félix was always cheerful and ready to prepare a special omelet or piece of chicken for one of us, and cook it as carefully as he would have for the most important VIP at Le Plaza. It was well executed, polished fare, the only way he knew to cook.

I may have been the highest-ranking first *commis* in one of the best restaurants in the world, but like any chef, I was still perfectly capable of producing a culinary disaster. Fortunately, one of the worst of these happened well out of the sight of M. Diat. On my days off I worked — usually thanks to the Société — in an incredible array of restaurants from the Salvation Army's soup kitchen to the three-star Maxim's. The short stays were unbeatable experiences. Arriving at a restaurant at 9:00 A.M., I was sent to one department or another by the chef and, within seconds, was working to earn my day's pay. There was no time to get accustomed to the habits of the house or acquainted with fellow workers. One day I worked the rotisserie, the next the fish department, and the next the *garde-manger.*

Passing through so many kitchens, I acquired taste memory. I identified each restaurant by specific smells, looks, and tastes: the lobster soufflé at Le Plaza Athénée, the whitefish at L'Hôtel d'Albion, the crayfish gratin at Le Grand Hôtel de l'Europe. All had some peculiarity, some flavor, some aroma. These tastes went beyond recipes; there was a *tour de main,* a sleight of hand, and a spirit in each dish that made it unique.

The Bible of all these tasks was *Le Répertoire de la cuisine,* a pocket book measuring seven by five inches and less that one-half inch thick. I still use it today. First published by Gringoire and Saulnier in 1914, it contains more than seven thousand recipes. All the known garnishes used in the professional pre–nouvelle French kitchen cuisine are there. The recipes are usually explained or defined in one line — an elliptical set of chefs' crib notes: "*Armenonville.* Artichoke bottom, *cocotte* potatoes, *concassé* tomatoes, and string beans." When confronted with an unknown or forgotten recipe, I pulled *Le Répertoire* surreptitiously from my pocket and consulted it before I started ordering the ingredients needed for the dish.

These shifts as an extra were great learning experiences, but they could lead to colossal mishaps. I spent a couple of days once at Fouquet's, the famous restaurant at the corner of the Champs-

Elysées and avenue George V. The chef sent me to the fish department as first *commis*. There the *chef de partie* ordered me to make hollandaise. I put forty egg yolks and a cup of cold water into a sturdy saucepan and started beating the mixture on the stove. I was terrified of overcooking the yolks and ending up with scrambled eggs, so I kept sliding the saucepan from the hot center to the cool side, whisking furiously to achieve the desired frothy texture without curdling the eggs. I did not give the yolks enough heat, and the mixture started foaming and rising in my pan, finally overflowing onto the stove. At this point, I added clarified butter, but instead of turning the mixture velvety and creamy, it liquefied it into a mess.

~~~~~

BY MODERN STANDARDS, the fare we produced daily at Le Plaza seems rich, arcane, and overly ornate. But this was nothing to the baroque feasts the brigade was capable of producing when M. Diat decided that the theme of a dinner should hark back to the culinary extremes of nineteenth-century classic French cuisine. M. Dupré, the owner of Le Plaza, ordered just such a meal when he invited a hundred of his friends, which was to say *le tout Paris,* to a banquet to celebrate the Prix de l'Arc de Triomphe, France's answer to the Kentucky Derby, Preakness, and Belmont rolled into one. Our formally attired guests seated themselves in a private salon and started with a truffled consommé, followed by lobster *en Bellevue,* which technically should consist of medallions of lobster meat decorated with truffles and glazed with shellfish aspic. But M. Diat had wanted the presentation of the dish to take the form of an underwater still life. Lobster shells were positioned atop rounds of bread shaped to imitate rocks on the ocean floor. *Barquettes* (boat-shaped pastry shells) filled with smoked salmon mousse, artichoke bottoms stuffed with red beet purée, eggs mimosa (stuffed eggs), and croustades of foie gras were arranged at the base of the rocks to resemble colorful corals, anemones, and other bottom-dwelling lifeforms.

M. Diat chose pheasant *en volière* (in aviary) as the main course. The presentation called for us to create a true-to-life diorama worthy of a major natural history museum. Each pheasant would appear to be tending two nests, one full of eggs, one cradling newly hatched chicks. As a first step, Chef Duclos had slowly dried the colorful male pheasants' tails, heads, and wings, with feathers still attached, in an oven, and then secured them with large wood skewers into roasted loaves of bread, to reconstruct the bird. He placed a hot roasted pheasant on the bread in the center of the feather decorations. Surrounding the pheasant were nests made of waffled potatoes and straw potatoes secured on small bread pedestals. We filled the nests of waffled potatoes with small *pommes soufflées* (potato soufflés), imitating eggs, and the nests of straw potatoes with roasted ortolans, which are tiny, fatty buntings, each about the size of a chickadee.

As a sweet finale, M. Diat had the kitchen make *ananas voilé en surprise,* a "veiled pineapple surprise." The pastry cooks filled whole hollowed pineapples with pineapple sherbet, arranged them on rolling tables, and surrounded them with slices of fresh pineapple macerated in sugar and kirschwasser. They piled apples, peaches, bananas — all made of brown sugar — between the pineapples and draped ethereal strands of pulled sugar, known as angel hair, over all. Lights in the base of the tables gave the sugar an incandescent glow.

Having access to an expertly staffed (and free of charge) dining room was only one of the many perks that came with working at Le Plaza Athénée. I didn't earn a lot of money, much less than I would have made cranking out pig's feet at a neighborhood bistro. Most months, I spent my entire paycheck within a few days of collecting it. But I was rich in other ways. In addition to having five weeks of vacation a year, we received not one, but one and a half days off a week. Medical and dental care were paid for, and Le Plaza employed a full-time nurse to tend to minor illnesses and to treat the inevitable cuts and burns of our trade. The hotel gave us uniforms, and we had spacious and clean rooms in which to shower and change. We could play on Le Plaza's soccer and basketball teams or paddle a little canoe reserved for our use down by the Seine.

To me the biggest perk of all was that we had access to Le Plaza's private library, whose shelves bulged with the best in classic and modern literature and philosophy. One of the older *commis,* Lucien Vergé, befriended me and became something of an informal tutor, suggesting books that I should read and inviting me to join in serious discussions with a group of young people who gathered nightly at the cafés.

Decked out in tailor-made suits that cost far more than I could rightfully afford, I became a regular at the "in" spots. One evening at Café Cyrano in place Blanche, an older guy asked if we minded his taking a vacant seat at our table. There was nothing unusual in this. Nor was there anything out of the ordinary in his immediately joining the conversation, which concerned a play we'd recently seen. Our newfound companion was a wonderful addition to the table. Not only did he spring for drinks (always welcome), but he spoke eloquently and knowledgeably about all aspects of the theater. He seemed to know everybody who was anybody. I listened to him, transfixed.

Too transfixed. It soon became obvious that he misunderstood my intentions. During a lull in the conversation, he brushed my arm and quietly suggested that we depart together. I begged off, and the evening progressed with the same engrossing conversation and steady flow of wine.

On the way back to the room I kept in a small hotel on rue des Abbesses in Montmartre, I commented to a friend about the stranger.

"He knew everything about the theater," I said.

"You don't who that was?"

I shrugged.

"That," my friend said, "was Jean Genêt."

Café Cyrano was a far cry from the lecture halls at the Sorbonne, but I was picking up an education. I became a voracious reader, an avid participant in late-night philosophical conversations. True, my motives were not always pure. I liked to show off a bit, particularly when a couple of girls joined us. At some level I was overcompensating. I felt embarrassed that I had so little formal education.

A good number of the girls who befriended us were hookers, anxious to spend some no-strings-attached time with boys their own age by watching a movie or going dancing. They had a lot more disposable income than we did and no qualms about picking up the tab. These encounters were usually but not always platonic.

All in all, I was working hard and living well. Life was good until my concierge handed me an official-looking letter: my draft notice.

Gnocchi à la Romaine

(ROMAN GNOCCHI)

YIELD: 4 SERVINGS

*A*LTHOUGH MOST PEOPLE associate gnocchi with the Italian kitchen, *gnocchi à la parisienne* (little dumplings made with choux paste) and *gnocchi à la romaine,* made from *semoule des blé dur,* called *semolina* in Italian, were standards on the menu of Le Plaza Athénée. I still love semolina gnocchi and make them a few times a year for family and friends. They make a great starter to a meal and are just as good as an accompaniment with poultry or veal.

> 2 cups whole milk
> 3/4 teaspoon salt
> 1/4 teaspoon freshly ground black pepper
>   Dash of grated nutmeg
> 1/2 cup semolina (granulated hard durum wheat flour)
> 2 large eggs
>
> 1 teaspoon good olive oil
> 3/4 cup grated Comté or Gruyère cheese (2 ounces)
> 1/4 teaspoon salt
> 1/4 teaspoon freshly ground black pepper
> 1/2 cup heavy cream

Bring 1 3/4 cups of the milk to a boil in a medium saucepan with the salt, pepper, and nutmeg. As soon as the milk boils, pour the semolina into it in a steady stream while mixing it in with a whisk. Reduce the heat to low, and cook for 1 to 2 minutes, stirring occasionally with the whisk. The mixture should be very thick and smooth.

Meanwhile, break the eggs into a small bowl, add the remaining ¼ cup milk, and beat with a fork until smooth. Add to the semolina in the pan, and mix in well with a whisk. Cook and stir for about 30 seconds, until very thick. Set aside while you line a 9-×-6-inch baking dish with plastic wrap, so the ends overhang the sides of the dish. Pour the mixture into it, and using the plastic wrap liner, press on the dough so that it is about ¾ inch thick. Let cool.

Preheat the oven to 425 degrees. Cut the cold gnocchi dough into 3-inch squares (you will have 6 squares), oil a gratin dish with the teaspoon of oil, and arrange the gnocchi in the dish, leaving a little space between them. Sprinkle the grated cheese, salt, and pepper on top, and bake for about 15 minutes, until lightly browned and hot. Remove from the oven, and move the oven shelf 6 to 8 inches from the heat source. Pour the cream over the gnocchi, and return the dish to the oven. Immediately switch the oven setting to broil, and broil the gnocchi for about 5 minutes, or until nicely browned on top. Serve.

7

Cooking for Presidents

IN THE SPACE of a few weeks, Jacques Pépin, first *commis* at Le Plaza Athénée and would-be boulevardier, became Jacques Pépin, sailor third class. The French navy, mindful of the morale-boosting role that good food could play in alleviating the dreariness of months spent at sea, was always on the lookout for professional chefs and had a friendly arrangement with la Société des cuisiniers de Paris. The Société alerted the navy whenever a professional chef was about to be drafted, and somehow the navy found a way to bend its usual volunteer-only policy.

With my tailor-made suits replaced by olive green fatigues and my Jean-Paul Belmondo–like locks trimmed to a uniform half-inch brush cut, I joined hundreds of other young men for ten weeks of basic training in Hourtin, a small town and navy base in the southwest of France near Bordeaux. At the time, France was involved in the Algerian War, a bloody, unwinnable military quagmire. The enemy was tenacious, fighting on its own soil and often invisible among the civilian population. Thousands of young French soldiers were dying in the deserts of North Africa.

Every morning before dawn — the hour at which I had once gaily made my way home from the cafés — we rolled out of our hammocks and ran for five miles through the gloomy pine plantations that line the coast in that part of France. An hour of push-ups, sit-ups, and chin-ups followed. Then more running. And when that was over, more calisthenics. I was miserable.

The time came for us to receive immunizations for who-knows-what dreaded desert diseases. Their symptoms must have been truly awful to justify the pain inflicted by those veterinary-grade stainless steel syringes wielded by an assembly line of sadistic medics. My shoulder still throbbed the next day when our drill sergeant lined us up and asked if anyone in the regiment knew how to drive. Two recruits stepped forward, no doubt expecting that their prowess behind the wheel would get them out of a morning on the obstacle course. Smiling, the sergeant pointed toward two shovels.

"Clean out the shithouse," he said. And thereby he imparted the two most important military lessons of all: keep your head low, volunteer for nothing.

Years in various kitchens had kept me in surprisingly good shape, which turned out to be a mixed blessing. I passed all aspects of my physical training and was deemed worthy to serve both aboard ships and in the navy's land-based commando units, meaning that the sands of Algeria were very likely to be my next stop.

The only blot in my near-perfect boot camp record came completely by surprise. Despite my professional status, I had to pass the official navy cook's exam. True to the spirit of bureaucracies everywhere, the test was given by a petty officer (*petty* being an especially appropriate word) who fancied himself a professional cook. He ordered me to prepare eggs *bénédictine*. I had prepared this dish in most of the restaurants where I had worked. The versions served at Le Meurice, Le Plaza, and La Maxéville were basically the same: a poached egg placed on a toasted slice of brioche lined with ham, napped with hollandaise sauce, and, as a final touch on top, a slice of black truffle. I had made eggs *bénédictine* dozens if not hundreds of times, without a word of complaint from the most discriminating palates in the world.

The petty officer took one look at my preparation and snorted. "You call yourself a cook?" he said. "Everyone knows eggs *bénédictine* calls for poached eggs to be served with a purée of salted codfish and a cream sauce."

Salted codfish? Cream sauce? I had never heard of that version and never met a cook who prepared eggs *bénédictine* that way. The petty officer had found this archaic variation of the dish, viewed as a quaint curiosity by all professionals, in my precious Escoffier's *Le Guide culinaire*. It was a trap, but the damage was done. I flunked. Algeria beckoned.

I was spared that fate, thanks to my brother Roland.

Following the slaughter of an entire family of brothers, the government had enacted a policy that prohibited draftees from the same family from serving in Algeria at the same time. Roland had been called into the air force and was part of the ground crew at a base near Algiers. So I was assigned to go to Paris, where I was to work as a cook for the officers' mess at the Pépinière, the navy's headquarters.

There, I was put under the command of a Breton who must have attended the same cooking school as the guy who had flunked my eggs *bénédictine*. But my failure in boot camp was forgotten the moment my new boss heard that I had worked at Le Plaza Athénée. He knew as much about cooking as I knew about skippering a destroyer, but like so many talentless bureaucrats, he had a cockroach-like sense of survival. He realized that he needed young draftee-chefs who had been properly trained in the great houses and restaurants of Paris to cook the quality food demanded in the Admiralty mess — cooking that he, of course, took complete credit for.

Left on his own, he would have been put on a troop transport ship destined for Algeria before the officers finished his first soup course. He needed us desperately to make him look good, but his dependency on us made him resentful of our ease in the kitchen and our familiarity with the big city and its ways. A small, rotund man with piercing, porcine eyes and a pointed nose, he always wore a wary scowl. In him the Napoleon complex was carried to perfection, especially when he had imbibed too much of the ordinary red wine at the canteen, a daily ritual.

He rarely ventured near the stove. But once, when he had had more than his usual allotment of wine, he became confident enough to butt into a discussion we were having about the precise way to prepare the mousseline sauce that was going to accompany a dish of asparagus. A classic mousseline is light and frothy, made with hollandaise sauce combined with whipped cream.

"Mousseline sauce," he slurred. "What do you sissies know about mousseline sauce?" He stood behind the stove, flicked his wrists, and proceeded to cook the asparagus in a rusty iron pan. Instead of throwing the spears into rapidly boiling salted water, he dropped them casually into barely hot, unsalted water. After a few minutes, the beautifully green asparagus started to turn a faded khaki color. I covered my mouth and barely succeeded in suppressing a laugh.

After draining the spears, he used the same pan for his sauce, first placing some fat and flour in the bottom of it and cooking them, then adding water to make a thick glue, which turned beige when he deglazed his pan of its rust deposits. Whistling tunelessly, he added a dozen eggs, brought the mixture to a boil, and kept it on the heat long enough for the eggs to scramble nicely. Finally, he folded the slop into egg whites that were already grainy from overbeating. The entire mixture liquefied into a lumpy, brownish soup, which he proceeded to ladle over the asparagus, proclaiming, *"Voilà!"*

The laugh could no longer be suppressed. It burst from me, and of course that got the two other chefs going.

Those little eyes for a moment looked crestfallen. But then they became mean. I knew I was permanently on my superior's bad side. The lessons of my doomed relationship with old Chef Cram-pette had taught me that this was a situation that could only deteri-orate. I had to find a way to get out of his kitchen. Fast.

THE FIRST INKLING that perhaps I had a military career as a chef beyond the Pépinière came one afternoon when a fellow dressed in the uniform of a sailor third class stopped by the kitchen. The other draftees greeted him warmly and began to make small talk.

"Hey, Jacques," said one of my comrades. "This is Georges Roussillon. He used to work here before he got too good for the likes of us."

"You got that right," said the newcomer, winking. He stuck out his hand. "Good to meet you. Don't listen to these clowns."

"Gave that up a long time ago," I said.

"Wise move. So how you like working for Brittany's answer to Escoffier?"

"I try to keep reminding myself it's better than Algeria."

Georges poured himself a cup of coffee. "So where were you before you got drafted?"

I gave him a thirty-second biography, which ended with my saying that I had come to Paris from Lyon, where my mother ran a restaurant.

Georges brightened. "I thought I recognized the accent. I'm from Lyon, too. Did my apprenticeship there and worked there until I was called up. Used to cook here, but someone must have been watching over me. I got assigned to be the private chef of the secretary of the Treasury."

"I'd kill for a posting like that," I said.

Georges thought for a moment and smiled faintly.

A few days later the Breton commander accosted me, obvi-ously angry. "Report to the secretary of the Treasury's kitchen im-mediately," he said, trying to make it sound as if the order was coming directly from him. "They need extra help there today for a banquet tonight."

The Office of the Treasury was, and still is, on the rue de Rivoli in the former Palais Royal. One aisle of the palace overlooks the Seine and houses the Louvre. The other aisle accommodates the Treasury department within magnificent apartments that once belonged to French kings. The kitchen I wandered into was certainly fit for a king. It was constructed of enormous stones, had a vaulted ceiling resplendent with royal fleurs-de-lis, and had been built to house more than 150 cooks. But the place hadn't been updated since Louis XVI was beheaded. Georges had succeeded in turning a corner of this huge place into a somewhat modern, efficient workspace, where he officiated in chef's clothes, not a navy uniform. And that was only one of the job's perks. He could live in his own room in Paris, coming to work each morning and returning each night just like a civilian, only getting into uniform once a month to go over to the Pépinière to collect his paycheck. His typical workload was preparing simple lunches and dinners for six to ten people.

Georges labored under one disadvantage. As skilled as he was, he was still a regional chef who had never worked in Paris or in any high-class restaurant. He had been assigned to his lofty position without being consulted and was the first to admit that aside from the provincial cooking he had done in Lyon in a couple of family restaurants, he had no knowledge of classic French cuisine. He was at a loss when he had to prepare a special banquet or a meal for dignitaries from other countries.

"I'll tell you what, Jacques," he said. "You want to get out of the Pépinière. I need someone with classical experience to help out here full time. I'll get you transferred."

"Our Breton friend will never let me go. Might mean he'd have to learn to cook. He was mad enough about my coming here for one banquet."

"Is that so," said Georges.

Later I learned that the request for a specific chef — me — went from Georges directly to the secretary of the Treasury, who buttonholed someone at the Admiralty, who passed word down the line until it reached my commander at the Pépinière. He all but fell over himself in an effort to comply when he learned that the order had come from on high. Thanks to Georges, I'd escaped.

Paul Ramadier was the secretary of the Treasury at the time. He was an old, large, garrulous man — how Walter Matthau would have turned out if he'd been a French public servant. Despite his façade of perpetual grumpiness, M. Ramadier was well liked by the employees, even though his only means of addressing his staff (or wife, for that matter) was in a tone somewhere between a growl and a bark. Our duty consisted of serving lunch and dinner to the minister and his family, along with any guests they might invite, which occurred four or five times a week. We shopped at the local markets on rues St. Honoré and St. Roch each morning, purchasing fresh, fine products.

That summer, Georges was released from the armed services. I found myself in the right place at the right time. Not wanting to mess with a good thing, particularly something as important as the food he ate, the secretary retained me. I was given Georges's job and was able to wear civilian clothes again, to my delight, and moved back to my small room at 48, rue Pierre Charron, in the center of Paris. I had responsibilities but was allowed to do as I pleased in my work without military supervision and was master of my free time.

Georges had never really adjusted to life in Paris. He made it clear to me that as soon as his stint in the armed services was over, he was going to return to his roots in Lyon where all he wanted was to resume cooking the food he loved: good, straightforward, regional fare. But he didn't have a job lined up. I was able to return Georges's favor of rescuing me from the dreaded Pépinière by pulling a few modest strings of my own. Through connections back home, I found him a position at a busy little place in the city that provided just the sort of work atmosphere he craved and whose owner desperately needed the services of an energetic young chef. I was even able to put in a good word for Georges with the proprietress, a woman named Jeanne Pépin.

~~

UNDER THE Fourth Republic, governments rapidly replaced one another. It's a testament to the shakiness of the regime at that time that being a chef gave me far more job security than my cabinet minister bosses had. But regardless of whether their persuasion was socialist, liberal, or conservative, these guys all loved to eat, and most of them were used to eating very well indeed. A few weeks after I came to help Georges at the Treasury, the government changed and Félix Gaillard became the secretary of the Treasury.

The dishes I served were classics that I interpreted in the traditional fashion. Gradually, however, I began to impart nuance to each dish without straying from the strict recipe or altering its classical status.

Four months later, the government, headed by Guy Mollet, toppled, and my boss, Gaillard, was suddenly the prime minister of France. And I was suddenly France's "First Chef." Not that I had any time to savor my lofty new position. I got the news early in the morning, when one of Gaillard's assistants came into the kitchen and told me that I had to get over to L'Hôtel Matignon, residence of the prime minister, and have lunch for six ready within the hour. I ran out to the markets, which, fortunately, were good and plentiful in that neighborhood. In a completely unfamiliar kitchen, I threw together a lunch of thick veal chops, which I pan-fried in butter and shallots; a thin *galette* (a flat cake) of raw potatoes sautéed with mushrooms; and a Boston lettuce salad, followed by cheeses. It was a simple lunch, but it was my first meal as chef to the leader of my country.

Matignon, which is still the residence of the French prime

minister, is located on the Left Bank at 57, rue de Varennes, a beautiful street lined with old residences. The kitchen was small, efficient, and modern, and I had only a helper-dishwasher with me. Carême, the greatest French chef of the nineteenth century, worked in the same kitchen, where he prepared the most elaborate dinners served during the reign of Napoleon Bonaparte. Napoleon himself reportedly gulped down his meals while standing. Although he liked Chambertin, the great wine of Burgundy, he diluted it with water. He had so little interest in cooking or in entertaining that he assigned his ministers, Talleyrand, the famous diplomat, and Cambacérès, who devised the French code of law, the task of hosting the state banquets.

Even though his place of business was Matignon, Prime Minister Gaillard, who had a vast personal fortune, spent most nights and evenings at his own splendid mansion on avenue Foch near l'Arc de Triomphe, where he employed another chef and household staff. I cooked lunch for the president, but most dinners were prepared for a man I knew only as M. Aicardi, his cabinet director and one of the president's key advisers. M. Aicardi lived in the presidential quarters, and the dignitaries he'd been assigned to entertain dined with him.

Aicardi was a short, jovial man, somewhat of a hedonist and certainly a gourmand. He loved food passionately and had dined at the best tables of Paris. He knew that I had worked at Le Plaza Athénée, and one day he asked me to reproduce a jellied beef dish, *le boeuf daube en gelée*, which was a specialty of Le Plaza. He loved it, which turned out to be a mixed blessing. True, it was nice to be liked and respected by my superior. But when Aicardi saw what I could do in the kitchen, his demands grew. He kept asking for more and more complicated dishes. I had to comply.

I should have known that potential trouble lay ahead when he asked me to provide him with some cookbooks. Except for my dog-eared little *Répertoire,* I possessed no cookbooks, so I was delighted to oblige and acquired two large, lavishly illustrated volumes, one by Henri Paul Pellaprat and one by Curnonsky (whose real name was Maurice Edmond Sailland). Pellaprat was the founder of the Cordon Bleu school of cooking in Paris, and he taught there for more than thirty years. In 1935, he published one of his largest and best books, entitled *L'Art culinaire moderne.* My second pick was *Cuisine et vins de France* by Curnonsky. A famous gastronome and author, Curnonsky was elected "prince of gastronomy" by a jury of chefs, caterers, cookbook authors, and famous gourmands in 1927. One of the first traveling epicures, he was known for a series of small books published yearly and called *France gastronomique.*

Occasionally, M. Aicardi sent for the books and me. He peered in silence at the color plates with great concentration before pointing to a dish — often one that was unusual, expensive, and elaborate — and saying, "This one!"

That is how I ended up preparing a *capon Régence,* which is stuffed with a mousseline of crawfish and garnished with small shells of puff pastry filled with whole cooked truffles and foie gras. This was served with three different small dumplings, one green (flavored with herbs), one red (flavored with chopped tongue), and one black (flavored with chopped truffles).

One Sunday, M. Aicardi was felled by a severe attack of gout. He called for me, and I went up to his sickbed to take his order for dinner. He requested *les oeufs du Périgord* to start. Created to resemble giant black truffles, *les oeufs du Périgord* consisted of spheres of goose liver pâté the size of Ping-Pong balls, rolled in finely chopped black truffles, glazed with a translucent meat aspic, and presented in an elaborate edible basket. The base of the basket was a large slab of raw potato. To make the "wicker," I poked raw spaghetti into the outside edge of the slab to create the vertical ribs and wove thin ribbons of potato through them. I then fried the basket, cooled it, and filled it with my glazed "eggs." This recipe represented hours of work. M. Aicardi ate three entire basketsful, followed by a poached salmon trout served with mousseline. A salad and cheeses were served next, and he finished with a rice pudding garnished with steamed fruits. No wonder the poor man had gout!

And no wonder that I started to feel overwhelmed cooking everything from first courses to desserts for M. Aicardi every day. I needed help in the worst way and approached my commanding officer.

"I need someone," I said. "I'm getting more and more work and I'm alone here."

He seemed unimpressed.

"If the situation gets worse, the quality is going to suffer," I said.

That got his attention. Like most members of the household staff, he had a direct interest in the quality of my leftovers. "I'll see what I can do," he said.

"It would be great if the guy was a pastry chef," I said. It didn't hurt to try.

C~~

WHEN I FIRST saw my new associate, I thought I had been made the butt of somebody's joke. Or had someone in the military bureaucracy completely screwed things up, as usual? I'd asked for a chef. The gawky kid who slunk into the kitchen looked more like a recently drafted poet, and a starving one at that. He had delicate features and a full head of hair, and he was skinny to the point of being skeletal. His army recruit's khaki uniform was so stiff and new that it could well have been donned for the very first time that morning.

He gave a nervous salute and stammered, "Reporting for —"

"Sit down, my friend," I said, trying to get the poor guy to lighten up a bit. "Tell me where you're from."

"I honestly don't understand why they sent me here," he said. "I mean, the prime minister's . . ."

I wanted to do something, anything, to put him at least a little at ease. I gave him a bang on the shoulder. "Don't worry. Things are going to be great."

His name was Jean-Claude Szurdak, and he was a couple of years younger than I was. As he spun out the details of his training, I realized that the commander could not possibly have found a better partner for me in the kitchen. What I first took to be shyness turned out to be soft-spoken reserve. He was actually spirited, quick, and easygoing when you got to know him. True to his looks, Jean-Claude had the sensitivity of an artist. He had completed two full apprenticeships, one in pastry, the other in cooking, at a well-known restaurant north of Paris called L'Aubergade. The two of us created splendid meals.

Ours was a heady position but, paradoxically, in the context of that time, not prestigious in any way. Chefs, even those who worked for the president, were not looked upon as artists. We were employees of the household, important and well liked, for sure, but at the most, artisans. This condition afforded us a certain freedom without the pressures of recognition and the obsession to create, too often the lot of the present generation of chefs.

We had both been taught well and in a very structured way and were comfortable with what we knew. As young chefs, we didn't have elevated opinions of ourselves. We did a *cuisine soignée* (a tasteful, polished cuisine), but we did not try to "create," if creation is understood to be the invention of a dish using techniques and combinations of ingredients not conventionally applied.

Matignon was a terrific training ground for our palates. Preparing the dishes that our bosses demanded was fascinating, time consuming, costly, and practically never done in a restaurant. No one whose livelihood depended upon turning a profit at the end of the month could have afforded the time and expense such dishes required. We were delighted to be in the service of connoisseurs. Once a foreign attaché came back from Russia with two five-pound cans of the best and largest beluga caviar I had ever seen. For several days, we not only served it in a variety of ways but consumed a great amount ourselves, spooning it into our mouths like two kids set loose on a container of ice cream.

Every morning a fresh tray of cheese was delivered from

Androuët, the famous Parisian cheese purveyor. The leftovers, often the entire untouched tray, were given to the employees the following day. When we served oysters, the *écailler* (oyster sheller) from Prunier, the most famous fish restaurant in Paris, arrived with prized green Marennes and his knife. He waited until the guests were seated and — at the last moment and with lightning speed — popped open the oysters and placed them on special plates for immediate serving with dark bread, cold butter, lemon, and, sometimes, shallot pepper sauce.

Typically, the prime minister's banquets were small, with between six and twelve guests, a perfect number. The largest meal Jean-Claude and I cooked was for twenty-eight guests and required several nights and days of preparation. The first course was a braised turbot, served *dieppoise*-style with a garnish of mussels, mushrooms, and tiny shrimp in a cream-cognac sauce. As a main course, we prepared small Prague hams braised in stock and Madeira, baked in puff pastry, and served with a truffle sauce and a *bouquetière* of vegetables. After the salad and the cheese courses came a *parfait au café,* a rich frozen coffee cream. Serving so many guests was unusual, and this was fortunate, because I believe that it is impossible to cook superlatively for more than ten diners.

Occasionally, for very special guests, we would use the government's treasured chinaware and vermeil platters. That old warning, "Don't break the china," took on new meaning for me one evening just before a state dinner. A functionary from the Department of Beaux-Arts came into the kitchen and gently placed a platter in my hands. "Careful," he said with a smirk, "it belonged to Marie Antoinette." He might as well have handed me a bomb. Cradling the platter in my hands, I lowered it to the counter, certain that it would shatter if I so much as looked at it hard. But somehow Marie Antoinette's platter and my nerves both survived the encounter. I won't say that handling national treasures once used by the likes of Mme. de Maintenon, the stern wife of Louis XIV; Mme. de Pompadour, the beautiful mistress of Louis XV; or Marie Antoinette and Louis XVI ever became second nature to me, but after a time my hands stopped shaking.

Circumstances at Matignon frequently put our classical training to the test as we tried to fit the meals we prepared into the busy and sometimes erratic schedules of heads of state such as Eisenhower, Tito, Nehru, and Macmillan. One day I was told to prepare a lunch for British prime minister Harold Macmillan. The first course was to be a poached *barbue,* or brill, a very delicate fish that I intended to cook whole, for carving at the table. It was a cold winter day, and London's Gatwick Airport was fogged in, so the time of the premier's arrival was, to say the least, uncertain. I didn't want to overcook my fish. Therefore, as an act of international culinary diplomacy, I asked the security officer at Matignon, Colonel Ribe, to establish a telephone link with his counterpart at the London airport. Standing in the kitchen, Ribe bent over the telephone receiver, grimaced, and yelled, "Could you repeat that." Grimaced again and said, "Chef, put the fish on. The plane is leaving!" Then, five minutes later, he said, "Remove the fish. The plane is on standby!" I put that dish in the oven and pulled it out several times that morning, based on garbled telephone instructions coming across the English Channel. Yet the end result was a perfectly poached brill.

Working for France's boss of all bosses had some advantages. One morning M. Aicardi came into the kitchen twenty minutes before lunch and offhandedly informed me that the number of guests had doubled. Fortunately, I had enough ingredients for the meal, but I was short of the small, crunchy rolls that we always served.

"I don't have enough bread," I said.

However, as usual, a couple of other members of the premier's household staff were hanging around the kitchen, including a chauffeur, who had frequently benefited from my efforts. He put down his coffee cup and said, "Come along, Chef."

I hopped in the back of a stretch limo bearing the presidential flag and proceeded through the streets of Paris at sixty miles per hour to my favorite bakery. At every intersection, police officers stopped traffic, snapped to attention, and saluted.

In the spring of 1958 France faced its worst crisis in postwar history. Gaillard's government fell. Within less than three weeks, the government formed by his successor, Pierre Pflimlin, also collapsed. The country hovered on the brink of revolution as a junta of disaffected military officers, including General Salan and Colonel Massu, unhappy about the political policy in Algeria, were poised to stage a coup. In this atmosphere, the politicians and people called for the return of General Charles de Gaulle, a national hero who had been head of the provisional government after liberation from Germany until he was pushed out by the Communists.

The crisis reached its peak on the evening of May 12, 1958. Dinner was over, and I was cleaning up in the corner of the kitchen when an aide to one of the cabinet ministers hurried to me. Gesturing toward the president's salon where politicians were negotiating our country's future, he said, "Chef, they're going to be at this all night. They need food. Can you stay?"

It was the longest night of my life, a night when no one knew who would be the leader of France when the sun rose. As French democracy hung in the balance, I did what I had been trained to do. I cooked.

There was plenty in Matignon's larder, from cold meats to cheeses, pâtés, and prosciutto. I began turning out sandwiches. The leaders of the country and representatives of the world's media swallowed my offerings as fast as I could make them. Once, in the early hours of the morning, as someone came in from the salon with an empty tray, I caught a glimpse of the pandemonium and confusion in the room. Fittingly, my vantage point to history-in-the-making was the crack between two swinging kitchen doors.

I was understandably groggy the next morning when Mme. de

Gaulle — called Aunt Yvonne by the entire nation — came into the kitchen and established the pattern that would be followed for the remainder of my stay at Matignon. Although My General (it was always My General, never Mr. President) remained aloof from what he considered trivial issues, such as establishing menus, Aunt Yvonne viewed it as her sworn duty to the nation to protect her husband's health and made that clear to me in her gentle but resolute manner.

"I was thinking of a leg of lamb," I said, when she inquired about dinner.

"That's good. The General loves lamb. But, Chef, you must be certain not to cook it too rare. He likes it rare, but he should not have it that way. It's not good for his blood."

Aunt Yvonne and I met several mornings a week. I usually proposed three menus for each meal; she selected one and provided whatever guidance she felt necessary. I could not have asked for a more gracious supervisor. Aunt Yvonne was a small, immaculately groomed woman, always soft-spoken and unfailingly polite, the perfect foil for her stern, larger-than-life husband. When she was not occupied with the details of her husband's home life, she worked tirelessly for an assortment of charities. No wonder the French loved their Aunt Yvonne.

The General was scrupulously fair-minded and detested favoritism, even when it came to the smooth operation of his household. So when Jean-Claude received orders to report for active duty on the staff of a general based in Oran, Algeria, there was no chance of fixing things so he could stay at Matignon. I said goodbye and good luck to a man who had not only become a trusted colleague but also my best friend.

Nor would I have the opportunity to use the back-door route to finding a qualified replacement for Jean-Claude that I'd used to get him in the first place. In the spirit of equality, de Gaulle insisted that Matignon be treated just like another government kitchen. So instead of sending me a recently drafted chef from a three-star restaurant, the army shipped over a pair of cooks who had learned their trade in small-town cafés and polished their technique in a series of military mess halls. To make matters worse, both of my new associates outranked me. Marcel le Servot was a chief petty officer, Jacques Waki a sergeant. Despite my tenure at Matignon, my rise up the naval ranks had been somewhat less than meteoric. I was a sailor first class, not much higher in rank than I had been on my first day of boot camp. Outranked by the newcomers, I had good reason to fear that my future would mirror my miserable existence under the petty officer back at the Pépinière. Matignon had been nice while it lasted.

The first night I worked with Waki, ostensibly the new pastry chef, he prepared a Bavarian cream, a standard dessert made with a custard cream, whipped cream, and a dash of gelatin. Waki added enough gelatin to make the dessert as firm as a basketball. It was inedible, and we served instead a caramel custard that, fortunately, I had made ahead.

Back at the Pépinière, such a situation would have been my undoing. But when I unveiled my backup dessert, Waki and le Servot smiled with relief. And then the truth came out. They felt overwhelmed to have been plucked from their army kitchens and ordered to cook for the president. They knew enough about cooking to understand the limitations of their skills. And they knew a good posting when they encountered one. They wanted to stay at their new jobs, but they needed me. So, in an ironic twist, they made it clear that even though I was still only an unranked sailor, at Matignon I was Chef. I remained in charge of purchasing, setting up menus, and teaching them the routine and habits of the house. We became friends.

On Sundays, we prepared a special lunch for the General's family. It was a private affair — no politicians, no foreign dignitaries. Just the de Gaulles' children and grandchildren. After attending church, the General and Aunt Yvonne met everyone for apéritifs in the salon and soon moved on to the dining room. The menu changed, but it was always simple, straightforward French cooking. The General was fond of lamb (which I now knew not to cook rare) and hake, which we poached and served warm with a light butter sauce or cold with mayonnaise. Another standard Sunday menu featured a mousse of sole with mushroom and tomato sauce, followed by a veal roast with braised endive or a gratin of turnips and potatoes, a salad, an assortment of cheeses, and, for dessert, a French apple tart or a fruit *coupe*. I kept experimenting. When guests of the General were invited to Rambouillet, the presidential hunting grounds, the kitchen benefited by the arrival of pheasants, grouse, and woodcocks, which we plucked, eviscerated, and dressed. We often accommodated these luscious game birds in pâtés and *salmis* (game stews), in addition to preparing them in roasts and other kinds of stew.

De Gaulle remained aloof from the kitchen. But on special occasions, such as Christmas, he met with Matignon's employees at small, informal gatherings. He was polite, remembering names and acting attentive and concerned. At the same time, he was stately and imposing in stature and voice, which made it difficult to feel completely at ease in his presence.

Although I took orders from Aunt Yvonne for all private meals, for formal government dinners, I dealt with a State Department protocol officer through an attaché to the president. When a foreign dignitary visited, someone on his staff synchronized the menus, so the visitor would not be served the same dishes at different venues. Furthermore, since I was not knowledgeable about the cultural traditions and taboos pertaining to a visiting head of state, the protocol officer ensured that nothing on my menu would give offense. Pork or wine sauces could never be served to a Muslim, nor beef to a Hindu, and shellfish would never appear on a dinner menu for a visiting Israeli. Within these parameters, however, I still served classic French cuisine. I would never have dreamed of making a curried chicken for a visiting Indian politician. His cook could do that much better than I. But I might roast him a wonderful bird from Bresse and season it with a bit of garam masala as a polite measure of congeniality.

The French say, *"L'éxactitude est la politesse des rois"* (Punctuality is the good manners of kings). That summed up de Gaulle. When dinner was scheduled for 8:00 P.M., at precisely 8:00 P.M. he moved to the dining room. Even if some of his guests hadn't arrived, he proceeded with Mme. de Gaulle to the table.

For me this was a happy change. With Gaillard, I had learned to compensate when meals were put on hold sometimes for two hours, which was not always easy. For a lunch starting with a cheese soufflé, a dish that Gaillard was particularly fond of, I had to have one soufflé ready at the appointed time, another ready to go into the oven when the first one showed signs of collapsing, and yet another in the making.

The General also was extremely honest — to the point of punctiliousness — in dealing with the budget allocated to the kitchen. My expenses were spelled out in a ledger, which I presented twice a month to a member of the cabinet to obtain money to pay my suppliers. However, under the General's orders, I had to keep a special account for the Sunday family meal because the expenses incurred for these were paid for from his personal fund. Even though he was not wealthy, he felt that the Sunday meal was his own responsibility. For de Gaulle, it was a question of ethics.

~~~

DESPITE HAVING SPENT nearly two years as chef for the head of state, I still preserved traces of my old mischievous self, especially when a ready audience and an opportunity too good to ignore presented themselves. One afternoon a chambermaid came into the kitchen with a pile of the General's clothes that were going out to be cleaned. Called away on another errand, she left the bundle on a counter. I promptly slipped into his shoes, hat, and greatcoat. It was quite a sight: at six foot four or five, the General was nearly a foot taller than I, so his coattails dragged on the floor; he had size fourteen feet, to my size eights; yet his head was so tiny that his hat perched on top of my mine like a precariously balanced demitasse.

I'm sure some official regulation forbids kitchen help from giving guided tours of the General's personal quarters, but when word reached me that my father was coming to Paris for the first and only time, the urge to show off a bit in front of the Old Man was too great to resist. The main reason Papa had made the journey to the city was to take in an international rugby championship game, but he did come by Matignon, and I was able to give him a full tour of the mansion. It was fun, and I'm sure he was impressed and proud of me and that he bragged about his visit to his friends back in Lyon. Yet as he walked down the sidewalk toward the Métro, Papa looked small. I had grown, and he had shrunk somewhat. The dynamic between us would never be the same.

A FEW DAYS before I was to be discharged from the military — and end my stint as Chef for the presidents — Charles, the maitre d' at Matignon, came into the kitchen. I was in the middle of preparing dinner, so I barely paid attention until I heard him saying, "The General and Madame would like to see you in their quarters after dinner."

I was so stunned, I nearly dropped a plated turbot. Me? Their personal quarters? This was unheard of.

Still dressed in my chef's whites, I approached the General and Aunt Yvonne after dinner. They thanked me for the quality of my work and wished me their best. With a gentle expression on his face, one of the most important leaders in the history of France shook my hand and then handed me a cigar.

"Good fortune and happiness to you," he said. "Smoke that to my health."

Gigot à la Provençale

(ROAST LEG OF LAMB PROVENÇAL)

YIELD: 8 TO 10 SERVINGS

A ROAST LEG of lamb is the typical centerpiece for a Sunday family lunch in France. I often served this classic to French president Charles de Gaulle, who after church on Sunday would always share his dominical lunch *en famille,* with his children and grandchildren. We used a *pré-salé* leg of lamb, a term that refers to lambs that graze on a salted marsh near the sea in Normandy. These small *gigots* were incomparable in taste. I often served this roast with a gratin made of potatoes, a touch of garlic, cream, milk, and cheese, which is called *gratin dauphinois.*

1 small leg of lamb (about 5 pounds), trimmed of most visible fat and with the pelvis bone removed (4 pounds trimmed weight)

2 tablespoons butter, softened

¹/₂ teaspoon salt

¹/₂ teaspoon freshly ground black pepper

TOPPING

1 cup (lightly packed) fresh flat-leaf parsley leaves

2 garlic cloves, peeled and coarsely crushed

2 shallots, peeled and thinly sliced

4 slices good white bread (4 ounces)

2 tablespoons good olive oil

About ¹/₃ cup water

Preheat the oven to 425 degrees. Rub the leg of lamb with the butter, and sprinkle it with the salt and pepper. Place in a roasting pan top side up, and bake for 20 minutes.

FOR THE TOPPING: Meanwhile, put the parsley, garlic, shallots, and bread into a food processor, and process just enough to finely chop all the ingredients, or chop them by hand. Transfer to a bowl, and mix in the olive oil, gently tossing it with the other topping ingredients until the bread mixture is coated. (This will help hold the topping together on the roast, and the oil makes the bread crumbs brown beautifully.)

After the lamb has baked for 20 minutes, tilt the pan, and use the fat that collects on one side to baste the lamb. Pat the crumb mixture gently but firmly over the top and sides of the lamb to make it adhere.

Return the lamb to the oven, and reduce the heat to 400 degrees. Cook for another 30 minutes or so, or until the internal temperature registers 125 to 130 degrees for medium-rare meat. Transfer the lamb to an ovenproof platter, and keep it warm in a 150-degree oven. It should rest for 15 to 20 minutes before carving.

Meanwhile, pour the water into the pan, and stir well with a wooden spatula to melt the solidified juices and mix the water with the drippings. Slice the lamb and serve it with these natural juices.

8

Home Again

IT IS NOT ENTIRELY ACCURATE to say that I returned to Le Plaza Athénée after my stint in the military. I had never really left. In keeping with its tradition of providing chefs with the finest fringe benefits in the business, the hotel allowed cooks who had been drafted to remain as members of the greater Plaza Athénée "family." Although our salaries stopped, we were welcome to play on the hotel's sports teams, borrow books from its library, and drop by the employees' dining room for meals.

Over the years, I struck up a friendship with the executive pastry chef, a soft-spoken man in his sixties known by the honorific "le père Vivian." He had worked in Washington, D.C., years before and was enthusiastic about America, boasting about the free spirit of the people and the endless possibilities there for a young chef. Listening to his tales, I realized that my years as a "young chef" were slipping away. My entire adult life (and a large chunk of my childhood) had been devoted to work and duty. Now my military obligation was out of the way. I was single. It was time for an adventure, time to see a bit of the world. Le père Vivian convinced me that the ideal destination would be the United States. Not that I needed a lot of convincing. Unlike England, Ireland, and Spain, where I had offers to work, America was far enough away to seem truly exotic. I'd be able to learn English — a language of which I spoke not a word. I never considered the possibility of moving to the States permanently. But for a year or two? What could I lose? A job at Le Plaza would be waiting for me upon my return. If not, there'd be a position at some equally prestigious kitchen. It would be like an extended version of the season I spent after apprenticeship at the resort in Aix-les-Bains.

I asked le père Vivian to help me find a sponsor willing to vouch for me and guarantee me a job in the United States. He contacted an old friend of his, an Alsatian named Ernest Lutringhauser, who owned a restaurant named La Toque Blanche on 50th Street and First Avenue in New York City. Ernest agreed to sponsor me, and I immediately applied at the American Embassy. Then I waited for my green card.

Back at Le Plaza, M. Diat promoted me to the post of *chef entremetier,* putting me in charge of all vegetable preparation. He assigned me a promising young first *commis* who had presented a truly confounding problem to the other chefs. It was not that the boy was underperforming. On the contrary, he was an excellent worker, one of the best in the brigade, punctual, fast, and thorough — an absolute joy. Laughing all the time, do anything for you, the nicest guy you could meet. Everybody from M. Diat on down loved the big, loutish fellow. They couldn't help it. But the *commis* was a complete klutz, totally uncoordinated. Any cook working beside him got covered in slopped sauce — albeit properly made sauce. He once plated a perfect gratinée and slid it toward M. Diat at the pass, but just a little too hard. The plate slid past M. Diat and shattered on the floor. The kid was the only person in the kitchen not terrified by M. Diat, greeting him each morning with a cheerful "Good morning, Chef!"

Chef Vendroux, M. Diat's second in command, had an annoying habit of sneaking around the kitchen, drifting up behind cooks as they worked, and eavesdropping on their tales of nocturnal exploits at the bistros. He did that once too often. The kid was peeling a potato, illustrating his narrative in the French fashion with sweeping hand and arm gestures. A particularly grand flourish sent the blade of the peeler into Chef Vendroux's nose, slicing neatly through one of his nostrils.

With me, M. Diat had finally found a supervisor who he figured knew how to handle the kid. I certainly had long experience. The kid was my little brother, Bichon, now a chef in his own right, four years my junior, a good head taller than me and thirty pounds heavier.

It wasn't long before Bichon became my neighbor as well as my assistant. He found a room around the corner from mine on rue Pierre Charron. I had lived on that street for five years. I consider myself an affable, reasonably outgoing guy, but this was the big city, so I had the usual nodding acquaintance with my neighbors and the local merchants. But by the time Bichon had been there for two weeks, he knew first and last names of everyone he passed — every retiree, every school kid, every merchant, every baby in every pram. And everyone knew Bichon. The owner of the corner bistro greeted him like a best friend and had his drink poured before he sat down. The baker saved special treats for "her Bichon." Little boys eagerly wanted him on their team for street games.

It was a good time. I was glad to be with Bichon and working again in a large kitchen. Things got even better when I was promoted to *chef de nuit,* putting me in charge of a team of five chefs whose responsibility it was to serve late diners. We worked from 6:00 P.M. to 2:00 A.M. Free from the scrutinizing eyes of M. Diat and Chef Vendroux, we had our own rules and habits. We functioned as a gang, covering one another's back. We even had our own late-night sports league. To convey orders from the upper floors to the kitchen, the room service department used wooden balls, each with a hole in the center. Rolled pieces of paper with orders were inserted into these holes by chambermaids or grooms. The meal-order balls clattered noisily through a system of metal tubes and ended up in a large wooden receptacle in a pantry near the coffee machines. During the night's slack time, we used them to play *pétanque*. While two cooks covered, the other four — two teams of two — rolled the balls in the back pastry kitchen, which was narrow and very long. Those who lost had to pay, with all the money going into a kitty. Once a month, we used the kitty to pay for a late meal at a brasserie that was open all night in Montmartre.

It was still dark when we finally went to bed — 6:30 or 7:00 A.M., and dark again when I got up at 4:00 or 5:00 in the afternoon. I lived by the lights of Paris for several weeks during that winter of 1958.

～

MY GREEN CARD arrived in the spring of 1959. I made plans to leave for New York at the end of the summer, but not before going back home for one final reunion with my entire family.

The occasion was the wedding of my big brother, Roland. It was held in my parents' huge new house in Neyron, the little town not far from Lyon where Maman's first restaurant, Hôtel L'Amour, had been. Despite the size of the place, it was filled with guests sleeping on every sofa and unoccupied patch of floor space, more than sixty people in all.

Roland's wedding party went on for three days and three nights. We sang and danced, and of course, we ate. We certainly had no shortage of qualified chefs in the kitchen, what with Maman, Bichon, La Marraine, my aunt Hélène from Port, and me on hand from the family, as well as Georges, my navy friend who had been working at Le Pélican for two years and had been all but adopted into the family.

We turned out capons, langoustines, whitefish, lamb, onion soup, and *croquembouche*, all washed down by glass after glass of Beaujolais drawn directly from the two barrels that Papa and Roland had rolled into the back courtyard and decorated with moss, flowers, and greens. It was Roland and Renée's wedding, but it was also a big send-off for me. I was going to America.

Maman's
Apple Tart

YIELD: 4 TO 6 SERVINGS

*T*HIS APPLE TART was a staple at Le Pélican, and my mother would prepare two or three every day. For Roland's wedding, she must have made one dozen. Most of the guests preferred her tarts to the elaborate *croquembouche* wedding cake, a tower of caramel-glazed cream puffs covered with spun sugar. Maman's method of making dough breaks all the rules that I learned professionally. Using hot milk? Stirring the dough with a spoon? Smearing it into the pie plate? Yet it comes out tender, crumbly, and light in texture, with a delicate taste.

DOUGH

1¼ cups all-purpose flour
1 large egg, broken into a small bowl and beaten with a fork
3 tablespoons unsalted butter, softened
3 tablespoons vegetable shortening (such as Crisco)
Pinch salt
1 tablespoon sugar
1 teaspoon baking powder
2 tablespoons hot milk

FILLING

4 large Golden Delicious apples (about 2 pounds)
3 tablespoons sugar
2 tablespoons cold unsalted butter, broken into pieces

FOR THE DOUGH: Preheat the oven to 400 degrees. Put all the dough ingredients except the hot milk into a bowl. Stir well with a wooden spoon until the mixture starts to combine. Add the hot milk, and stir until well mixed. Do not overwork. The dough will be very soft. Place it in a 9-inch pie plate (my mother used a fluted metal quiche pan) and, using your fingers and a little extra flour to keep them from sticking, press the dough into the pan until it covers the bottom and the sides.

FOR THE FILLING: Peel, core, and halve the apples. Cut each half into 1½-inch wedges. Arrange the wedges on the dough like the spokes of a wheel. Sprinkle with the sugar, and top with the butter, broken into pieces.

Bake the tart for approximately 1 hour, or until the crust is golden. Serve it lukewarm.

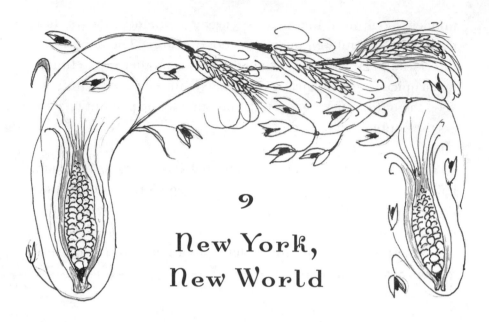

9

New York, New World

AT THE END of August 1959, I embarked from Le Havre on the *Ascania,* an old, converted luxury ship that was bringing home hundreds of American students. As the boat pulled away from the dock, I watched my mother and father, who had driven me there, standing immobile, getting smaller and smaller, and finally disappearing in the mist of Normandy.

It was a powerful feeling, a dual sensation of loneliness and excitement. On one side my parents and everything I had known, on the other side a boatload of vivacious young Americans, jabbering, strumming guitars, singing the latest folk and rock tunes. Although I was completely alone, not knowing one soul on board, and spoke only a few phrases of English, I was overcome with a thrilling sense of freedom. I was starting with a clean slate. Everything was possible.

I soon realized that the English they'd crammed into my head in a few lessons at the Gardiner School in Paris was, to say the least, rudimentary. I developed a habit of thinking through and rehearsing what I wanted to say several times before daring to deliver it to an English-speaking passenger, especially if that passenger was a pretty college girl; there were many aboard ship. However, everyone seemed sympathetic, unpretentious, and ready to accept my mistakes. I started to relax.

Perhaps too much. One morning, I got up early, took a good, long shower, and went up to the deck, where I met a group of students with whom I had spent time the night before. A flirtatious brunette greeted me, and we started a tentative conversation. She asked me why my head was wet. I wanted to tell her that I had just taken a shower but did not know the word for shower in English. I substituted the French word in my explanation, a subterfuge that often worked. It didn't this time. The French word for shower happens to be *douche*. Her face reddened, and she burst out laughing. This was my first — but unfortunately not my last — imbroglio with the intricacies of the English language.

After eleven days and two aurora borealis sightings, we disembarked in Quebec City. I flagged a cab at the pier and began to rehearse the English phrases necessary to get where I wanted to go.

"TRAIN — STATION — PLEASE — MISTER," I said as the cabby wrestled my luggage into his trunk.

The first words I heard on North American soil were the most bizarre French profanities I'd ever encountered, relics from the eighteenth century, most focusing on items found in a church.

"Tabernacle!" he grunted, lifting my heavy trunk.

His face reddened and he cut loose with *"Hostie,"* the French word for "Host." The cab driver was swearing like a bumpkin straight out of a Molière comedy.

MY TRAIN ARRIVED at New York's Grand Central Terminal on the evening of September 12, 1959. Lugging the large wooden trunk containing all my clothes and a small valise with personal papers and reading material, I eventually made it to La Toque

Blanche on East 50th Street, where Ernest Lutringhauser, my sponsor, was waiting. He and his wife showed me to an extra room in their apartment above the restaurant, and to my disappointment, Ernest informed me that I wouldn't be working with him at La Toque Blanche as I had expected.

"But don't worry," he said. "A guy I know up on 57th needs a *chef de partie*. We'll go see him in the morning." The name of the restaurant, Le Pavillon, and its executive chef, Pierre Franey, meant nothing to me. I made up my mind that I would have to make do.

The next morning Ernest led me down the long staircase to the basement under Le Pavillon, site of the kitchen. I was ready for the aloof dignity of M. Diat, but instead I met a guy wearing a chef's whites who greeted me almost as an old pal before ushering me into his office, inquiring about my voyage over, about where I was from, about where I'd worked. I prepared for the ritual presentation of my *certificats de travail*, or work certificates: one from each restaurant where I had cooked, including papers from the Gaillard and de Gaulle governments. I was eager to show them to Chef Franey.

I pushed the manila envelope across his desk. He could have cared less. Franey didn't need certificates or anything else to determine that I had the two qualifications he needed: I was French; I was a chef.

"Can you start tomorrow?" was the extent of my interview.

I accepted the job, but I was completely unaware of how prominent and important Le Pavillon was. For two decades, it had been recognized as the finest French restaurant in the United States. Le Pavillon set the standards and style for what Americans came to think of as classical French cuisine. Alumni from its kitchen spread Le Pavillon's philosophy when they left to open French restaurants of their own. Franey himself was regarded by his peers as the finest chef in New York, if not the entire country. He would go on to introduce the rest of the country to fine French cuisine through his cookbooks and column in the *New York Times*. He would also become my mentor, familiarizing me with all things American and profoundly influencing my approach to my trade.

As the name implies, Le Pavillon began as the restaurant of the French Pavilion at the New York World's Fair in 1939. The French government had designated Drouant, a famous restaurant in Paris, to set up the kitchen. The whole brigade — thirty-eight waiters and wine stewards and sixty cooks — arrived aboard the French liner *Normandie* on April 1, 1939. The French Pavilion restaurant became an instant success and the most popular restaurant at the fair during the springs and summers of 1939 and 1940. As the *New York Times* reported on May 10, 1939, "Every gesture of the staff, from the august Jean Drouant, director of the establishment, down to the most unobtrusive waiter, signaled the pride of the employees in what was instantly signed, sealed and delivered to the fairgoing public as a retreat for epicures."

As part of this assemblage of chefs, Pierre Franey, then an eighteen-year-old *commis poissonnier,* started his career in the United States. Franey worked at the fair during both the 1939 and 1940 seasons, after which it closed. By then, war had been declared in France, and like many other members of the Pavillon team, he enlisted in the American army and went back to France as an American GI.

Henri Soulé, Le Pavillon's maitre d', was ineligible for military service. He decided to stay in New York instead of returning to occupied France. In October 1941, he opened Le Pavillon on East 55th Street. At this time, there were only a few great French restaurants in the city, such as Le Chambord and Lafayette. Better known were little bistros, such as Larré and Du Midi. Under the tyrannical leadership of Soulé, Le Pavillon produced extraordinary classical cuisine, among the best in the world, and Soulé became New York's most famous restaurateur.

A few years later, Soulé opened his second Le Pavillon, at 57th Street, between Lexington and Park Avenues. He retained the first restaurant, but renamed it La Côte Basque. When Franey was de-mobilized after the war, he returned immediately to Le Pavillon's kitchen and rose steadily through Soulé's brigade. By 1959, Franey had ascended to the top as executive chef.

ALTHOUGH THE QUALITY of the cooking at Le Pavillon was high, it differed from what I had been accustomed to in France. I had worked, in my opinion, in more sophisticated kitchens in Paris, although the kitchen of Le Pavillon was great fun. The work-ing arrangement was not as structured as it was at Le Plaza Athénée or Le Meurice, nor did the restaurant employ nearly as many cooks in proportion to the number of meals served. It had a much less rigid way of operating, with the chefs moving from one station to another.

The ingredients — produce, meat, herbs, fish, and fruits — tasted different from those in Paris. Fruits, vegetables, mushrooms, and herbs tended to be milder. Beef and lamb cuts were larger and more tender, and the poultry plump, juicy, and delicate. The pun-gent fish of the Mediterranean were nowhere to be seen; instead, we had striped bass. Lobster replaced the more familiar French langouste. I had to get used to new tastes and new combinations and compensate to reach the tastes that I had in my memory. A large, powerful broiler cooked meat and fish, but there was no grill with wood charcoal underneath, like the one at Le Plaza Athénée. The *entremetier,* or vegetable department, one of the largest depart-ments at Le Plaza, with a *chef de partie* and five *commis,* was reduced to one lowly assistant cook at Le Pavillon; he produced a limited repertoire of vegetable gratins and creamed dishes that customers ordered à la carte, if at all. Who would have known at this point in time that the grill and vegetables would eventually come to define the new American cuisine?

One specialty was *poulet Pavillon,* a harmonious, rich, glisten-ing roast chicken. We flavored the chicken simply with thyme, salt, and pepper and roasted it on high heat, basting regularly to give it a deep brown, crisp finish. Then we made a sauce of reduced chicken stock, Champagne, and cream, finishing it with cognac, and drizzled the reduced natural juices over the sauced bird. Classical dishes like these were less complicated and more straightforward than the overwrought food often served in restaurants today, even those that are falsely labeled "country" or "simple."

My salary at Le Pavillon was astronomical: $86 a week, as opposed to a monthly salary of $140 in Paris. I was easily able to afford to move out of my temporary lodgings and, for $20 a week, into my own quarters. The common toilets and shower stood in the hall next door, and I could distinctly hear the noise of the dining room below — a familiar, comforting sound that reminded me of boyhood nights falling asleep above Maman's restaurants. My room in the back of the building was large and comfortable. I didn't mind that the window overlooked a trash-clogged alley. I had two days off a week, and on my working days I worked eight hours only in a straight shift. Considering what my schedule had been in Paris, I was living like a king.

~~~

IN THE BACK of my mind, I had always had a latent desire to go back to school. Coming to another country gave me a chance to see if my long-dormant classroom skills could be revived, or whether they had died along with my youth. And now I had the time. And a good excuse, if I needed one: I wanted to improve my English.

On the *Ascania,* I had conversed with a man who taught school in New York state, and when I asked him to identify the best school in New York, he answered, without hesitation, "Columbia University."

I didn't know anything about Columbia or American universities in general, but forty-eight hours after I arrived in New York, I went to Columbia and struggled through one office after another until I arrived at General Studies. I applied to enroll in the English for Foreign Students program. This wasn't an accredited course, but nevertheless I was back in school. I was going to learn to speak English from the best.

I took a placement examination, ended up in an intermediate class and immediately realized I was in over my head. Although I found reading and writing English within the realm of possibility, understanding the spoken language was another matter. I comprehended maybe one word out of ten when people talked to me. I labored through that first course. Eventually, my ears started to cooperate, and it got easier.

On my days off, I furthered my English studies by heading to Times Square. The Paramount on 42nd Street offered two or three movies in a row for the price of one, enabling me to spend most of the day there, immersed in my new language. Between the movies, I walked the streets. The wind from the sea mixed with the sweet smoky aromas of hot dogs, hamburgers, popcorn, pizza, pastrami, roasting chestnuts, cinnamon buns, and apple pie — whatever vendors were selling from carts or the open windows of coffee shops. As a chef and a Frenchman used to the planned ritual of the meal, I found it liberating to eat on the spur of the moment and to be served within a few minutes of ordering.

The teacher I had met on the *Ascania* had invited me to his home in New Rochelle, and I took him up on it one Sunday a few weeks after my arrival. It was my first trip out of the city, and I traveled by train to spend the day with him and his family at their cottage by the sea. His two teenage sons invited me to go to the beach with them and, as it was close to noon, they made sandwiches and ate them standing up. They offered me one, which I refused, deciding that I didn't want to spoil my lunch. This, of course, *was* lunch — a far cry from the two hours we used to spend at the table in Neyron. Fortunately, dinner was served much earlier than I was used to, because I was starving by then. We all sat down outside to a meal that included pot roast, carrots, and mashed potatoes. Everyone else dug in. I waited, assuming that they had forgotten the bread and wine. After a few minutes, I realized that these staples would not be forthcoming.

On weekends, I often visited Pierre Franey and his wife, Betty, at their cottage in the Hamptons. On one Saturday morning when Betty was giving their teenage daughters breakfast, I was introduced to those little individual boxes of corn flakes lined with wax paper, which can be opened down the center, to add milk directly. I loved the fun of this, and, surprisingly, the taste; the flavor reminded me of the country bread that we had cut into pieces and soaked in ice-cold milk during the war. Over time I was exposed to other distinctly American foods. I never got used to root beer or marshmallows, but I loved — and still do — Oreo cookies, Jell-O, and iceberg lettuce.

I helped Pierre in his garden, put the boat in the water with him, went fishing and water skiing, and caught tiny *friture,* or whitebait, with a net. We walked through the marshes to catch eels at night, using flashlights and special nets. We dug for clams, which were a new taste for me and a treat on the half shell or in fish stews.

A COUPLE OF MONTHS after starting at Le Pavillon, I got good news from France. Jean-Claude Szurdak, my best friend and cooking partner when we worked for General de Gaulle, had survived his tour of duty in Algeria and had just been discharged from the army. It had always been our plan to be reunited in New York. I wrote back, saying that I had approached Ernest, my sponsor, to see if he would provide sponsorship for Jean-Claude, as he had for me. No problem. Like most French restaurant owners in New York, he was always anxious to expand the pool of Gallic kitchen talent.

Jean-Claude's ship, *Le Flandre,* docked at the 53rd Street pier in late June 1960, and I was there to meet him. It was a typical New York summer afternoon — which is to say about ninety-five degrees and so humid and hazy that you could see only two blocks in any direction. Jean-Claude arrived with plenty of luggage and dressed in the heavy clothes appropriate for an Atlantic crossing.

Naturally, there were no cabs to be had, so I suggested we head toward 10th Avenue in search of one. Jean-Claude began sweating profusely. His breathing was labored. We trudged through heaps of ankle-deep litter, and the glares we got from some of the residents made me glad it was broad daylight. For his part, Jean-Claude was shocked by the garbage in the streets and understood how that neighborhood came to be named Hell's Kitchen.

But his opinion of New York improved dramatically when we finally hauled ourselves up the stairs to the marvelous new apartment I had secured in anticipation of Jean-Claude's arrival. Ernest not only owned La Toque Blanche, but the five-story building it occupied, and he rented an apartment to us for $75 a month.

It was a very old building, with the sort of cockroach population that can only thrive one floor above a restaurant. When I came home from work at 2:00 A.M. and flipped on the lights, the walls crawled with scurrying brown bugs. But this didn't bother me. The apartment was palatial, extending the entire length of the building, with three windows on the street side and three out the back, overlooking a courtyard with a garden. We had three separate bedrooms, one large living room, a kitchen, and a bath. With a bedroom to spare, I asked another friend who was working at Le Pavillon to join us, and the rent went down to $25 per person between the three of us.

We cleaned, we painted, we caulked, we plastered, we fixed the floors, and we furnished the apartment with furniture from the Salvation Army and Good Will, gifts from friends, and discards in alleys. We reupholstered and refinished. I found out, to my surprise, that I was pretty good at repairing and mending old chairs and dressers. I wished Papa could have seen my handiwork, and for the first time, I felt like the son of a cabinetmaker rather than the son of a cook. The three of us were proud to have what we thought to be the greatest apartment in the world. We were rich! Jean-Claude capped it all off when he got hired at La Toque Blanche, securing one of the shortest commutes in the entire city — all of thirty steps.

The nearby A&P was my first supermarket. In France, I shopped at open-air markets and in individual shops that specialized in one product: a *boulangerie* for bread, a *boucher* for meat, an *épicerie* for dry goods, and a *marchand de légumes* for vegetables and fruits.

At our A&P, it was all under one roof. Everything was boxed or wrapped in plastic, as if the contents were something to be ashamed of: packages, packages, and more packages. There were not many types of oil, vinegar, or mustard. There were only two types of salad greens: iceberg and romaine. There were no leeks, no shallots, no Swiss chard or purple garlic, and no fresh herbs, except for curly parsley. When I asked for mushrooms, I was sent to aisle five, where the canned mushrooms were shelved. After much searching, I finally located ordinary fresh white mushrooms in a specialty store. However, I did see beautiful steaks for very little money, a large variety of packaged bread — albeit not French bread — and a staggering amount of cookies and candies. We bought everything in sight, with varying degrees of success. What we thought were cornichons, tiny pickling cucumbers in vinegar, turned out to be sickeningly sweet and startling to our palates. We sampled an orange-colored, presliced cheddar cheese, a far cry from the Camembert of my youth.

We divided the household chores equally. Cooking and shopping were never a problem. But enthusiasm could not always compensate for my still-shaky command of English. One day, when it was my turn to shop, I hunted through several aisles for paper napkins. We had a couple of friends over for dinner that evening. As I set the table, one of our American guests burst out laughing. There, enblazoned on the side of the package, were the words *napkins* and *sanitary*.

The early 1960s seemed a gentle time in New York — no iron grates on doors and windows and no graffiti in the subway. When we spoke to strangers, they did not recoil, and we walked the streets at night without fear. After evening classes, my fellow Columbia students and I thought nothing of strolling in the dark through Riverside Park, emerging onto bustling 125th Street, the throbbing heart of the Harlem music scene. We'd move along, listening to jazz riffs drifting through the open doors of the many small bars and clubs, until we heard a tune that drew us into some joint's smoky interior.

On one of these late-night shambles, I passed the display window of a small grocery store and stopped in my tracks. There, in a refrigerated case, was a cornucopia of the sort of wonderful offal that I had never been able to find in my Upper East Side A&P. Tripe, pig's feet, kidneys of both veal and lamb, chicken feet, liver, sweetbreads, brains, you name it.

As soon as I got off work the next day, I hurried back to the store. That fabulous offal counter was overseen by an enormous African American wearing a bloodstained white apron. I took my place in the scrum that was gathered in front of the display — men, women, kids, and me, the only white face in the store. When my turn came, I realized to my horror that I hadn't a clue about the English names for my favorite pieces of offal. It wasn't the sort of place that had little plastic signs informing customers what each tray contained, so I was reduced to pointing and smiling. The guy manning the display picked up a half-dozen lamb kidneys with his hand, plopped them onto a sheet of butcher paper, folded it over, and handed my package to me with a nod toward the woman who sat near the door behind a cash register. It seemed that the culinary African American culture had common roots with French country cuisine. Both traditions originated among poor rural people who wasted nothing. Everything had to be used, and over time, the resulting dishes became part of a culinary tradition. I may not have been able to converse with these people, but I felt an immediate affinity for their way of looking at food.

~

MY CAREER at Le Pavillon ended abruptly eight months after I came to the States.

Soulé, still the maitre d' there, might have been accorded the status of a culinary god by most New Yorkers, but I was under-whelmed. My years under M. Diat at Le Plaza Athénée had taught me that extraordinary talent and civility were not mutually exclu-sive. Soulé struck me as a bombastic tyrant. He constantly yelled down the stairs at us in the kitchen. He treated Pierre Franey, who had now become a friend of mine, with no more respect than he accorded to the most recently hired pot scrubber.

Years had gone by without salary increases for the kitchen staff. Soulé maintained that severe cash flow shortages prevented him from giving raises. Yet when a movie star or some minor Euro-pean royal came into Le Pavillon, Soulé comped everything — the Champagne, the caviar (several pounds of it in one instance), nu-merous entrées that were often custom-made to order, rare wines, the best cheeses in the house, every item on the dessert menu.

The situation finally strained Pierre's loyalty to the breaking point. Howard Deering Johnson — the original Howard Johnson — was a frequent diner at Le Pavillon. He had made Pierre a stand-ing offer to join Howard Johnson's as a vice president, with a vice president's salary and all the accompanying perks and fringe bene-fits. Pierre had resisted, but when he realized that he could not get decent wages for his brigade, he took Johnson up on his offer.

Soulé was shocked. He thought Pierre would never leave. He still viewed him as that eighteen-year-old *commis* who had shipped over on the *Normandie* two decades earlier, not as a talented chef who had earned his position through skill, hard work, and loyalty.

I was the one who suggested a mass walkout to protest this treatment. In France, such events were so common that there was a special term denoting when an entire kitchen brigade quit: *la bri-gade saute* — "the brigade explodes." Cooks owed allegiance to the chef, not to the owner or maitre d'. With my big French mouth, I became the ringleader, and the brigade was ready to follow.

That evening a pair of large Italian gentlemen who were asso-ciated in some capacity with Local 89 of the restaurant employees union dropped by Le Pavillon. I can assure you they were not there to sample our *poulet Pavillon*. Accompanied by a snitch from the kitchen, the goons cornered me in the cooks' dressing room. The snitch closed the door and stood against it as one of the union guys lifted me off the floor and slammed me against the wall, pinning me there.

He said something in English I didn't understand, but the snitch provided translation.

"What's the problem with you?"

I couldn't have spoken even if I had known what to say.

"You better watch your step, understand? Think you're a big shot, just off the fuckin' boat? Keep it up and you'll get hurt."

He let go. I fell to the floor.

"And you'll never be able to find work in a New York kitchen again."

The union enforcers might have been able to stop us from quitting en masse, but there was no way they could force us to work overtime. Or make us work if we were sick, or keep us from ignoring an order from the dining room that required careful, very lengthy preparation. And there was no way they could prevent us from leaving one by one, which we did.

Within a few days, Soulé didn't have enough cooks to continue serving customers. He was forced to close Le Pavillon. The culinary feud was prominently reported in the *New York Times* the following day. I had won a victory of sorts. But the cost was high. I suddenly found myself in a foreign country and out of work.

Braised Striped Bass Pavillon

YIELD: 4 SERVINGS

I HAD NEVER SEEN or tasted striped bass before I worked at Le Pavillon. It is similar, however, to the *loup de mer* of the Mediterranean, one of the most prized fish of that region and a standard menu item in restaurants along the Côte d'Azur. With flesh that is slightly softer and moister than its European cousin, striped bass was a specialty of Le Pavillon. The braised wild striped bass would be presented to the patrons whole and carved at tableside.

The following is a simple, elegant, and mouth-watering adaptation of the recipe from Le Pavillon. The fish, gutted with head on, is braised with white wine, shallots, and mushrooms in the oven, then coated with the cooking juices enriched with butter. This dish is excellent served with tiny steamed potatoes or sautéed cucumbers.

- 1 striped bass, gutted, with head on (about 3 pounds)
- 2 cups thinly sliced mushrooms
- 1/4 cup chopped shallots
- 1/2 teaspoon salt, plus more to taste
- 1/2 teaspoon freshly ground black pepper, plus more to taste
- 1 tablespoon good olive oil
- 1 teaspoon fresh thyme leaves
- 2 bay leaves
- 1 cup dry, fruity white wine (Chardonnay or Sauvignon Blanc)
- 8 tablespoons (1 stick) unsalted butter, at room temperature
- 1 tablespoon fresh lemon juice
- 1 tablespoon minced fresh chives

Preheat the oven to 400 degrees. Place the fish in a gratin dish or stainless steel baking dish that is narrow enough to prevent the garnishes and the wine from spreading out too much. Sprinkle with the mushrooms, shallots, 1/2 teaspoon salt, 1/2 teaspoon pepper, olive oil, thyme, bay leaves, and wine. Cover tightly with a piece of aluminum foil so the fish will cook in its own steam.

Bake for 35 to 45 minutes, or until the fish is cooked through. Check by inserting the point of a small knife into the flesh. It should be tender, and the flesh should separate from the central bone when pierced with the knife. Reduce the heat to 150 degrees. Using a large hamburger spatula, transfer the whole fish to an ovenproof serving platter, and set aside in the warm oven while you complete the recipe.

Pour the fish's cooking juices and vegetable solids into a small saucepan, and discard the bay leaves. You should have 3/4 to 1 cup of liquid; cook down the liquid or add water to adjust the yield to this amount. Bring to a boil on top of the stove, and add the butter spoonful by spoonful, incorporating each piece into the mixture with a whisk before you add another. Remove the saucepan from the heat, and add the lemon juice, chives, and additional salt and pepper to taste.

At serving time, pull or scrape off the skin on top of the fish with a small paring knife. Coat the fish with the sauce, and sprinkle the chives on top. Bring to the table, and carve for the guests.

Reuben Sandwich

YIELD: 4 SERVINGS

*W*HILE LIVING in New York City, I became a sucker for sandwiches, which for me represent the American spirit and lifestyle: easy, unstructured, and casual. They are convenient, fast, and mess-free and may well be the most versatile of all foods. Sandwiches can be healthful or decadent, light or heavy, with ingredients to please vegetarians and carnivores. Made with pita, regular bread, tortilla wraps, or baguettes, they can reflect different ethnic traditions. I believe it was James Beard who said not many people understand a good sandwich. I like to think that I still do.

I first tasted this sandwich in a restaurant near 42nd Street a few weeks after I arrived in New York. With a cold beer and a bit of salad, it makes a perfect meal for either lunch or dinner.

You can use commercial Russian or Thousand Island dressing on the sandwich or create your own Russian dressing. I sometimes make the Reuben with pastrami, although corned beef is the traditional choice, and I use rye as well as pumpernickel bread. Be sure to use good Swiss cheese (Emmenthaler or Gruyère). I prefer the sauerkraut available in plastic bags to the canned varieties.

RUSSIAN DRESSING

$\frac{1}{2}$ cup mayonnaise

3 tablespoons ketchup

1 tablespoon fresh or bottled horseradish

1 teaspoon Worcestershire sauce

   Good dash Tabasco hot pepper sauce

SANDWICHES

8 large slices pumpernickel bread (each about 6 by 4 inches in diameter, $\frac{1}{2}$ inch thick, and weighing about 1 ounce)

6 ounces Swiss cheese (preferably Emmenthaler or Gruyère), cut into enough slices to completely cover the bread (about 1$\frac{1}{2}$ ounces per sandwich)

1$\frac{1}{3}$ cups drained sauerkraut

8 ounces thinly sliced corned beef (not too lean)

2 tablespoons unsalted butter

2 tablespoons corn or peanut oil

FOR THE DRESSING: Mix all the dressing ingredients together in a small bowl.

FOR EACH SANDWICH: Spread 2 pieces of the bread with 1 tablespoon each of the Russian dressing, and arrange enough cheese slices on both pieces of bread to cover them. Measure out about ⅓ cup of the sauerkraut and spread half of it on top of one of the cheese-covered slices. Cover with 2 ounces of the corned beef, then spread the remaining half (⅙ cup) of sauerkraut on top. To finish, top with the other cheese-covered slice of bread.

Repeat with the remaining ingredients to make 3 additional sandwiches.

At serving time, melt the butter with the oil in a nonstick skillet, and sauté the sandwiches, covered, over medium to low heat for about 8 minutes, 4 minutes per side, until the cheese on the sandwiches has melted and the corned beef is hot. Serve immediately.

10

Only in America

I SOON FOUND MYSELF in a conundrum, with job offers from two of America's most visible businessmen: Howard Deering Johnson and Joseph P. Kennedy. Both men had been regulars at Le Pavillon, and both were looking for a French chef. Johnson, who had hired Pierre Franey, wanted me to join him in improving the food at the chain of restaurants. Kennedy, whose son was campaigning for the presidency, sought a future White House chef. It was Camelot versus HoJo's.

The Kennedys had been patrons of Le Pavillon since the early days of the restaurant. They were always seated at La Royale, the name of the most prominent and visible table, which was reserved for those whom Soulé deemed VIPs. In the spring of 1960, the whole Kennedy clan gathered at La Royale for lunch to discuss strategy for John's planned presidential bid. Somehow, a news photographer sneaked into the restaurant and began snapping pictures. Joseph called Martin Decré, the manager, and asked that he get rid of the annoying photographer. Soulé, who happened to be nearby, heard the request.

"Decré!" Soulé said.

The Kennedy table went so silent, you could hear ice cubes tinkling against the sides of the crystal water glasses.

"You'll do no such thing." Every head turned. "At Le Pavillon, only Soulé decides who is or isn't accepted in the dining room." He lowered his voice but still quite audibly said, "The campaign has not even begun, but some people already think they are running the country."

The Kennedys never came back and began patronizing the newly opened La Caravelle, which was mostly staffed, to Soulé's vexation, with former employees of Le Pavillon.

Later that summer, Joseph Kennedy asked the owner of La Caravelle, Robert Meyzin, former general manager of Soulé's La Côte Basque, to recommend someone for the White House chef position. Meyzin, in turn, asked the executive chef, Roger Fessaguet, former sous-chef at Le Pavillon, to help, and Roger called and urged me to take the job.

Meanwhile, Pierre kept regaling me with stories about the good life at Howard Johnson's. He needed an assistant and offered me a 30 percent pay increase, to $120 a week. More important, I would have regular hours, 7:00 A.M. to 3:00 P.M., with Saturdays and Sundays off and vast test kitchens in which to experiment with recipes.

It was an appealing offer. After the debacle at Le Pavillon, I had pretty much had it with fancy French restaurants. Besides, my visit to the States was supposed to be both a lark and an opportunity to learn. Buried in the basement of yet another French restaurant, I would neither have fun nor learn anything about America. Some guys at Le Pavillon had worked there for fifteen years and spoke English no better than I did after six months in the States. Finishing their eight-hour days in a Francophone kitchen, they spent their leisure hours drinking *vin ordinaire* and smoking Gitane cigarettes with other French immigrants at brasseries on the West Side. They might as well have stayed in Paris, for all their exposure to the American way of life. Before I returned to France,

I wanted to learn about American culture and work in a truly American environment. What better place than HoJo's for a crash course?

My training as a chef had taught me that being a chef — no matter where — was a blue-collar job. Period. A respected job, to be sure, but there was not much difference between a short-order cook at a corner diner and a cook at Le Pavillon; both were just working stiffs in my eyes. For that matter, at this time in New York, so were the dishwashers, who were in the same union as the chefs. I did not feel that I was taking a step down the social ladder to go from the kitchen of Le Pavillon to the experimental kitchen at Howard Johnson's. I would be getting into new territory. Besides, I would be in the States only for a year or so. What did I have to lose?

To be honest, I had absolutely no idea how much publicity and exposure being the White House chef under the Kennedys could have generated. After all, I had been chef under three governments in France, and I had never so much as been interviewed by a newspaper, much less interviewed on radio or television. In France, cooking for heads of state was recognized in the trade as a good job. However, it wasn't considered as prestigious as working as chef in one of the famed one-, two-, or three-star restaurants.

But something else had happened to me in the months since I had walked down the *Ascania*'s gangplank. I had made friends in New York. I had a nice apartment. And I was enrolled in Columbia's English for Foreign Students program. In New York, my life was starting to move in a direction that I liked very much.

A few weeks passed before I received a second, more urgent-sounding summons from Roger. "The Kennedy job is still open. It's yours, if you want it. But they need to know soon."

"I don't know . . ."

"Are you crazy? You have to take this job. It's a great opportunity for you."

He may well have been right. But I turned him down and a few weeks later found myself the only white guy in a brigade of African

Americans, flipping burgers and deep-frying potatoes at a busy Howard Johnson's out in Queens.

To JUDGE from the glares that greeted me, my new coworkers were anything but predisposed to embrace somebody who spoke with a funny accent. But Mr. Johnson rightfully felt that if I was going to be designing menus for his chain, then I should have a firsthand understanding of how things worked on the line in the biggest and busiest HoJo's in the company.

Fortunately, I knew the cardinal rule of getting on with one's fellow cooks. It applies in any kitchen and can be summed up in two short words: *bust ass*. Restaurant kitchens are the ultimate levelers. When you're slammed and orders are starting to back up, you could care less about the color of the hands of the cook who is working next to you, as long as they are moving fast and effectively. Personal life, sexual preferences, accent, addictions, criminal record — none of them matter. Conversely, if he isn't holding up his end, he could be your blood brother and you'd fire him in a second. That I had been chef at the "French White House" didn't mean anything to these HoJo line chefs. Not one of them had heard of Le Pavillon. So I showed them what I could do. I not only learned how to flip a hamburger the second it had sizzled to a perfect medium-rare (a skill not taught in Parisian kitchens), but I was soon able to hold my own with the other guys on the grill. The cuisine may have been at the other end of the culinary spectrum compared with what I'd made at Le Plaza, but the frenetic pace was the same. As was the sweat that ran in streams down my face. Within a few days I was producing food as fast or faster than anyone else in the kitchen. I was in and getting respect.

As I got to know my coworkers on the line, I discovered that we had the same basic approach to cooking. They hadn't gone through years of classical training — or any formal training at all — but they cooked with natural grace and gut-felt understanding drawn from a well of deep culinary tradition. Food was as important a part of their culture as it was of mine. I barely understood their accents and they mine, but I felt an affinity for these men.

Ironically, the biggest personality clash I had out in Queens involved the only other Caucasian there, the general manager, an arrogant kid just out of hotel school who seemed to think his Cornell degree conferred on him the right to treat the kitchen staff as his own personal servants, men who had been in the business before he was weaned. One day he went too far, and I found myself hollering at him, using a few basic Anglo-Saxon terms that I had picked up from my workmates.

"You're fired," the twerp said.

I suggested he do something anatomically impossible.

"Get out of here," he said.

"You can't fire me."

"We'll see about that." He retreated to his office and picked up the phone. I imagine it was then that he learned who had personally assigned me to the restaurant job — one of those lessons not found on the curriculums of Ivy League universities.

But I also learned something from the kid: having a couple of letters after your last name can work magic. It was the first time in my career that I had come in professional contact with someone with a college education. All of my other bosses had left grade school as I had, to begin the decades-long process of mastering a trade: busboy to waiter to maitre d' to restaurant manager; apprentice to *commis* to *chef de partie* to sous-chef to executive chef. Because of his education, the Cornell boy had skipped all the steps, beginning at the top of the restaurant business, with a future that would doubtlessly hold promotion upon promotion. As big a jerk as he was, he had something I did not.

AFTER MY INITIATION to the world of Howard Johnson's, I began working at the company's central commissary, a vast complex of modern warehouse-like buildings, also in Queens. In this suitably industrial setting, Pierre and I played a role in one of the major shifts in Americans' eating habits. Working under Mr. Johnson, we became pioneers in the technology that could produce food of a consistent quality that in turn could be prepared by relatively unskilled cooks toiling in outposts of the chain far from the commissary kitchens in which the dishes were originally made. Today we take it for granted that we can eat the same shrimp scampi dish in Red Lobster restaurants at opposite ends of the country; that a Friday's hamburger is always a Friday's hamburger whether it's served in Boston or Miami; that the fries at one McDonald's will be identical in quality to all other McDonald's fries. At the time, however, the concept was revolutionary.

This was Mr. Johnson's vision as he began to shape a single-ice-cream-scoop shop in Massachusetts into America's first large restaurant chain, with over one thousand outlets — far bigger than were Kentucky Fried Chicken, McDonald's, and Burger King combined, at the time. He realized that he would have to recruit the nation's top restaurant talent if he was to succeed in his mission to give traveling American families a restaurant where the atmosphere was friendly and the food delicious in every location. He gave Pierre and me a simple mandate: improve the stuff HoJo's already served, and introduce new dishes that the customers would like. Issuing those instructions, he had the good sense to set us free, imposing no limits and adopting a completely hands-off management style, although he attended every test kitchen tasting and had an astounding food memory. "I liked the way you did it the last time," he would say, even though the last time might have been several months and who knows how many business trips and board meetings earlier. "There was less salt in it and the sauce wasn't as thick."

One of Howard Johnson's most popular standbys was clam chowder. People loved it. Most restaurateurs would have told us not to try to fix what was not broken. But Mr. Johnson gave us carte blanche to tinker. Out went the chowder's dehydrated onion flakes, and in went fresh onions. Real potatoes replaced frozen ones. We put in garlic instead of garlic powder, butter rather than margarine. The texture became lighter and livelier with the addition of real stock. Fried chicken underwent a similar metamorphosis. Instead of being precooked in an oven and then breaded and reheated in oil, the raw chicken was battered with good bread crumbs, fresh eggs, and real cream and then deep-fried in a pressure cooker so it was both crisp and moist.

Everything about my new surroundings was Brobdingnagian. Trained to nurse delicate consommés in one-pint quantities, I suddenly faced stockpots that held 500 and 1,000 gallons. Imagine above-ground swimming pools, and you'll get a feel for the proportions in that kitchen. Where I had formerly made dishes such as beef Burgundy in batches of maybe a dozen servings, I had to learn to make 2,500-portion batches. Instead of measuring in cups, ounces, and teaspoons, I began dealing in gallons, tons, and bushels. The ingredient list for our standard veal stock recipe called for roasting 3,000 pounds of veal bones, to which we added 200 pounds of onions, 150 pounds of carrots, 100 pounds of celery, 12 gallons of canned tomatoes, a couple of sacks of salt, and a pound of black peppercorns. We boned out and prepared 1,500 turkeys a day. It was enthralling and absorbing work, an assembly-line process that yielded good results at record speeds.

All of our experiments began with small, easy-to-manage quantities of a few servings at most. Once we had it right in miniature, we began the trial-and-error process of upsizing a dish so a batch could serve thousands. As anyone who has tried to double or triple the most straightforward cookbook recipe knows, this involved much more than simple multiplication. And even once we had gotten a recipe to work in large volume, the food chemists on our staff sometimes nullified weeks of work by informing us that we couldn't leave the food at the required temperature for the necessary time because their tests indicated that bacteria would develop. Our dishes not only had to taste right, but they had to freeze fast and thaw in reasonable time in the restaurants' walk-in refrigerators.

We never succeeded in making some dishes work. Shrimp or

scallops in puff pastry shells seemed like a natural for HoJo's. In blind tastings, our small trial batches got Mr. Johnson's enthusiastic approval. But we were never able to create a mass-produced dish that could be replicated in the company's restaurant kitchens. The chefs there would overcook the shellfish in an attempt to get the pastry right or end up with raw, mushy pastry and nicely cooked shellfish. Pierre decreed that the margin of error was unacceptable.

I concocted all kinds of sauces, such as fish sauce with tomato, mushrooms, herbs, and white wine, which is a classic of the nineteenth-century chef Adolphe Dugléré, as well as a Burgundy sauce. I had to adjust their ingredients and preparation so they could be frozen or preserved in cans. My products went out to the regular Howard Johnson's restaurants and a fancier, upscale restaurant line owned by the company, called the Red Coach Grill. The grocery division also sold the Howard Johnson's brand to supermarkets.

~~~

LIKE ALL Americans of a certain age, I remember precisely where I was and what I was doing on the afternoon of November 22, 1963. I was working at the Howard Johnson's commissary in Queens Village when I learned that President Kennedy had been shot. We were packaging chicken pot pies. Ten women worked on the line, two spooning the proper amount of cooked chicken meat per pie into individual plastic bags, two adding pearl onions and cooked carrots, two adding peas and button mushrooms, two adding the proper amount of cream sauce, and two sealing and packaging the bags. When we got the news, the whole production line stopped, and everyone — me included — fell silent, then began to weep.

~~~

IN MY TEST KITCHEN, I started to understand what happens chemically to food during preparation and cooking. My vocabulary increased with my understanding of terms such as *bacteria and coliform counts, the specific gravity of sauces, emulsion,* and *total solids,* and I learned what could and could not be frozen and how to freeze and defrost foods properly so as to retain maximum flavor and texture.

Another mandate from Mr. Johnson was to test the latest up-to-date equipment to see if it would help us in our drive for consistent quality. My first exposure (and *exposure* is the right word) to microwave technology was an encounter with a large, noisy contraption made by Amana called a radar-range and billed as the latest technical wonder for the kitchen. The demonstrator showed us that if a certain amount of leakage occurred at the seam of the door, a small neon-light tube that he held in his hand would light up as he stood a couple of feet in front of the operating machine. Escaping microwaves agitated electrons in the lamp and made them glow. His demonstration so thoroughly scared me that even now I refuse to stand in front of a microwave oven when it is operating.

Occasionally, a food snob took a cheap shot at what we did for a living. For that reason, Pierre and I always got a kick out of serving our creations, most of them reheated from the frozen state, at home to other famous French chefs. André Soltner (the star chef of Lutèce) came over to my place one evening, and I served some fish stew I had picked up frozen on my way out the door of Howard Johnson's commissary. Needless to say, Soltner has a discriminating palate, and I was interested in using him as an unwitting guinea pig. I figured that if the stew was good enough for Soltner, then it was good enough for the middle-class Americans who dined at Mr. Johnson's restaurants. As we ate, I casually asked him what he thought.

"Hmmm," he said, nodding. "Quite good."

He sputtered on his wine when I revealed the truth.

"How could you make this? Frozen. Impossible. You're lying. No way was that frozen."

Those preparations were so good that I was even able to slip them past Jean-Claude when it was my evening to cook in our apartment.

In the spring of 1962, Jean-Claude, who was still at La Toque Blanche and still my apartment mate, pointed out that our planned lark in the United States had now extended to almost three years and that we hadn't been home or even had more than two days off in a row since arriving. To rectify this situation, he suggested that we both quit our jobs and take the entire summer off to return to France, visit family, and maybe tour a few of the bordering countries.

We'd managed to accumulate considerable savings, $3,500 in my case. Our plan was simple. Go home and blow every cent we had. Live like the idle rich. Actually enjoy our money for once. Two New York friends mentioned that they wanted to buy new European cars and ship them back to the States. They could realize huge savings in import duties if the cars came into the country as used vehicles. Would we mind putting a few thousand miles on a couple of nice cars that had never been off a dealer's lot?

But there was this little issue about our jobs. Jean-Claude had put in his time at La Toque Blanche, and he'd be able to get a similar job when he came back. But I was reluctant to leave my post at Howard Johnson's, and I certainly didn't want to go back to the drudgery of a restaurant kitchen. In the end, I figured that a footloose summer in France, Italy, and Spain was worth more than any job. I gave Pierre my notice.

"Take the summer off," he said. "Your job will be waiting when you come back."

~

AFTER PICKING UP my friend's new car, a gleaming red VW Beetle, I drove directly home to Neyron. In honor of my return, Maman took time off work. For the first time since signing the papers that finalized her purchase of Le Pélican, she closed the place and taped a sign to the door informing her customers to come back in two weeks.

The Pépin clan was going on a road trip, and I was footing the bill. There would be eight of us in two cars: Maman and Papa, Roland and his wife, Renée, Bichon and his new fiancée, Loute, our housekeeper Paulette, and me. We drove across France, into northern Spain, and down the coast to Valencia and Granada. I was pleased to see that, despite her inexperience with the concept, Maman had no trouble adjusting to leisure time. One sun-drenched day followed the other in a predictable routine that suited us all. Up none too early after a night in a small hotel in a village — never a city. Stop at every market (Maman refused to pass a single one by) until our vehicles became laden with local vegetables, cheeses, breads, meats, fish, and of course, wines. At that point, usually midafternoon, we pulled off the road under a tree and set up a portable grill. After lunch, and maybe a swim or snooze, we'd push on, scouting for another inn in another small village.

No one enjoyed himself more than Papa, who fit in so well, he might have been a closet Spaniard. We had barely crossed the border when he discovered that wonderful Spanish invention, the wineskin, and kept all of ours supplied with each region's offerings. His greatest pleasure came from finding bargains.

"Look," he said, brandishing a bottle, "two francs is all this cost. It would be worth ten francs at home. I've saved eight francs."

No one bothered to mention that he was more than making up the difference in price in quantities consumed. We were on vacation. And besides, the family doctor had recently diagnosed Papa as having extremely high blood pressure, for which at the time there was no medication — only dieting, which wasn't in line with my father's lifestyle. The doctor had confided in Maman that her husband probably had only a few years to live. At home, Papa was beginning to slow down. But in Spain, he was the gregarious father I had known as a boy.

That family trip pretty much set the tone for the summer. After Spain, Maman and Papa went back to the restaurant, Bichon and Roland to their jobs. Jean-Claude and I met up and visited Italy and Switzerland together, doing exactly what we'd planned. As we loaded the cars aboard the ship for our return voyage to New York, Roland and I hugged, and I promised to return home for at least a couple of weeks every summer.

But you know what happens to those pledges. Three more years would pass before I returned to France. And when I did, it was to say goodbye to Papa, who died while I was there.

IN MR. JOHNSON I found a second father figure. He was a charismatic, powerful, and yet soft-spoken man. In business matters he was straightforward, candid, and always open to new ideas. Occasionally, Pierre and I prepared private parties for Mr. Johnson and his wife at their apartment on Sutton Place in New York City (often using our frozen commissary fare). But it wasn't a master-servant relationship. We always joined the Johnsons and their guests at the table and became friends, a relationship that was new to me, because the social structure in France would not have permitted a lowly cook to befriend the chairman of the board. Even so, I feared I would experience Mr. Johnson's wrath one evening after Pierre had gone hunting, bringing back three pheasants we planned to serve. I plucked them and pushed the feathers down that marvelous new invention — the garbage disposal. To my dismay, the machine stalled, totally clogged. Embarrassed, I confessed to Mr. Johnson, who laughed wholeheartedly and then poured a glass of wine to console me.

One weekend Mr. and Mrs. Johnson joined us for dinner on Long Island, and I went to pick them up in Sag Harbor, where they had moored their yacht. Mr. Johnson was waiting for me on the dock, seated comfortably on a case of Dom Perignon. We had a great evening together, and the following day he invited all of us to cruise on his lavish 120-foot boat, with a crew of eight. We drank cocktails, and Mr. Johnson served all of us himself from the buffet that his cook had prepared. I was embarrassed as he served me.

With a big smile he told me, "Young man, you are being served by the chairman of the board." This was Mr. Johnson, one of the best businessmen that America ever produced.

AFTER TWO YEARS of study at Columbia University, I completed the English for Foreign Students program that I had started two weeks after my arrival in New York. My grades were good, and that inflated my spirits and my ego. I wanted desperately to further my education, but since I hadn't even started high school, let alone graduated, I lacked the qualifications to be admitted to the university as a matriculated student. My option was to try for admittance to the School of General Studies, a school for adults, where students had to be at least twenty-one years old.

An adviser at the university explained my options. Either I could go to night school to earn a high school equivalency diploma, which would take a couple of years, or I could take an entrance examination. If I passed, I would be allowed to take courses over the next two years as long as I maintained a B average. If I succeeded, the classes taken in the validation program would earn credit, and I would be admitted to Columbia's School of General Studies.

Using a headset, I took the very general, lengthy entrance exam in a large room with four hundred other hopefuls, knowing that most of us would fail. Many subjects were covered: English, philosophy, mathematics, geography, and history. After a week or so of tense waiting, I got the results. Somehow I had passed.

But the exam was only my first step, and as it turned out, the easiest. Once in the validation program, I became a model student by necessity. Each time I started a new subject, it took me two or three weeks just to absorb the vocabulary and jargon before I could begin to figure out how to do the actual work. Whenever I had a spare moment — on the subway, during breaks at work, nights, weekends — I had a textbook open in front of me. Despite my efforts, I was falling behind in mathematics, a notoriously difficult course that covered everything a university-bound student would take in high school over four years: algebra, plane and solid geometry, and trigonometry. More than half of those who took the course flunked. My odds did not look good.

Desperate, I turned to Jack Bixgorin, the office manager at the Howard Johnson's commissary. Before becoming an office manager, Jack had been a high school math teacher. He was generous and patient, and — most important — he loved good food. I gave him cooking classes and fixed lunch for him on weekdays in my test kitchen. Through a full mouth most of the time, Jack tutored me in the complexities and intricacies of mathematics. I passed that class.

There were a few moments of levity during the ordeal of validation classes. In one biology lab, my group was presented with a rabbit that we were expected to dissect. While the professor rambled along, pointing to a diagram in front of the room, I took a scalpel in hand and to my lab partners' amusement, deftly boned out our lab specimen.

I got through validation with the required B average and was admitted to the School of General Studies as a matriculated student.

I STAYED at Howard Johnson's throughout the 1960s, a decade that changed my view of food along with my view of the world and of the restaurant business, a time in which I became immersed in the American lifestyle and came to understand American eating habits. Howard Johnson's was a platform for Pierre and me during the 1960s and led us to become thoroughly involved in America's culinary revolution, as foot soldiers, not as chefs working in an elitist restaurant, serving food to only a few privileged people. Perhaps the most important thing I came to understand during my decade at HoJo's was that Americans had extremely open palates compared to French diners. They were willing to try items that lay out-side their normal range of tastes. If they liked the food, that was all that mattered. I wasn't constantly battling ingrained prejudices as I would have been in France, where doing something as simple as adding carrots to *boeuf bourguignon* could have gotten me guillo-tined, not because carrots make the dish taste bad (they are great), but because it wouldn't be the way a *boeuf* was supposed to be made. In France, unless a dish was prepared exactly "right," people would know and complain. In the States, if it tasted good, then fine, the customer was happy. A whole new world of culinary possi-bilities had opened up before me.

New England
Clam Chowder

I DON'T REMEMBER ever eating clams when I was in France. Oysters and mussels, yes, but not clams. Fried clams and New England clam chowder were popular menu items at Howard Johnson's, and I soon learned to love them. Although HoJo's clam chowder recipe was made in 3,000-gallon amounts and canned, it was quite good. I reproduce that taste at home when a bit of Howard Johnson's nostalgia creeps in.

- 5 quahog clams or 10 to 12 large cherrystone clams
- 4 cups water
- 4 ounces pancetta or lean, cured pork, cut into 1-inch pieces (about ¾ cup)
- 1 tablespoon good olive oil
- 1 large onion (about 8 ounces), peeled and cut into 1-inch pieces (1½ cups)
- 2 teaspoons chopped garlic
- 1 tablespoon all-purpose flour
- 2 sprigs fresh thyme
- 1 pound Yukon Gold potatoes, peeled and cut into ½-inch dice (2¼ cups)
- 1 cup light cream
- 1 cup milk
- ¼ teaspoon freshly ground black pepper

Wash the clams well under cold water, and put them in a saucepan with 2 cups of the water. Bring to a boil (this will take about 5 minutes), and boil gently for 10 minutes. Drain off and reserve the cooking liquid, remove the clams from their shells, and cut the clams into ½-inch pieces (1½ cups). Put the clam pieces in a bowl, then carefully pour the cooking liquid into another bowl, leaving behind any sediment or dirt. (You should have about 3½ cups of stock.) Set aside the stock and the clams.

Put the pancetta or pork pieces in a large saucepan, and cover with the remaining 2 cups water. Bring to a boil, and boil for 30 seconds. Drain the pancetta, and wash it in a sieve under cold water. Rinse the saucepan, and return the pancetta to the pan with the oil. Place over medium heat, and cook gently, stirring occasionally, for 7 to 8 minutes. Add the onion and garlic, and continue cooking, stirring, for 1 minute. Add the flour, mix it in well, and cook for 10 seconds. Add the reserved stock and the thyme, and bring to a boil. Then add the potatoes and clams, bring to a boil, cover, reduce the heat to very low, and cook gently for 2 hours.

At serving time, add the cream, milk, and pepper, bring to a boil, and serve. (Note: No salt should be needed because of the clam juice and pancetta, but taste and season to your liking.)

11

Cooking with Friends

I HAD BEEN in the country just two weeks when Pierre Franey introduced me to a friend of his, a dapper, drawling Mississippian named Craig Claiborne. A graduate of a Swiss hotel school, Craig was thoroughly trained in classic French cooking and eager to get to know anyone with a similar background. Although our ages and upbringings (not to mention sexual orientations) could not have been more different, our serious interest in all aspects of food drew us together.

To most Americans in the 1960s, food was sustenance, full stop. Viewing it as something important, as integral to a nation's culture as its music, art, and literature, made you a member of a small, oddball minority. In the early 1960s, the term *foodie* had yet to be coined. There were no culinary institutes, few cooking schools, no celebrity chefs. The country supported only one small-circulation food magazine, *Gourmet.* The *New York Times* and other prominent newspapers had yet to break out special sections dedicated to cooking and dining. Not only was there no Food Network — no food programming existed anywhere on TV.

But a few people loved food, thought about it all the time, and naturally gravitated toward one another. Although small, the food world was by no means a closed clique. On the contrary, new members and new ideas were not only welcomed but actively courted. It also helped that there were no unapproachable superstars in the group.

Craig, who had just been appointed the food editor of the *New York Times,* had met Pierre after doing a review of Le Pavillon. He and Pierre became friends, cooking together and sharing information about food, laying the foundation for their later professional relationship as a cook and writer team. Craig was surely the most easygoing, generous, socially active person I had ever encountered. He raised the concept of mixing business and pleasure to an art form, especially when the *New York Times* was picking up the tab, not only for Craig but for any friend fortunate enough to be in his entourage. If you had dinner at Craig's, you knew that recipes for the dishes he served would soon appear on the food pages. If you and he went to a restaurant, you'd read a replay of tidbits of the evening's conversation a few days later in a review. If he asked you a question about technique as you cooked together at his stove, your suggestions would form the basis of a *Times* article.

Craig's finest achievements in blending the two aspects of his life were played out in the home he built at the Springs near East Hampton on Long Island, not far from where Pierre had his summer place. I became a regular weekend visitor to the Hamptons and a major beneficiary of Craig's largesse.

Craig owned two large lots overlooking Gardiner's Bay; he built his house on one and dug a beautiful swimming pool on the other. The whole first floor of the house faced the sea, and that was where the large kitchen, dining room, and living room were situated. Except for a counter between the kitchen and dining room, the floor had no dividers, which gave the space a comfortable, easy air.

I was conditioned to a French way of dealing with guests,

which was much more formal and regulated than the hospitality found at Craig's. When family and friends came to our house in France, we fussed over them from the moment they came downstairs for café au lait and croissants in the morning to their last long yawn at midnight over a snifter of cognac. Every moment was scripted and orchestrated for their pleasure, so much so that our efforts often backfired. A visit became an ordeal, overwhelming for guests and hosts alike. But at Craig's, I felt free to get up in the morning whenever I wanted to, to eat breakfast or not, as I desired, to swim if and when I cared to. There was great freedom to enjoy oneself without the burden of an overzealous, oppressive host. The experience coincided with the way I felt about America.

This freedom was also reflected in the food that we experimented with each weekend, sometimes preparing Chinese, Mexican, Italian, or Indian, as well as pure, simple American fare, along with French concoctions. Typically, our Saturdays began with a trip to the open summer market. We started cooking seriously in the afternoon, always joined by Pierre, an expert fisherman and a dependable source for fresh lobsters, striped bass, bluefish, eels, whitebait, and clams.

Craig was unsurpassed at harnessing the divergent energies of chefs to create memorable parties. One of his greatest efforts, in the summer of 1965, was what he billed as the grandest picnic of all time, to be held on Gardiner's Island, which was owned by Craig's friend Robert Gardiner. Pierre, Roger Fessaguet (the chef at New York's La Caravelle), Jean Vergnes (the chef at New York's Le Colony), René Verdon (the chef at the White House), and I got together to prepare the meal.

Most of the picnic food came from Gardiner's Island or the waters around it. We cooked mussels ravigote, a pâté of veal, a seviche composed of different local raw fish, a green salad, a bluefish cooked in vinegar and white wine, a poached striped bass with *rouille* sauce, grilled squab, cold stuffed lobster, a mixture of different berries, cheese, French bread, and several cases of fine wine.

We ferried equipment and food from the mainland to the island in small boats, most of them provided by Pierre and his neighbors. Heavier items we loaded into a pickup truck and drove to the marina where Robert Gardiner and his wife waited with their thirty-foot, 500-horsepower yacht, the *Laughing Lady.*

Craig put me in charge of setting up the buffet. I decided to arrange the food on driftwood gathered from the beach. We scavenged weathered planks and logs to create the buffet table. An old cable wheel became a graceful pedestal. Our collection of flotsam was covered with white, starched tablecloths and napkins.

Naturally, such an event called for Champagne. And because this was Craig, the brand was to be Dom Perignon and the flutes that were to contain it were to be Baccarat. Crystal of that quality was well beyond our budget, but Craig had gone to Baccarat's shop on 57th Street and asked to borrow the glasses for a special party that, he explained, would be featured prominently in the *New York Times,* a party where the famous chefs of President Kennedy and General de Gaulle would cook along with chefs from New York's best restaurants, Le Pavillon, La Caravelle, and Le Colony. Despite Craig's sales pitch and the power of the *Times,* Baccarat refused to lend the flutes, saying that even their own managing director would have to buy the glasses at regular price, $50 each. However, as a special favor, Baccarat told Craig that he was welcome to buy the glasses, two dozen in all. After the party, they would repurchase at the same price any he returned undamaged.

By the end of the picnic, we were all stuffed with wonderful food and more than a little tipsy, thanks in no small part to the contents of those precious flutes. In the darkness, we had to cross between Gardiner's and the mainland a half-dozen times with leftover food, partially empty cases of wine, and soiled eating and cooking utensils. Despite the favorable odds of one of us tripping, slipping, or mistakenly putting a glass down on an uneven surface, only one flute got chipped. Fifty bucks did not seem too onerous for the *Times*'s accountants to swallow in the interests of a great food story. Back on shore, I cautiously washed and rinsed the twenty-three surviving glasses. Craig placed each one on a counter between the kitchen and dining areas. We were safe.

I slept in the living room at Craig's that night and at around 3:00 A.M. was jerked out of bed by a crash, followed by a tinkling sound as shards of the world's finest lead crystal showered onto the floor. A large oval fish platter that had hung for years on the wall just above the glasses had chosen that night to come loose. Not one glass escaped. Craig's article ran on August 5, 1965, no doubt the most expensive food piece that the paper had ever published.

But a little thing like trying to slide a $1,200 bill for smashed glassware past his editors was not about to dampen Craig's enthusiasm for bigger, better, and more expensive celebrations. He decided to organize the clambake to end all clambakes. I had no idea of what a clambake was, though the name conjured unappetizing images. Craig explained that the clambake was part of a New England tradition, which came from the American Indians, who used to cook fish, shellfish, corn, and potatoes between seaweed and hot rocks buried in the sand. The pièce de résistance would be, of course, the lobsters. We planned to cook sixty, along with fifteen chickens, two bushels of cherrystone clams, fifteen pounds of sausages, several bushels of husked corn, Long Island potatoes, and large local onions.

Two days before the event, we dug the pit, which measured twenty feet long, fifteen feet wide, and two feet deep. We lined the bottom of the pit with large stones, which were, fortunately, plentiful on the beach, and gathered wood — tons of it, ranging from twigs to tree trunks — enough to create a five-foot-tall pyre on the rocks. Next, we collected seaweed, again plentiful along the beach, heaping it into what looked like a dark, soggy haystack. Rockweed was the preferred variety. With its many small, bubble-like pods, it created the most steam, according to Craig. We requisitioned four bed sheets and a sturdy tarpaulin, and we were ready.

I have never been an early riser, but on the day of the clambake I saw a stunning sunrise above the Atlantic. Coffee mug in hand, I helped light the fire at around 5:30 A.M. My next assignment was a critical one. I was to help Pierre secure the sixty lobsters. The previous day, Craig had informed us that he had arranged for an added twist. Not only did Pierre and I have to catch the main course, but our efforts at hauling up lobster traps were to be filmed by a television crew.

We didn't know a thing about television, but Pierre understood enough about the habits of Long Island's lobsters to have taken the precaution of buying a couple of bushels of them the previous evening at Grossman's fish market on Montauk Point. In the semidarkness, we loaded the store-bought crustaceans aboard Pierre's boat, used them to supplement the grand total of five lobsters that had wandered into his traps on their own, and then lowered gear and captives back to the ocean floor.

At filming time, we pulled up the cages and started removing the lobsters and placing them in a bin — all with exaggerated gestures of surprise and happiness. The lobsters, even those we had purchased at Grossman's, seemed to know their parts, slapping their tails and brandishing their claws. All of a sudden, Pierre stopped laughing. His eyes got larger, and he gestured with his chin to a store-bought lobster. I squinted and realized that we'd forgotten to take the rubber bands off their claws. The cameras rolled on.

Back on the beach, Pierre seared the chicken pieces on the grill, seasoning them with herbs and pepper. Other guests husked the corn, washed the clams, and wrapped all the food, except the lobsters, in cheesecloth. By 11:00 A.M., the fire had burned down to white ashes between rocks so hot I couldn't get closer than four feet from the pit. Craig decreed that the time had come to start cooking, and he threw a layer of seaweed about a foot deep on the hot stones. The rockweed turned from dark brown to light green, emitting a geyser's worth of steam. We placed bed sheets rinsed in seawater on top of the seaweed to prevent dinner from disappearing, and everyone present, including the kids, began tossing lobsters and bundles of food into the pit. Two more wet sheets were spread over the food, followed by the large tarpaulin. Finally, a half-dozen of us took shovels and heaped sand on top to secure the tarpaulin and prevent precious steam from escaping.

The meal baked for about two hours, while we enjoyed apéritifs and made sauces: plain rendered butter, herb butter, tartar sauce, and ravigote sauce, a spicy vinaigrette with mustard, capers, and herbs. We prepared salads of local tomatoes and greens and set up the desserts, which included chocolate and vanilla ice cream and local strawberries and raspberries.

At the appointed time, we brushed the sand away, and four of us lifted the tarpaulin and sheets to expose the steaming, bright red lobsters. My face was warmed by a potent fragrance of the sea, mingling with smoke, onions, and chicken. We served the food, ate, and drank wine until nightfall. That was the way Craig threw a party.

BUT LIKE ANYONE involved in cooking, Craig hosted his share of disasters. One of them stands out as being so truly monumental that I shudder to think about it even now. It started when Pierre and I were at Craig's, complaining about how difficult it was in the States to secure the offal common in French markets, from the spinal cord (*amourette*) to kidneys, brains, sweetbreads, feet, and, especially, calf's head (*tête de veau*), which Pierre loved. In France, calf's head is a classic bistro dish and is often served with calf's tongue. The skinned and cleaned head is usually poached *au blanc*, meaning in a mixture of flour and water to which are added a dash of lemon juice, onion, thyme, and a bay leaf. The meat is simmered until it falls from the bones, then sliced and served hot with a rémoulade, a light mayonnaise with a lot of chopped onion, garlic, herbs, hard-cooked eggs, capers, and pickles. It was puzzling to us that even though veal was easy to get in America, and of great quality, it was impossible to purchase heads. What happened to all those calves' heads?

You never knew whom you'd be partying with at Craig's — except that the person would be involved deeply with food. As it turned out, one of his guests was a meat supplier, and he told us that he had plenty of calves' heads and would send us some by the following week.

The next Saturday, three large cases bearing the return address of the meat supplier arrived. We were ecstatic, until Pierre tore open the first case. Craig's meat purveyor friend had obviously meant well. And he'd certainly lived up to his promise. The crate contained calves' heads all right — but in exactly the same condition they had been in when lopped from their owners' necks, which is to say with hair intact. Even after our decades in French kitchens, where sheep, ducks, chickens, and rabbits regularly arrived in their fur and feathers, neither Pierre nor I had ever dealt with a hide-covered calf's head, and twelve of them were literally eyeing us now.

Still, the meat man had gone to a lot of effort, and I was salivating at the thought of my first real *tête de veau* since I'd left Paris — so temptingly near yet so disgustingly out of reach. Surely the hair problem could be overcome. I recalled that in France, butchers usually removed the hair at the processing plant by dropping the head in scalding water and scraping the fur off the skin. Pierre wasn't so sure. He thought he remembered hearing something about a waxing process. Lacking wax, we scalded one head. At the end of a smelly, messy half-hour, every hair remained firmly rooted in its follicle. In desperation, Pierre requisitioned one of Craig's razors and tried to shave the head. He destroyed a few razorblades but put barely a scratch on the head. Our other attempts met with similar results.

So instead of enjoying a taste of home, Pierre and I were stuck with the problem of how to dispose of a dozen rapidly decaying calves' heads in the Hamptons. Pierre came up with what struck us as an ideal solution, and an environmentally sound one as well. The heads would make a feast for the lobsters and crabs crawling across the bottom of the Atlantic. Just before sunset, like mafia hit men disposing of evidence in the time-honored New York fashion, we piled all three cases of calves' heads in his little boat and furtively motored out until the shore of Long Island became a hazy smudge on the darkening horizon. Wishing the creatures of the deep *bon appétit,* we dumped the heads and watched them slowly disappear into the blue-green water.

For a couple of days, it looked as if our calves' heads were, indeed, sleeping with the fishes, and none of our tony neighbors were the wiser. We'd gotten away with our crime against Hamptons sensibilities. Or so we thought.

Then, thanks to prevailing currents, our heads resurfaced. The *East Hampton Star* ran a front-page article that ranted about a cultist group that had murdered calves, probably as part of some diabolical ritual, and thrown the heads on the town's beach in plain view of bathers. Foreseeing headlines about the arrest of a couple of crazed French chefs in subsequent editions of the *Star,* Pierre and I thought it prudent to maintain our own version of omerta.

The calves' heads incident was not my only brush with culinary crime. Craig was always scouring New York for hard-to-find ingredients. One weekend he arrived in the Hamptons bearing a true prize, a jar of gourmet-quality *glace de viande* he'd found at a place in New York aptly called La Maison de Glace.

"You've got to try this," he said, opening the small jar, which, he told us, had cost four dollars.

I was very interested in tasting Craig's discovery, but not for the reasons he thought. Although Craig did not know it, I had made this particular *glace* but had never sampled the final product. The idea had come to me at the Howard Johnson's commissary when one of my associates was about to dump three thousand pounds of used beef-stock bones in the refuse container. Back at

Le Plaza Athénée in Paris, beef-stock bones were viewed as treasures by the *saucier* and his *commis*. They were the raw materials for a tidy second income made by selling *glace*. Why not duplicate my old Parisian sideline, but as with everything at Howard Johnson's, on a gargantuan, New World scale? Instead of discarding the cooked bones, I covered them again with cold water and recooked them gently overnight. The liquid was then strained into a two-hundred-gallon kettle, reduced to about forty gallons of beautiful, syrupy essence, and, finally, transferred to a fifty-gallon kettle where it was further reduced to a powerful *glace*. A ton and a half of bones yielded between ten and twelve gallons of *glace* of the best possible quality. We sold it to La Maison de Glace for ten dollars a gallon. Packaged in the store's pretty little jars, it retailed at a profit margin of about 800 percent.

Craig presented me with a spoonful.

I all but spat the stuff out.

He'd been gypped. My beautiful, concentrated glaze had been diluted and extended by at least three times its volume for extra profit. This was fraud, and the end of my stint in the *glace* trade.

～

TOWARD THE END of the 1960s word reached North America about a revolution in French cooking. Just rumors at first, and like all rumors, the information was both fragmented and contradictory. Our East Hampton group of French chefs were excited and unsettled about the concept, without knowing specifically what it was. One chef would tell us that everything was to be served on large plates, another that meat, poultry, and fish were always served boned, while a third would define it as a cuisine with flourless sauces. Other theories spread about a cuisine with a lot of raw fish and mixtures of sweet and sour tastes. We had endless discussions but remained puzzled.

I thought I would get the definitive answer directly from the source when Craig invited me out to his place on Long Island to cook dinner with Paul Bocuse. The great Lyonnais chef made his famous truffle soup, a consommé with diced foie gras and truffle slices, covered with a piece of puff pastry and baked. I prepared lobster from the area in a light sauce *américaine,* with butter, tomatoes, garlic, and cognac. While we worked in the kitchen, we discussed the cuisine that was creating such a stir. Bocuse admitted that he didn't really understand what it was. It seemed to amount to a few dictums: to simplify cooking while staying true to the taste of what one was preparing (lobster had to taste like lobster), to replace fancy sauces with mostly natural juices, and to shorten cooking times, especially for fish and vegetables. Neither of us guessed that this nouvelle cuisine would change all restaurant fare, from starred restaurants to bistros to single-family eateries.

For me and other cooks of my age, who were trained in the autocratic and disciplined old style, nouvelle cuisine was truly nouvelle. Nouvelle cuisine was, and would remain, the biggest revolution in my culinary life, bringing sweeping changes to my way of cooking and my approach to food. With its advent, I felt validated to start using new ingredients, different techniques, and different procedures in ways that were my own. I felt free to combine new tastes with old ones in combinations that were more personal than anything I had done in the kitchen before. I could break the old rules, and that liberation from the confinement of classic French cooking opened my eyes to a new cuisine that was more in tune with the freedom that I was experiencing in my New World.

Nouvelle cuisine was soon popularized by food writers eager to discover something new, and by journalists, who overpraised it. It became the rage, a new creed, and the intellectuals of the movement were the French journalists Gault and Millau. They not only extolled this new way of cooking but set down the cuisine's bylaws with the help of some of the great chefs of France, particularly Bocuse and Michel Guérard.

Chefs were instructed to obtain the freshest possible ingredients and to create shorter menus in order to focus on a few specific dishes. Chefs were also directed to reduce cooking times, especially for fish and vegetables; to avoid, whenever possible, complicated cooking procedures; to investigate regional recipes but be open to preparing them with new techniques and new equipment, such as the food processor; to make leaner sauces; to be mindful of the health of their customers; and, especially, to create new dishes with an open mind to ethnic influence. All of these were good rules, but rules that would lend themselves to many misunderstandings.

I WAS ROLLING out dough for an apple tart at Craig's apartment three months or so after my arrival in the States when I met the woman who would become one of the most important figures in my life, a friend, mentor, and surrogate "American mother," all in one. A tiny lady, with her gray hair tightly wound into a bun, scurried into the kitchen. She paused, sized me up, and said, "How do you do, young man," formally extending a hand encased in a kid glove that even then was decades out of fashion. "My name is Helen McCully."

Today, the name Helen McCully is unknown even to most Americans who are active in the culinary world. But in the early 1960s, this feisty Nova Scotia native was as influential in American cuisine as James Beard, Julia Child — or anybody. Not because of her writing, although she published several cookbooks and authored a long-running food column; not because of *House Beautiful,* the magazine she edited; but because of her personality. Helen knew everybody in the country who had a passionate interest in food, and she made it her life's mission to bring us all together, to encourage us, to boost our careers, and when occasion demanded, to scold us like the children she never had. Helen's apartment on the Upper East Side became a culinary salon. In her small kitchen the food revolution gained the critical mass necessary to take off in this country. If a foreign chef was visiting New

York, he'd show up at Helen's for dinner. A food person in town from the West Coast or Deep South occasioned an impromptu gathering at Helen's. If the Buddha-like Jim Beard was not stationed at her table in the evening, you knew that they had spoken earlier that day on the phone for at least an hour, gossiping, exchanging recipes, swapping stories about restaurants, anything concerning the one subject that interested them.

From the moment we met at Craig's, Helen assigned herself the task of polishing me and directing both my career and my personal life.

"You wear your hair too long about the collar," she said.

It was gauche, I was informed, to wear European-style socks that left a little bare calf showing below my trouser cuffs. I must be sure to wear tie and jacket and always send formal invitations and thank-you notes.

And she was forever setting me up with young ladies that met her rigid definition of eligible. These were generally recruited from the ranks of editorial assistants at the magazine and possessed all of the qualities any young man's mother would want in a daughter-in-law: pretty, poised, polite, educated. But there was always a certain lack of chemistry — on my part and theirs. Unfortunately, Helen also had an uncanny ability to pick women who lived in the remote corners of Queens and Brooklyn. I, as Helen's budding gentleman in training, had to escort them home in my recently acquired Beetle. Following one particularly unsuccessful date, I spent the wee hours of a morning trying to find my way out of an unfamiliar maze of streets in some distant part of the boroughs.

She had her shortcomings as a matchmaker, but Helen and I worked well together developing recipes and working on articles, even though we sometimes had violent and lengthy arguments that left us stubbornly refusing to talk to each other for days at a time.

One such rift developed over asparagus, which she liked to eat slightly crunchy.

"These are not cooked properly," I said.

"They taste better when not overdone."

"You're saying I don't know how to boil asparagus?"

"Precisely."

Another long silent period followed an occasion when she used my recipe for a génoise in *House Beautiful* and followed it with a suggestion that a Betty Crocker box cake was an acceptable substitute.

"How can you do such a thing? It's an outrage!" I said.

"The cake mix is fine."

"Not in the same article as my génoise."

"A lot of my readers will never make a proper génoise. Some might want to try. Your recipe is there for them. For the rest, I had to give them something."

"You gave them trash."

"You are a stubborn Frenchman."

We met several times a week in her apartment on East 52nd Street, and we — although mostly I — cooked for guests and friends. True to her Nova Scotian heritage, Helen was very thrifty. She ate little and, consequently, when we prepared dinners at her home, the portions were always minuscule. Once when she invited Jim Beard for dinner, I was to cook quail. Helen decided that one quail per person would be quite enough, thank you. There was no sense in trying to change her mind.

Jim could have single-handedly devoured an entire turkey and then sopped the roasting pan clean with a loaf or two of bread. His allotted quail disappeared in one nibble, and he spent the rest of the meal with the pleading, disappointed face of an old St. Bernard hoping someone might toss him a table scrap. Afterward on the street outside, Jim turned to me and said, "So where are we going to go for dinner?"

One day Helen insisted that I drop by her apartment on my way home. There was a note of urgency in her voice.

When I got there, she said, "I have something I want you to

read." She presented me with a cardboard box filled with typewritten pages.

"A woman up in Cambridge wrote it," Helen said. "She's been trying to find a publisher, but they're all rejecting it. I think it's an amazing piece of work. I want to know what you think."

I lugged the box back to my apartment, mercifully just around the corner from Helen's. Jean-Claude was sitting at the kitchen table when I entered.

"What's that?" he asked.

"A book manuscript," I said.

He looked at the box suspiciously. "A very long book," he said.

I put the box down and opened its flaps. The page on top read, "*Mastering the Art of French Cooking,* by Julia Child . . ."

An hour later, I was still reading, passing the pages to Jean-Claude, who became as engrossed as I. Someone had taken the training and knowledge that Jean-Claude and I had acquired as apprentices and *commis* and codified it, broken it down into simple steps that someone who had never boiled a kettle of water could follow. I was a little jealous. This was the type of book I should have written.

Moules Ravigote

(MUSSELS RAVIGOTE)

YIELD: 6 FIRST-COURSE SERVINGS

*M*OULES RAVIGOTE is a standard at most good French bistros and brasseries and was a regular dish at Craig's and Pierre's in the summer. The juice of the mussels, not used in this recipe, can be transformed into a velouté, a poaching stock for fish or shellfish, or, with the addition of heavy cream, chives, and black pepper, into a delightful cold soup called Billi-Bi.

3½ pounds medium-size mussels, preferably heavy ones, which are usually fuller and better
1 cup dry, fruity white wine, such as a Sauvignon Blanc
¼ cup extra-virgin olive oil
1½ tablespoons Dijon-style mustard
1 tablespoon red wine vinegar
3 tablespoons chopped fresh parsley
3 tablespoons finely chopped mild onion
1 tablespoon drained small capers
1 teaspoon finely chopped garlic
¼ teaspoon salt
½ teaspoon freshly ground black pepper

1 hard-cooked egg (see page 22), cut into slices with an egg cutter, then turned 90 degrees in the cutter and cut again into ½-inch pieces
6 large leaves Boston lettuce, washed and dried

Put the mussels in a large bowl of cold water, and rub them against one another to clean them. Transfer the mussels to a clean bowl of water, repeat the washing, then lift them from the water, and put them in a stainless steel saucepan with the wine. Cover, and bring to a boil over high heat. Cook the mussels, tossing them occasionally, for about 3 minutes, or until almost all the shells have opened. Drain in a colander, reserving the stock for soup or freezing it for future use.

Remove the mussels from the shells, discarding any that did not open, and put them in a bowl.

In a separate bowl, mix the rest of the ingredients, except for the egg pieces and the lettuce. Stir the dressing into the mussels. Arrange a lettuce leaf on each of six plates, and spoon the mussels into the leaves. Top with the hard-cooked eggs, and serve at room temperature.

12

Gloria

JEAN-CLAUDE SAYS that the object rolling downhill toward the lift line resembled a one-man avalanche, a whirling blur of skis and poles and boots, tumbling end over end, gaining momentum, bearing down on the innocent skiers clustered at the base, who were waiting for their turn on the T-bar. The object scored a near perfect strike, knocking down about half a dozen of the skiers before coming to an abrupt halt against a steel pylon.

The advanced trail at Sterling Forest ski area had looked like a cinch — from the bottom. I'd been on skis once before and figured I'd pretty much mastered the sport, so I took the lift to the top and launched myself fearlessly downhill, forgetting that during my previous day of skiing I had spent most of the time on my back. On that occasion, stopping was something that had happened naturally, gradually, and in accordance with the laws of physics when I reached the bottom of the slopes and the terrain leveled.

But this hill kept getting steeper. I was flying, utterly out of control. Luckily, I didn't kill anybody, myself included. As it was, I ended up with torn ligaments in my knee, an injury that definitely stopped my exploits on the slopes for the rest of the ski season.

Given that inauspicious beginning, it's surprising that I returned to the slopes the following winter and became a competent skier.

I might not have, except a couple of our buddies from Le Pavillon had opened restaurants in the Catskills around Shandaken and Hunter Mountain and spoke highly of the area, so Jean-Claude and I, along with a few other friends, rented a place there to use as a weekend retreat. We often had Karl Plattner, the ex-Olympian who ran the ski school at Hunter, his wife, Margot, and a few other ski instructors to dinner, and Karl reciprocated with free lessons. Eventually, he invited me to become an instructor. It sounded like a pretty good deal to me: a small stipend, free lift tickets, no lines, and, best of all, a snazzy uniform that drew a very positive reaction from the young, single females on the slopes of Hunter.

I had my eye on one young woman in particular. She had short, dark brown hair that went well with her winter-tanned skin and the handful of freckles that were sprinkled across her cheekbones as if to advertise the fact that their pretty owner possessed a perky and ever-ready sense of humor. I figured I was in luck one afternoon when she joined a large party of us who regularly gathered in the bar to unwind after a hard day on the slopes. But then I saw there was a man with her.

"Who is the guy?" I asked Margot, Karl's wife.

"Her husband."

One Saturday morning a month or so later, Margot, who ran the administrative side of the ski school, told me that someone had signed up for a private lesson with me. Private lessons were expensive — twenty dollars an hour — so it was an honor and a testament to one's teaching skills to be requested as a private instructor. Plus, it was a lot more pleasant spending an hour one-on-one than dealing with a half-dozen novices who hadn't learned to snowplow. I strode out into a sunny winter morning to meet my new student.

It was the brown-haired woman.

I always took a serious approach toward my responsibilities as a teacher. Perhaps because of my pupil's marital status, I went out of my way to comport myself as a professional for that hour, pushing her hard, correcting her every flaw, no matter how minor. I barked at her to turn into the hill. I tapped on her legs with my pole when her form slipped. I exhorted her to keep her knees slightly bent. It was a good lesson. She definitely got her twenty bucks' worth.

A week later, Margot approached me, shaking her head. "Gloria has signed up for another private hour with you," she said.

"She seemed to have made good progress last week," I said.

Margot looked at me with exasperation and put her hands on my shoulders as if about to shake a little sense into a child. "Jacques," she said, very plainly, "Gloria and her husband have separated."

Observing my blank expression, Margo said, "What if I were to tell you that Gloria is an expert skier? A member of the Ski Patrol."

Ever so slowly the message sank in.

But I still had a problem with the concept of her being separated. Did that mean she was single and available to be asked out? Or was it more like being married, which is to say monogamous but living apart while certain marital problems were resolved? I didn't want to appear forward, but I wanted to show interest. So as I left the bar that evening, I dropped the cover of a matchbook with both my home and work numbers on it onto her lap, saying, "Give me a buzz."

Sunday passed without her calling. Monday came and went. No Gloria. It was Tuesday afternoon when the phone in my office finally rang. After consultation with all of her friends, she decided to relent and give the idiot one more try.

And I even managed to blow that one.

"You want to get together for a drink?" I asked.

After accepting my invitation, Gloria skipped lunch and called a friend to walk the dog that evening, certain that "drink" was a euphemism for drinks, dinner, and who knows what else.

I had something more literal in mind and escorted her directly to my apartment, uncorked a bottle of red wine, poured us each a glass, and then drank. When our glasses were empty, I checked my watch and said, "I have to get to a class in ten minutes. You can make your way home by yourself, can't you?"

Gloria promised herself never to speak to me again.

Somehow I convinced her to come over to my place for dinner on Valentine's Day. As a first course I prepared scallops poached in white wine and butter, which I presented in a delicate puff pastry shell. For a main course, we had beef stroganoff on satiny noodles. She loved the meal. I didn't think it necessary to ruin the ambience of the evening by telling her that the entire production had come packaged and frozen in ready-to-heat plastic pouches from the commissary out at HoJo's. Besides, I had made that dinner in an indirect sort of way. And I was proud of it.

Gloria was so impressed with my culinary skills that she became afraid to cook for me. As we began to spend more time together, I started to drop by her place on 83rd Street after classes at Columbia, inevitably famished. To my delight, Gloria always maintained a fridge full of fine deli meats — salami, pastrami, corned beef — which I loved. Her fridge was a late-night cornucopia, particularly because such treats were costly and well above my budget. I didn't realize it, but Gloria was making a financial sacrifice in order not to have to make dinner for me.

One evening, I swung open the door of her wondrous refrigerator and saw that she owned a thick slice of Virginia ham along with a half dozen eggs. I got an instant craving for the sweet, smoky, salty richness of ham and eggs, one of my all-time favorite dishes.

"Would you mind frying these up for me?" I asked.

There was a pause. Gloria muttered, "Sure," and scooped a dollop of butter into the pan, added the ham, got out two eggs, and stopped.

She looked at me a little awkwardly. "Jacques," she said. "I'm going to have to excuse myself to go to the washroom. Would you mind . . . ?" She held up the eggs.

"No problem," I said.

I am of the opinion that temperature and texture win out over appearance and other purely aesthetic considerations when it comes to a plate of ham and eggs. I like my yolks hot, but I also like them runny. To achieve that almost contradictory state, I puncture the yolks with a fork and then smush them around for a minute with the whites. I dump the resulting concoction directly from pan to plate. *Et voilà!*

By the time Gloria came back from the bathroom, I was happily seated at the table, scooping up runny bits of egg on slices of ham.

She glanced at the partially coagulated mess on my plate and made a face as if she just had seen the results of someone being sick. "You eat that?"

I nodded, chewing.

"It's disgusting. I wouldn't touch it," she said.

Gloria had overcome her fear of cooking for me.

GLORIA, Craig, Helen, and my coworkers at HoJo's were helping me overcome my Old World prejudices and become more open-minded and American in my social dealings. But it was one of my fellow students at Columbia who inadvertently taught me what it was like to think like an American.

Foreigners constituted about 75 percent of the student body at Columbia's School for General Studies. Most spoke Spanish or Asian languages; others were from the Eastern European bloc countries — immigrants like me. We were diligent, enthusiastic, curious, and demanding. Except for the requirement that you be at least twenty-one years old to enroll, there was no age limit at the School of General Studies, no class system, no shame in having a humble background or a lack of formal education. It was truly America as I had envisioned it.

In France at this time, the class system was such that it would have been all but impossible for someone like me to go back to school at twenty-six and be accepted. Ridicule kills in France, and the worst possible situation for a student is to ask a question deemed stupid. Such students become the butt of derision and jeering from the class and, often, even the professor. In many cases, particularly the professor.

I overcame my fear of asking questions during an intermediate English class. The teacher was explaining some abstruse rule of the language to us. To demonstrate his logic, he mentioned Beethoven.

A Chinese student shot up his hand and asked, "What is a Beethoven?"

In typical French fashion, I inhaled a mighty breath to join in the peals of laughter.

There were none.

No one except for me had so much as cracked a smile, and the prof was explaining — without irony — who Beethoven was. I felt ashamed, realizing that if the professor had made reference to a Chinese composer from the first half of the nineteenth century, my hand would have shot up just as fast as the Chinese student's.

~~~~~

I PROPOSED TO Gloria five months after we started seeing each other. The wording of my actual proposal was, "As long as Maman's coming over for a visit, we may as well get married."

It may have been a little light in the heart-stoppingly-romantic department, but I got the answer I wanted.

After my father's death, Maman had sold Le Pélican to my old army friend, Georges. Free from work responsibilities for the first time in her life, she decided to come over with my cousin, Merret, a formidable cook in her own right, to see America. They greatly enjoyed the summer weekends we spent in Woodstock, so Gloria and I decided to hold our engagement party there with just our small group.

Jean-Claude and my other apartment mate, a chef named Michel Keller, both on vacation from their jobs, were there, along with three other friends, Charlie and Anita Odeurs and Michel Bonnettat. It was early summer and we planned a feast from the neighborhood — everything was going to be gathered from the woods, fields, ponds, and rivers.

We picked wild leeks in the forest and boiled them until they were tender enough for serving with a mustard vinaigrette. Fresh eggs from a nearby farm were turned into eggs Jeannette, my mother's specialty. Jean-Claude caught enough trout to provision a small village. We grilled some of them and finished them in the oven with cream. We smoked others and served them with soft scrambled eggs. We caught frogs from the ponds and prepared them in the classic way, with garlic, shallots, herbs, and a little white wine. Michel, who may have been ignorant of local hunting seasons, bagged a couple of pheasants that had meandered out into a neighboring hay field. We roasted them with herbs and wild mushrooms from the forest. We picked fresh corn, and someone turned several quarts of wild blackberries into sherbet. A generous backyard tree yielded the peaches for a tart. About the only items on the menu that weren't hunted, hooked, picked, or scavenged were the numerous bottles of wine.

To match our engagement party, our wedding feast was going to have to be truly special. As soon as Gloria and I told Craig that we planned to get married, he insisted that the wedding be held at his home in East Hampton. Gloria spent the night before the wedding in a motel nearby. I slept at Craig's. Or, rather, tried to sleep. Sensing that it wasn't quite right for me to be a cook at my own wedding, I went to bed early so I would be fresh and thoroughly rested on the big day. Who was I kidding? Lying in bed, I heard the amiable buzz of my friends cooking in the kitchen. I felt left out. So I came down and joined Jean Vergnes, Jean-Pierre Lejeune, Roger Fessaguet, Michel, Pierre, Jean-Claude, and Craig. I was still in the kitchen an hour before the ceremony.

We prepared a buffet-style menu, which started with a salad of striped bass mimosa, a poached bass served with homemade mayonnaise, herbs, and shallots and garnished with sieved hard-cooked eggs and chopped parsley. It was followed by a fricassee of chicken prepared in the style of old France, with cream, white wine, and spring vegetables. We had a rib roast with a red wine Chambertin sauce that we served with a stew of rice and a jardinière of vegetables. Someone made a whole ham braised in port and served it with a garnish of zucchini and tomatoes. A salad and a tray of French cheeses preceded the big wedding cake, a five-tiered génoise filled and decorated with buttercream and royal icing and topped with almond paste roses and the traditional bride and groom figures; Jean-Claude had baked the cake at Craig's. The cake was served with Bollinger Champagne, one of my favorites. After dinner, we did what we always did when we were together: we drank, sang, danced. The evening's only casualty was the justice of the peace who had officiated at the service. He indulged a little too freely in Champagne and had to stumble home supported by his wife, but not before she had taken advantage of his less-than-alert condition to make a flagrant pass at me.

That night marked the beginning of a very special partnership, although Gloria still insists that I owe her forty dollars for two completely unnecessary ski lessons.

There was a certain advantage to getting married with only Maman, my aunt, and a cousin who was traveling with them representing the Pépin side of the family. My bride might have had second thoughts had she been overwhelmed all at once by her clan of in-laws. Still, she was going to have to meet them eventually, and on their own turf. My two brothers, sisters-in-law, cousins, aunts, and uncles were all anxious to entertain us, which meant that they were going to feed us. I had some doubt that Gloria's constitution could handle all the food and drink.

We headed over in the summer of 1967. After a few days in France, Gloria came to realize that my family was totally obsessed with food. It wasn't enough that everyone plied us with food and drink at their homes. Maman insisted on redoing our wedding in Neyron, so she could invite the whole family to a giant celebration: squab and blood sausage, along with a whole ham, roast chicken, *gratin dauphinois,* fish and vegetable terrine, and more. We had great cheeses and fruits, and for the wedding cake, my mother prepared a *croquembouche,* a pyramid of cream-stuffed profiteroles. It may have been my wedding, but that was no excuse to relax. I was drafted into service behind the stove to help Maman, Bichon, La Marraine, and my aunt Hélène. In Jeannette Pépin's kitchen, some things never changed.

Roland organized the champagne and wines. He set up three small barrels of wine, each containing about fifteen gallons, one of white and two of red, along the stone wall of the garden high enough so the wine would be easily accessible and flow freely. He decorated his barrels with flowers, and we were ready for the feast, which lasted for forty-eight hours.

Still stuffed from our visit home, Gloria and I set off on a trip with Roland, Bichon, and their wives through the south of France, up to Brittany, reaching Nantua, where an aunt of mine had a restaurant, and finally arriving at Valence, where my godmother, who was a cordon bleu, lived. Although we occasionally peered briefly into a church or museum, more often than not we headed straight to the open market, looked at the food, then went out for apéritifs and a long lunch — our appetites having been stimulated by the market. Any meal was reason enough to taste the local wines. Then we got back into the car and continued on to our next destination. Pretty soon, one of us would start perusing the *Michelin* or another food guide to know where we would have dinner that same night.

Gloria was a real trooper — tasting, commenting, and eating. But when we came back to Neyron, she went on an ascetic diet of fruits and vegetables.

~~~○

IN THE MONTHS that followed, Gloria and I began to develop an approach to cooking together. There were inherent difficulties in learning how to share a household kitchen with a professional chef. For some couples, the kitchen can become an emotional battleground littered with unintended slights and hurt feelings. The nonprofessional partner often completely surrenders that terrain, which can cause resentment on both sides. Rather than being a war zone, however, the kitchen became the heart of our home, a room in which we both felt comfortable, the room in which we spent most of our time.

Gloria grew up in New York City, the daughter of a Puerto Rican mother and a Cuban father. She learned to prepare specialties from those two islands as a young girl and had a natural and easy way with them. Drawing from childhood taste memories, she cooked wonderful renditions of Caribbean classics such as rice and beans, fried plantains, and *arroz con pollo* (rice with chicken, tomatoes, and peppers). She also made delicious roast pork and a chicken soup that would have been the envy of any Jewish grandmother.

We established kitchen boundaries and ground rules early in our relationship. Perhaps because of the scarcity of food during the war years, or perhaps because I grew up in a series of small restaurants where recycled scraps and leftovers were often the source of our slim profits, I was obsessive about not wasting a morsel of food. During the early years, Gloria and I had several pitched arguments about leftovers. Returning after a brief business trip, I would open the refrigerator and see that the piece of chicken or pasta from a few days before still hadn't been used. I couldn't help bringing it to Gloria's attention, which aroused her feisty nature. Magically, the problem — and the leftovers — disappeared before long. Gloria was either eating or discarding them before my return, and I didn't ask her which.

I learned to recognize when she needed a clove of garlic peeled or a sprig of parsley stemmed, and when I should stay out of the way. If I came into the kitchen while she was preparing a meal and began lifting pot lids and sniffing the contents, as is my habit, I would be frequently met with the words, "Don't touch anything." On the other hand, sometimes my sniffing and peeking would elicit a question like "How long do you think that roast needs?" — an invitation for me to get involved in the cooking. Before too long, we developed an easy cooperation in the kitchen, working efficiently side by side without talking much.

I soon discovered that Gloria's preferences ran to extremes. On one hand, she loved sturdy and well-seasoned food: roast squab, lamb stew, mashed potatoes, pasta. But when the mood struck, she craved delicate salads, lightly cooked fish, and frothy omelets, and she never hesitated to tell me exactly what she thought of a dish, announcing categorically, "I don't like it" or "Great stuff." She is never impressed by fussy or overly decorated dishes.

She and several good friends of ours had a running argument over who cooked the best meat loaf. In order to put the question to rest, they decided to hold a bake-off. In a field that included many professional chefs, Gloria won by a unanimous decision. I happened to be traveling on business at the time, and upon my return, Gloria confided the secret ingredient that had put her recipe over the top. She had liberally wet the meat mixture with cognac.

"Which cognac?" I asked.

"That opened bottle you keep in the back of the liquor cabinet."

Gloria's secret ingredient was my prize 1914 Hine, worth more than one thousand dollars. She still has the trophy she won, a meat loaf pan mounted on a pedestal. She has never managed to duplicate the winning recipe, however. That may be because I decided to finish my bottle of Hine before she could get her hands on it again.

Gloria's skills eventually topped mine in a few areas of classical French cooking. Organized and tidy by nature, she makes a formidable consommé. She absolutely relishes preparing stock, which she cooks very slowly, strains, and defats and, with the addition of egg whites, herbs, and spices, transforms into a crystal-clear, ethereal liquid. She loves to make cassoulet, the white bean, duck, and sausage casserole from the south of France. She also became an expert at making *fromage fort,* a concoction put together from various leftover cheeses, which are puréed in a food processor with the addition of garlic and white wine. This "strong cheese" is excellent spread on bread, toasted under the broiler, and served with a salad.

Gloria's first introduction to the food world beyond our circle of New York friends came when she and I were invited to Julia Child's house in Cambridge, Massachusetts, on a January day in 1970. In the years since the evening when Jean-Claude and I had sat at our kitchen table, poring over the manuscript of *Mastering the Art of French Cooking,* I had become friends with Julia, thanks to Helen McCully, who introduced us at a dinner in her apartment in New York. Even though I'd read her book, I wasn't in any way prepared for the woman I met that night. With Julia, who could be?

First there was Julia's height; she all but had a foot on me. Then there's the voice, that trilled warble as instantly recognizable as the speaker herself. The introductions over, we did what food people always do, talked shop. And in the case of Julia and me, we did so in French because her French was far more fluent than my English. Julia had been to all of the major restaurants that I had worked at in Paris. She knew the names of all the chefs and maitre d's. But unlike me, she'd actually eaten at these bastions of haute cuisine. I'd never gotten farther than the wrong side of the swinging doors separating their dining rooms from their kitchens.

Gloria was excited and happy to be meeting Julia and her husband, Paul, and she was looking forward to seeing their house, particularly the kitchen. We had no trouble finding Cambridge, but became completely lost the minute we crossed over the town line. After a half-hour of driving along one-way streets that ended at other one-way streets, we somehow found Julia's house on Irving Street. We entered through the back door, which was the real entrance to the house, and led, fittingly, directly into the kitchen.

Julia enveloped both of us simultaneously in a big bear hug. This was somewhat awkward. If you allow for the considerable difference in our heights, you can guess approximately where my face fit when she wrapped me in her arms.

A large room with a big, old Garland stove, pots hanging on the wall, and a grand center table, the kitchen was a place of comfort and conviviality. Everything conformed to Julia's larger-than-life personality. The pans were huge, the counters and table higher than normal, and the atmosphere festive. Paul, an adventurous amateur mixologist, greeted us and offered us a cocktail. His favorite drink at the time was a kind of reverse martini. A martini in France is a glass of Martini-Rossi, the sweet red vermouth from Italy. With a dash of gin on top, it is called a Martini-gin. Paul used bourbon instead of gin and added a twist of lemon, calling it a reverse Manhattan. It was one of the best drinks I'd ever had.

"So-o-o-o-o-o," said Julia, as soon as Paul equipped me with a glass. "What do you want to cook?"

She had bought a rack of pork, which I cut into pork chops and simply pan-fried. We served the chops with string beans and little red potatoes sautéed with rosemary. Salad and cheeses followed, and Julia had made stewed fruit for dessert, which she served with ice cream. Paul brought a Chambertin from the late 1950s, a very good wine, from his cellar. We ate at the kitchen table.

Gloria's Pork Ribs and Red Beans

YIELD: 4 SERVINGS

*B*EFORE I MARRIED Gloria, I knew nothing about Caribbean cooking — Puerto Rican or Cuban. She introduced me to many dishes that through the years we have transformed into our own family recipes. When Roland, my brother, came to visit, one of the first dishes that Gloria would prepare for him was pork shoulder ribs with red beans, which she usually serves with rice and onion pilaf.

This dish is great when made ahead, and any leftovers can be served with fried eggs for breakfast, a type of huevos rancheros. With the bones removed, it can be puréed into a sturdy, flavorful soup in a food processor. Although dried beans are typically presoaked in water before cooking, this is not necessary if the beans are started in cool water.

2 tablespoons good olive oil

4 shoulder pork chops with the bones or country ribs (about 1 1/2 pounds)

1 pound dried red kidney beans

2 cups fresh diced tomato flesh or 1 can (14 3/4 ounces) whole Italian tomatoes, with juice

3 cups sliced onions

1 1/2 tablespoons chopped garlic

1 jalapeño pepper (or more or less, depending on your tolerance for "hotness"), finely chopped, with or without the seeds (about 1 tablespoon)

2 bay leaves

1 teaspoon *herbes de Provence* (available in many supermarkets) or Italian seasoning
6 cups cold water
1¹/₂ teaspoons salt
1 small bunch cilantro

Cooked rice, for serving (optional)
Tabasco hot pepper sauce (optional)

Heat the oil in a large saucepan (I like enameled cast iron), add the pork chops or ribs, and sauté gently, turning once, for 15 to 20 minutes or until they are browned on both sides. Meanwhile, sort through the beans and discard any broken or damaged ones and any foreign matter. Rinse the beans in a sieve under cold water.

When the chops or ribs are browned, remove them from the heat, and add the tomatoes and their juice, onions, garlic, jalapeño, bay leaves, herbs, and water. Stir in the beans and salt, and bring to a boil. Meanwhile, pull the leaves from the cilantro stems. Chop the stems finely (you should have about ¹/₄ cup), and add them to the beans. Reserve the leaves (you should have about 1 cup loosely packed) for use as a garnish. When the bean mixture is boiling, reduce the heat to low, and boil very gently, covered, for 2 to 2¹/₂ hours, or until the beans and pork are very tender.

Divide among soup bowls, sprinkle the cilantro leaves on top, and serve with rice, if desired. Pass the Tabasco sauce for those who want added hotness.

13

Living off the Land

"HANDYMAN'S SPECIAL" was an understatement, even by the relaxed standards of rural real-estate ads. Perched on the top of a hill at the end of a steep, dirt driveway, the farmhouse had been unoccupied for several years. After his wife had died, the former owner simply closed the door behind him and never returned, leaving a lifetime of furniture and personal possessions at the mercy of the Catskills' winter blizzards and summer thunderstorms. Several holes gaped in the roof. The glass had long been smashed out of the windows. Rain had stained the interior walls with grayish swaths of mildew. Deer mice had chewed most of the upholstery. The furniture that thieves hadn't carted away was covered in several layers of chipped paint. And the beams supporting the floor bowed like the spine of a long-overburdened draft horse.

The real-estate agent shuffled his feet impatiently. To him, we were another pair of well-to-do city slickers looking for a country home, and this one didn't have the white-painted fence and well-maintained horse barns most New York lawyers, doctors, and me-

dia barons seek in a rural getaway. But we weren't your typical pur-
chasers of recreational property. I was still working in the Howard
Johnson's commissary and Gloria was an assistant at a Manhattan
company that produced jingles for radio and television advertise-
ments. We'd become addicted to escaping our cramped Queens
apartment for weekends in Hunter and were determined to acquire something there more permanent (and roomy) than the seasonal cabins rented by our pack of friends. We were motivated but
constrained by a lack of capital.

"What do you think?" I asked Gloria.

"I'm not sure," she said hesitantly.

I loved it and saw that it had potential. For all its faults, the
place had the great bones and the comfortable spaces of a well-
used family home, one whose roof and walls had sheltered births,
weddings, celebrations, and funerals. It was located near the village, and had one of the finest views in the Catskills: Schoharie
Creek glittering at the base of our hill, blue-green peaks tumbling
away toward the western horizon. And the asking price was only
$10,000.

By the late 1960s, the Woodstock-Hunter area had become an
enclave for expatriate French chefs, many of whom, like me, were
drawn to the area because its hills, streams, villages, and small
farms reminded them of home. In addition to the old ski-house
crowd of Jean-Claude, Michel Bonnettat, Jean-Pierre Lejeune,
Michel Keller, and Charlie and Anita Odeurs, chefs such as André
Soltner (of Lutèce fame) and Pierre Larré (from the family that
owned the well-known New York restaurant of the same name) also
had bought homes there. The Jamet brothers, Lucien and Louis,
whom I'd known as waiters at Le Pavillon, had opened La Cascade,
a restaurant and inn near Hunter Mountain, and on the pretext
of making extra pocket money — but mostly as an excuse to get
out of the city — I worked there a few weekends each summer. To
have a house in the Catskills was a dream for the food lovers we all
were.

But before that could happen, the place had to undergo extensive renovations, most of which Gloria and I undertook by ourselves. I shoveled two hundred wheelbarrow loads of dirt from the cellar to increase the overhead clearance from five feet to a more comfortable and much dryer six and one-half feet, and I lined the floor with flat blue stones from the creek, creating a perfect place to store my homemade wine, cider, *saucisson,* and prosciutto. After sledgehammering used telephone-pole ends under the joists to level the floor and provide support, we ripped out walls to create a 1,200-square-foot kitchen–dining room–living room space, covering the floor ourselves with red quarry tile left over from a Howard Johnson's renovation. I built the fireplace myself, facing it with round stones from the Schoharie, and I also made the furniture that went around the hearth. The application of several coats of paint remover, followed by countless afternoons of sanding, revealed that, along with the ramshackle house, we had acquired some well-crafted antiques made from walnut, bird's-eye maple, and golden oak.

Every summer Gloria gathered tiny gherkins from our garden and placed them in jars with vinegar, tarragon, cocktail onions, and black pepper, to be used throughout the year. She made an extraordinary strawberry jam that was "cooked" in the summer sun. The berries were added to a sugar syrup and boiled for a couple of minutes, then the whole mixture was poured into a roasting pan, covered with a screen to keep out insects, and left in the sun for several days until the moisture evaporated and the berries reached an almost candied state.

Autumns in Hunter were dedicated to a critical endeavor that enhanced our revelries year-round: the fermenting and bottling of apple cider. I made it together with André Soltner, who came from Alsace, and Jacques de Chanteloup from Normandy, who was another chef colleague at Howard Johnson's. We designed a label for the bottles and gave the cider a name that was a composite of ours: La Cuvée de Chanpesol. We each filled about a hundred bottles every fall, using mostly the unpasteurized juice of Russet, Golden Delicious, and New York Imperial apples from a nearby farm. After allowing the cider to ferment for a couple of weeks in five-gallon jugs, we drew it carefully into Champagne bottles salvaged from a friend's restaurant in New York, corked the bottles, and secured each cork with a metal wire.

The cider rested in my cellar over the winter — undergoing a second fermentation to produce a hard, sparkling beverage. Every bottle was different. Sometimes it came out just right: a golden color, with beautiful, sparkling bubbles; a clean, dry, slightly sweet taste of apple, honey, and apricot, with the scent of apple blossoms and honeysuckle. At other times it was hard and rough, with such a high carbon dioxide content that the corks, despite being secured with wire, burst out of the bottles during the peak of the second fermentation. Precious cider was lost on the floor and walls of the cellar. Opening a bottle became so unpredictable that after a few sticky showers in the kitchen and dining room, Gloria insisted that I perform that chore outside.

With the house renovated, Hunter became our year-round weekend retreat. A couple of weeks after we bottled the last of the cider, snow began flying, and it was time to have the skis tuned for another winter on the slopes. We got in the habit of loading the car early Friday morning to ensure a speedy 5:00 P.M. getaway from the city. But on the weekend of December 15, 1967, just as we were to get into the car for the trip north, Gloria announced an abrupt change in plans. We would be heading due south instead — to the Infirmary Hospital on 14th Street.

Her water had broken.

$\sim$

IN THAT ERA, obstetricians believed that the farther a prospective father was kept from the birth process, the better. Once I'd driven Gloria to the emergency room door, I had done all that was expected of me and was deemed superfluous to all further proceedings. As instructed, I took a seat in the fathers' waiting room and tried to concentrate on a magazine. Other would-be fathers were doing the same thing.

I didn't have long to wait. Gloria's doctor, looking anxious, put his head in and said, "Mr. Pépin, may I speak to you out in the hall?" He took me aside, saying, "The baby is breech."

I didn't know what he meant.

"The baby is upside-down. It could die," he said. "The safest thing for both Mrs. Pépin and the child is for me to perform a cesarean section. But we have to do it immediately."

I went back to the waiting room. An emergency cesarean. How long would that take? An hour? Two?

The population of the waiting room thinned as my fellow expectant fathers were singled out by happy-looking doctors and nurses.

"Congratulations, Mister . . . Your wife just gave birth to a healthy . . ."

I must have heard the refrain a dozen times. By 11:00 P.M. I was alone. Lights in the hallway dimmed. The hospital grew quiet except for the hiss of the heating system and murmured voices from the nurses' station.

Finally I caught sight of a familiar figure hurrying down the corridor toward the exit. Even though he was dressed in street clothes, there was no doubt the guy was Gloria's doctor.

I ran, calling to catch his attention before he stepped into the elevator. "Doctor, any word?"

He gave me a look of shock. "No one told you?"

"What's happening?" I said.

"I got called away on another emergency. I thought that the nurse was going to come out and give you the news. You're the father of a healthy five-and-a-quarter-pound girl. She and Gloria are doing fine."

A night nurse led me back into the maternity ward. My daughter, Claudine — we call her Titine — looked beautiful, asleep in her incubator. So did Gloria, who after her ordeal was as sound asleep as our new baby.

CLAUDINE WAS INTRODUCED to the food world when more than fifty of us, including Howard Johnson, Pierre Franey, and Roger Fessaguet, celebrated her christening at Helen McCully's apartment on the Upper East Side. The kitchen may have been no bigger than a good-sized shower stall, but we crammed into the space and produced a meal for the occasion. I prepared a whole ham, which I sliced, reconstructed, and glazed with aspic. The fish course was striped bass. For dessert we had puff pastry covered with pastry cream and various fruits.

After Claudine's birth, we began to spend even more time in Hunter, and I cooked a lot — alone, with Gloria, and especially with other chef friends. No meal was more memorable than the time we ate Billy.

Billy was a feral sheep that had escaped his pen as a lamb and grown up feeding himself on grasses and herbs on and around the mountain. As he matured, Billy became territorial. He decided that Hunter Mountain was his domain, off limits to all others, including the hikers and sightseers who paid the resort good money to enjoy a summer's day on the trails. By then, Billy had grown into a large creature and looked even more fearsome than he was, thanks to a heavy matted fleece that had never felt shears. After he chased a number of guests up trees and successfully head-butted an elderly gentleman into a patch of prickly wild raspberries, the management of Hunter issued a *fatwa* against the sheep. Ruddi, an Austrian skier and the summer foreman of the workers on the mountain, was ordered to have his crew dispose of Billy.

Ruddi decided to donate Billy to me, knowing that Billy would be put to good use in my kitchen. Unfortunately, I was visiting in France at the time, so Gloria was the recipient of the condemned animal. She drove a stake into the ground and attached Billy by a rope around his neck. He broke free and ate all of her flowers, along with most of the salad greens, vegetables, and herbs in our garden.

The second time he broke loose, Billy went on the offensive. When he backed off a few feet and scratched the ground with one of his front hooves, Gloria knew what was coming. She dashed frantically toward the house and made it inside just in time to close the door on his nose. Once Billy calmed down, Gloria affixed one end of a heavy metal chain to a tree and the other to Billy. By the time I returned, there was no vegetation within forty feet of the tree, and Billy had become fat on leftover bread and vegetables from the supermarket, along with grain and other food items contributed by friends who had a vested interest in maximizing his plumpness.

By summer's end, Billy weighed 130 pounds. My brother Roland and his wife had scheduled a visit to America, and in honor of their arrival, I decided to prepare a *méchoui,* a North African specialty featuring a spit-roasted lamb — in this case, Billy. My friend Loulou Latour, a chef whom I had worked with at Le Pavillon, was cooking at a camp in the Catskills that summer, and he did the dispatching with a .38 revolver. I took care of the skinning and gutting, chores I had performed many times in France. Dressed out and ready to roast, Billy weighed seventy pounds.

In preparation for the feast, I sautéed the kidneys and sweetbreads with lots of onion, garlic, and herbs, then mixed them with cooked couscous. We stuffed the lamb with this mixture and tied the cavity shut with wire. Roland took charge of building the fire, gathering enough wood to heat the house for an entire Catskills winter. He also cut down and trimmed a maple sapling to serve as a spit. As the lamb roasted slowly for hours, Roland turned it and rubbed it with a mixture of olive oil, paprika, cayenne, salt, rosemary, and sage, so that the outside crusted into a beautiful reddish mahogany color. We cut it up before our guests on a large wooden picnic table. The inside was pink and moist, the outside charred and crusty, and the couscous accompaniment flavorful, hot, and plentiful.

We also served tomatoes with basil from the garden, red beets with shallots, a pâté of chicken and duck livers, homemade *saucisson,* wild mushrooms *à la grecque* (marinated in olive oil and lemon juice with coriander seed), and breads that Loulou had baked fresh. We washed all of this down with cooled Beaujolais and half-gallons of Almadén white wine. For dessert, we had summer fruits with cognac, a chocolate mousse, and a pound cake made by Jean-Claude. Billy, who was doomed anyway, made a lot of Frenchmen very happy.

FROM THE TIME that Claudine was an infant, she saw me butchering deer carcasses, plucking pheasants, skinning frogs, or eviscerating rabbit or squab. She understood and knew naturally that there was nothing cruel or malicious in those processes. They were a normal part of life. In fact, most of the deer meat we enjoyed was road kill that otherwise would have gone to waste; we stewed it in red wine or roasted or grilled it, turning extra meat into sausages.

But even in a rural area, my attitude toward farm animals caused some misunderstandings with the neighbors. One fall day, I was mushrooming with Jean-Claude and his two young daughters, Natalie and Valerie. Driving along a little road, we passed a farm with a sign saying, "Ducks for Sale." What better on a brisk September night than a dinner of fresh duck accompanied by wild mushrooms? We pulled into the barnyard. A couple of dozen beautiful, white, plump Long Island ducks were feeding peacefully on worms and corn in the grass. Jean-Claude and I visually selected a couple of fat ones.

"Hello," said the farmer, emerging from her barn. She was a large, sunburned woman, whose hands were rough, with the fingernails cracked and black with dirt. Pushing a stray lock of hippie-length red hair back under a bandanna, she said, "What can I do for you folks?"

"We saw the sign," I said. "We'd like two."

She smiled, obviously delighted to make a sale. "Take your pick." She turned to the little girls. "Are these for you?"

Both nodded eagerly, all but licking their lips.

Jean-Claude backed up the car, opened the trunk, and grabbed the first duck by the throat. With a swift motion, he twisted its head to break the neck and tossed it into the trunk.

The farmer ran toward Jean-Claude, screaming, "Get the hell off this property! Murderer! Are you psycho? I can't believe what you just did. Leave! Now!"

We paid and departed, minus the second duck.

~~~

CLAUDINE BEGAN cooking with me when she was one year old. Stirring something in a pot or mixing a vinaigrette, I lifted her up, and she removed the lid, smelled what was cooking, gave her opinion, then tasted it or poked it a few times with a whisk or spoon. When I had a pastry bag filled with jam, pastry cream, or whipped cream, she stayed at my side until I filled her mouth with the contents of the bag.

She was still standing in her crib, not yet walking, the first time she sampled caviar, a beautiful beluga that I had spread on a piece of buttered bread. She licked off the caviar, handed me back the mushy bread, and said, "*Encore,* Papa."

She was about four when she went on her first sleepover at the home of a friend whose mother cooked asparagus as a first course that night. As everyone else began to eat, Claudine sat immobile in front of her asparagus.

In a gentle voice, the friend's mother said, "Claudine, these are asparagus. You don't like asparagus?"

With an earnest, serious look, Claudine replied, "I'm waiting for the hollandaise." It wasn't snobbery. The few times she had tasted asparagus in her short life, it had been served that way.

Sitting down for dinner around a well-appointed, well-set table was from the beginning part of our daily routine. It was a time when school and the other happenings of the day were discussed and debated — not always pleasant but essential in Claudine's growing up. Except for very spicy food, she was served exactly what we ate from the time she was an infant. When she didn't like something, we barely acknowledged the fact. Conversely, when she ate spinach, broccoli, or Swiss chard, we never congratulated her because we didn't want her to feel that she had done something special.

Ours was an open house. Guests dropped by at any time, but none quite so often as Michel Keller's father, JoJo, a truculent character who had retired to Hunter. A former pastry chef at La Caravelle, JoJo had an uncanny ability to arrive just as I was preparing a meal. Although he enjoyed a few glasses of red with us and was always up for a hand of cards, he never sat down at the table to eat, despite our entreaties, but preferred to snoop around the kitchen, tasting and offering his opinions and comments.

Gloria kept the cat's plate on the end of the kitchen counter, high enough so that Pastis, our rottweiler, could not get to it. One day a canned liver brand that the cat especially liked was in place, waiting for her. JoJo showed up as we were sitting down to eat. We went through the game of inviting him to join us, and as usual, he refused, so I poured him a glass of wine. While we ate, he shuffled around the kitchen, checking things out. Suddenly, he trotted back into dining room, gagging. He poured more wine and swallowed the entire glass in one gulp, sputtering, "Jacques, what in hell are you putting in your pâté?"

MUSHROOM HUNTING was the activity that brought me the most pleasure during our springs, summers, and falls in Hunter. I'd perfected my foraging skills during my apprenticeship at Le Grand Hôtel de l'Europe in Bourg-en-Bresse, picking mushrooms that I sold to the hotel. To be absolutely sure of my pick, I stopped at the drugstore next to the hotel and asked the pharmacists, who were trained mycologists, to check on our cache.

Most of the mushrooms that we picked in the Catskills were varieties familiar to me from Bourg, primarily different types of cèpes (porcini) and chanterelles. Pierre Larré was one of my most knowledgeable mushroom-hunting partners. We would go in his car directly to one spot and look around for five minutes before he said, "No, not here yet," and we would move to another place. His favorite recipe was perfectly simple. He would cook the whole cap of a cèpe, which sometimes weighed three quarters of a pound, in olive oil with whole garlic cloves in a low oven for forty-five minutes until the moisture evaporated. As the mushroom gently browned, the flavors became concentrated, almost like a piece of meat.

In addition to being a champion mushroom hunter, Pierre was our official trout-fishing teacher. No one could match the size of Pierre's catch or his casualness, gentleness, and generosity. Going to his house, you were assured that upon leaving you would find in your car a few bottles of wine or a ham he had cured himself in the style of Bayonne, in the south of France.

Life was good in Hunter. I loved the house we had put so much of ourselves into. I had dozens of wonderful friends in the area. Trout, frogs, mushrooms, and garden produce made Hunter a paradise for anyone who was passionate about food. At work, however, things were anything but good. Unfortunately, like so many sons of great men, the son of Howard D. Johnson, Howard B. Johnson, lacked his father's charisma and genius for business. The younger Howard Johnson surrounded himself with a coterie of university graduates who, like the manager back at the Queens restaurant, were "yes" men, with practically no interest in or knowledge of food.

It didn't surprise me that after Howard D. Johnson's death in 1972, his organization lost its raison d'être. The era of fast food had dawned, and Mr. Johnson's son, who took over management of the company, did not understand the forces that would eventually overrun the restaurant empire his father had built. Right up to the moment he died, the senior Johnson was open to change. He actively courted it. I'm certain he would have shifted the business approach of the company to compete directly in the booming fast-food market. In fact, we'd already opened a few outlets called HoJo's, which did precisely that. But the son and his band of business-school-educated henchmen chose to cut costs at the chain rather than alter the outdated way the food was served — on china and by waitstaff. Where we once served only prime beef, the accountants made the chefs substitute select beef, then choice beef, and finally precut, frozen portions of meat. The restaurants became obsolete, the food quality deteriorated further, and ultimately, the Howard Johnson Company went to pieces. Fortunately, by then I had decided to use the lessons I learned at HoJo's to take my career in a new direction.

~

I RECEIVED MY B.A. in 1970, writing an honors thesis on Molière, the great seventeenth-century French playwright, and I immediately applied to and was accepted into graduate school at Columbia's School of Arts and Sciences in a combined master's and Ph.D. program. I loved the study of philosophy and literature, and in graduate school decided to do my master's in eighteenth-century French literature. As a Frenchman, I was quite familiar with the names of literary figures such as Rabelais and Montaigne of the sixteenth century; Molière, La Bruyère, and La Rochefoucauld of the seventeenth century; and certainly, the eighteenth-century writers Diderot, Rousseau, and Voltaire, even though I had never read them.

By the time I had completed all but one of the required courses for my Ph.D., I was thinking about quitting the kitchen and becoming a university professor. But I faced one big dilemma. Although I viewed being a professor as prestigious, I still loved everything associated with food, so I made up my mind to blend my loves and proposed a doctoral thesis dealing with the history of French food presented in the context of French literature. There were plenty of literary references for me to explore, from Ronsard's "Apology to a Field Salad," to the wedding feast in Flaubert's *Madame Bovary,* to Proust's well-known madeleine.

But when I proposed the idea, my adviser, a Frenchman, shook his head. "The reason not much has been written on the topic, Mr. Pépin," he intoned, "is that cuisine is not a serious art form. It's far too trivial for academic study. Not intellectual enough to form the basis of a Ph.D. thesis." My proposal was turned down.

Perhaps I could have argued my point, but my adviser's curt dismissal of a field so important to me, to which I had dedicated my life, helped crystallize some doubts I was having about a career in academia. Though I enjoyed research, the last time I had participated in anything resembling a stimulating intellectual discussion with fellow students was back at the School of General Studies, when we met after class for drinks and conversation — people of many nationalities and all ages, a mini–United Nations. Now my associates were suddenly twenty-one- or twenty-two-year-olds whose only interest seemed to be grades. Far from being noble and high-minded, many of my professors were petty, focused on trivial departmental squabbles. When two or more of them gathered socially, the conversation was limited to university politics and junior-high-school-level gossip about other professors.

As much as anything, getting an education cured me of my complex about not having an education. Now that I was as well educated as anyone in the world of food, a piece of paper with my name and the letters *Ph.D.* on it seemed much less important. I was free to go back to my first love on my own terms, without feelings of inadequacy.

Cèpes aux Lardons

(WILD MUSHROOMS WITH LARDONS)

YIELD: 4 SERVINGS

I OFTEN MAKE this type of recipe in the summer when wild mushrooms are plentiful. I must emphasize that you should pick only those mushrooms that you can identify with certainty. Join a mycological society in your area if you want to learn about them. A reminder: wild mushrooms should be well cooked — some may cause intestinal problems unless well done — so be sure to cook them for a minimum of 15 minutes. If cèpes are unavailable, large white mushrooms from the supermarket will work well in this recipe.

- 4 ounces pancetta, lean cured pork, or salt pork, cut into ½-inch pieces (¾ cup)
- 2 cups water
- 3 tablespoons good olive oil
- 1 pound fresh cèpes, cleaned and cut into 1-inch pieces
- ⅓ cup minced scallions
- 1 teaspoon chopped fresh thyme
  Salt and freshly ground black pepper to taste
- 2 tablespoons chopped fresh chives
- 1 tablespoon unsalted butter

- 4 slices French bread, brushed with olive oil and toasted

Place the pancetta or cured or salt pork in a skillet with the water. Bring to a boil, boil for 10 minutes, then drain and rinse under cool water. Return these *lardons* to the skillet with the olive oil, and sauté them for about 1 minute.

Add the cèpes to the skillet, and cook them, covered, over high heat for about 15 minutes, stirring occasionally, until they are nicely browned on all sides and have a leathery, chewy texture. Add the scallions, thyme, salt, and pepper, and cook over high heat, uncovered, for 2 to 3 minutes.

Add the chives and butter, toss to combine them with the other ingredients, and serve immediately on the toasted bread.

Smoked Trout Gloria

YIELD: 4 SERVINGS

GLORIA BECAME PASSIONATE about trout fishing when we lived in Hunter. She would go to the river at an ungodly early morning hour, usually with Pierre Larré, and arrive back home, wet and exhilarated, with a bunch of fresh trout at about 9:00 A.M., when I was getting up. She liked them best smoked and served with creamy scrambled eggs on buttered toast, a dish that is a welcome treat for breakfast, brunch, lunch, or even dinner.

You can, of course, buy smoked trout, but we smoke our own. I first soak the trout for 2 hours in a brine made of 1 cup of kosher salt, 2 cups of water, and 2 tablespoons of sugar; then I wash and pat it dry. I spread a handful of hickory chips or sawdust in an old roasting pan and add some crumpled pieces of aluminum foil to the pan to support a wire rack, on which I arrange the trout. I cover the pan tightly with a large piece of foil and place it on a small electric burner over medium heat for 10 to 15 minutes, until the trout is golden. After it rests for an hour or so, I remove the skin and head, and the moist, fragrant flesh slides off the central bone. Smoked trout is best served lukewarm or at room temperature.

8 large eggs

1/2 teaspoon salt

1/2 teaspoon freshly ground black pepper

4 large slices country bread

4 tablespoons (1/2 stick) unsalted butter for cooking the eggs, plus extra for spreading on the toast

2 to 3 tablespoons cream or milk

4 smoked trout, 6 to 10 ounces each, with skin and head removed and the flesh separated from the bones

Beat the eggs in a bowl, and add the salt and pepper. Toast the bread, and coat it with butter. Heat the 4 tablespoons of butter in a sturdy saucepan. When it is hot, add the eggs, and mix them gently and continuously with a whisk to create a creamy mixture with small curds. Keep cooking for about 2 minutes, until the eggs are thick and creamy but still slightly runny. Do not overcook.

Remove the pan from the heat, and add a few tablespoons of the cream or milk to stop the cooking and keep the mixture from becoming too tight. Place a slice of toast on each of four plates, spoon the eggs on top, and surround with pieces of smoked trout. Serve immediately.

14

Soup's On

I QUIT Howard Johnson's to open a soup restaurant, really nothing more than a glorified cafeteria, on Fifth Avenue, between 45th and 46th Streets. After working in the commissary for a decade, I had learned everything that Howard Johnson's had to offer. The job there had become boring and was made more so when the younger Mr. Johnson took over and began to run the place in a more corporate manner, which meant meeting after meeting, layers of bureaucracy, and a decision-making apparatus designed precisely to prevent decisions from being made.

A group of entrepreneurs who had start-up capital and the bare bones of a concept approached me. They saw a market for a Midtown place that sold only soup, but plenty of it, to time-pressed New Yorkers. Although my backers had money, they had very little restaurant experience and no idea of how to overcome the practical challenges of designing a kitchen and cooking system that would permit a small number of nonprofessional cooks to produce a great quantity of top-quality soup in a minuscule space. Thanks to my years of working with Howard Johnson's–size ingredient lists, I was fairly certain that I could design a workable system. We struck a deal. I would get a tiny share of the business, along with a yearly salary of $23,000, far more than the $15,000 I was getting at HoJo's. In return, I would design and set up the restaurant, putting in seven-day weeks, if necessary, during the launch phase, with the understanding that I could step back and assume a part-time managerial role at my full-time salary if the concept succeeded.

The challenge was to bring form to their rough idea. I baptized the restaurant La Potagerie, hoping that the Continental overtones of the name would suggest sophisticated fare. Although it was going to have the functional soul of a cafeteria, La Potagerie's design was anything but institutional. The space was filled with large plants, and a waterfall tumbled down the back wall. The menu featured soups as main dishes — robust, hearty selections prepared daily with only fresh ingredients. Somehow I would have to produce them profitably at a price of around two dollars a serving.

But before the first bowl could be ladled out to a customer, I faced some real problems. The kitchen was located underneath the dining room in a small, narrow hallway-like area. I had chosen the equipment I needed so no space was wasted, but it was a tight squeeze. The vegetables, which came in crates, would be cut, washed, and stored in different plastic containers, ready to be measured and cooked for a recipe. The finished soups were to be placed on the shelves of the walk-in cooler so the older soups were used first.

On paper, it looked like a workable plan. Yet after a week, I realized we had a serious problem. Demand would require that we produce 150 gallons of hot soup each morning, but the containers couldn't go directly into the fridge because their heat would quickly turn the fridge into a sauna. We didn't have the money or the space for special equipment to cool the containers rapidly.

This called for innovation. As an experiment, I prepared a fifty-gallon batch of black bean soup, making it as I always did but adding only half as much chicken stock so the yield would be thirty-five gallons. I divided my soup concentrate, which was thick and salty, among ten five-gallon containers. Then I filled the rest of the space with ice, which melted into the hot soup, cooling it quickly and giving it the right taste and consistency. My soups — and the nascent business — were saved.

When La Potagerie opened in the spring of 1970, we set a standard price of $2.25 for the entire meal, including tax and tip. That sum, modest even at the time, entitled customers to a large bowl of soup, a croissant, a piece of black bread or a slice of baguette, a beverage — coffee, tea, or soda — and a dessert. The desserts consisted of fruit and cheese, usually a piece of Gruyère and an apple, a fresh brown betty made with homemade brioche or leftover croissants, or a homemade chocolate mousse. The business became an instant success.

I developed about thirty recipes, some with the consistency of stews, some lighter and more elegant, some cream soups, and some country-style. All had simple, straightforward preparation steps and timing. To ensure quality even when I wasn't on the premises, I set up a training program for the employees, especially the kitchen staff — young, willing people with no previous restaurant experience. Within a few weeks, they were preparing my recipes with splendid results. I was finally using my American as well as my French training.

Initially we were open for breakfast, lunch, and dinner. Our breakfast menu featured some special soups, including a spicy tomato mixture with fresh oysters, a light cream of potato soup with a poached egg, served with crisp, buttered toast, and a creamy oatmeal soup with chicken stock and sliced leek and crisp bacon tidbits. However, after about a year of experimenting, we concluded that the best times for the restaurant to be open fell between 11:30 A.M. and 8:00 P.M., so we eliminated breakfast.

Each day offered three soups: one with meat, one with legumes, and one with fish, shellfish, or poultry. Our menu might include, for example, a creamy veal goulash with cooked *spaetzle,* a chunky bouillabaisse seasoned with saffron, and a hearty lentil soup garnished with sliced sausages, croutons, and Gruyère cheese. Every day we also prepared three dozen individual gratinées of onion soup, each with a golden crust of bread and cheese, which usually sold within twenty minutes of the restaurant's opening.

People started arriving outside the restaurant at about 11:00 A.M. and waited in lines that sometimes extended halfway around the block. The soups were served out of beautiful copper pots and were ladled into red earthenware crocks. Red wine, white wine, and beer were offered at an additional charge of sixty cents a glass. When all the selections were made, a waitress in a long hostess dress took the tray and led the customer to a table, where other customers might be already seated.

We served from four to six hundred people each day, and on holidays the number climbed to eight hundred. La Potagerie became a very profitable operation, with low food and payroll costs. It even brought a measure of fame. In my first exposure to that most American of media, television, Kitty Carlisle and Gene Shalit grilled me on *What's My Line?* but they never discovered my identity as "the soup chef." Appearing as one of two contestants claiming to be the former chef to General de Gaulle on *To Tell the Truth,* I — young and trim at the time — was passed over, and the other contestant, older and fatter, was selected.

Organizations such as Marriott, Coca-Cola, and General Foods showed interest in purchasing La Potagerie. I dreamed of opening a small commissary and a dozen Potagerie restaurants throughout the New York City vicinity. Unfortunately, my partners always demanded that they be given high-ranking corporate positions as a condition of any sale. Although the companies wanted to hire me, they already had plenty of overpaid executives of their own. Because of my partners' stubbornness, we missed several opportunities to make a financial killing. The business was succeeding, but the relationship between me and my partners had begun to show signs of strain.

When Claudine became old enough to attend school, we decided to reverse our lifestyle. Hunter would be home. I would commute to work in New York and sleep there during the week in a small apartment. I was content. For the first time, my life was progressing along a clear path: husband, homeowner, father. A man secure in his profession.

That all changed in a fraction of a second on July 21, 1974.

C~~~

IT WAS LATE and I was eager to get home. Too eager. I pushed my old LTD station wagon to the limit, but I wasn't worried. I had been over that stretch of highway hundreds of times and under all conditions. I had memorized every curve, pothole, and bump, and I knew how fast the wagon could take them.

The deer materialized so fast it looked as if it had suddenly been airlifted onto the highway. Where there had been nothing but empty asphalt bisected by a double line, two glowing, yellow-green eyes appeared.

I hit the brakes and cranked the steering wheel.

And suddenly I was spinning. There was a sickening, hollow crash. The car began to roll.

The next thing I remember was a smell. Faint at first, then stronger, an acrid odor of burning oil and rubber. I heard voices. There were lights. I reached out to pull myself toward the only opening big enough for me to squeeze through and saw the white glow of my arm bone protruding through my skin.

I lost consciousness.

Split Pea Soup with Ham and Croutons

YIELD: 6 SERVINGS

*T*HIS WAS ONE of the favorite winter soups at La Potagerie. I serve it as a whole meal with a thick, crusty bread, a salad, and a few glasses of red wine. The base soup can be frozen and reheated as needed, and the garnishes can be varied or omitted.

1/4	cup good olive oil
2	cups diced (1/2-inch pieces) onion
1	tablespoon chopped garlic
8	cups chicken stock
1	pound dried split peas, rinsed under cold water
2	cups peeled, diced (1/2-inch pieces) potato
2	teaspoons salt
1 1/2	teaspoons *herbes de Provence* (available in many supermarkets)
1	teaspoon Tabasco hot pepper sauce
1	large ham steak (about 8 ounces), cut into 1/2-inch dice (2 cups)

GARNISHES

2	cups croutons, cut from 1-inch-thick bread slices, browned in the oven
1 1/2	cups grated Swiss cheese, preferably Gruyère (about 5 ounces)
2	tablespoons minced fresh chives

Heat the oil in a large saucepan, and add the onion and garlic. Sauté for 1 minute to soften. Add the remaining ingredients, except for the garnishes, and bring to a boil. Reduce the heat to low, cover, and boil gently for 1 hour, stirring occasionally to prevent scorching. Stir well, and add more water if the soup gets too thick.

At serving time, add the ham to the soup, and heat to the boil. Serve with the croutons, cheese, and chives, and sprinkle on extra Tabasco, if desired.

Oatmeal Breakfast Soup

YIELD: 6 SERVINGS (ABOUT 8 CUPS)

*B*REAKFAST was the inspiration for this soup, which has become a favorite at our house. Bacon, oatmeal, and milk are breakfast ingredients. And leeks? Well, I always put leeks in my soup.

I microwave the bacon until crisp because Gloria always does so with good results, but it could be cooked in a skillet as well. Although I use coarsely granulated Irish oatmeal, which is chewy and flavorful, the soup is good made with quick-cooking oatmeal, provided you reduce the preparation time and the liquid accordingly.

The first part of the recipe — bacon, leeks, and oatmeal — can be prepared ahead. It is better to add the milk and half-and-half at the last moment, however, for a fresher, cleaner-tasting soup. Finishing the soup with both milk and half-and-half is best, although using milk only is fine.

6 slices bacon (6 to 7 ounces), preferably maple- or honey-cured
2 small leeks, trimmed, with most of the green left on, sliced thin, and washed (2½ cups)
5 cups water
1 cup Irish coarse oatmeal
1½ teaspoons salt (less if bacon is highly salted)
1 cup half-and-half
1 cup milk
½ teaspoon freshly ground black pepper

Arrange the bacon on a microwave oven tray, cover with paper towels, and cook on full power for about 4 minutes, or until the slices are crisp and brown. Reserve about 2 tablespoons of the bacon fat, and transfer the bacon to a cutting board. Cut the bacon into ½-inch pieces, and set it aside.

Put the reserved bacon fat in a saucepan. Add the sliced leeks, and cook over medium heat for 5 to 6 minutes, until softened. Add the water, and bring to a boil. Add the oatmeal and salt, stir, and bring to a boil. Reduce the heat to very low, cover (with the lid placed slightly ajar, so the oatmeal doesn't boil over), and cook gently for 25 to 30 minutes, or until the oatmeal is tender. (The recipe can be made to this point up to 24 hours ahead of time.)

At serving time, add the half-and-half, milk, and pepper, and bring to a boil. Serve hot with the bacon pieces sprinkled on top.

15

Teaching

I SHOULD HAVE DIED. Once the paramedics had extracted me from the wreckage of the car, I was rushed by ambulance to Columbia Memorial Hospital in Hudson, New York. My prognosis was anything but good. The tally of my injuries from the accident included a broken back, two broken hips, one broken arm, one broken leg, and a pelvis that was broken in three places. In the first days after the accident, the doctor told Gloria that I would probably never walk again. My left arm was so badly fractured that he had no doubt it would have to be removed — if I lived and gained enough strength. Fortunately, he felt that I was too weak to survive an amputation.

But I was also too weak for them to risk moving me to a hospital with better facilities than Hudson's. For two and a half weeks, I lay there, drifting in and out of consciousness.

Dr. Johnson, my physician at Columbia Memorial, approached a former associate of his, Dr. Arnold, a surgeon at New York City's renowned Hospital for Special Surgery, one of the best hospitals in the world for treatment of injuries like mine and with a waiting list months long that included more than its share of dignitaries, politicians, and noted philanthropists. I was allowed to move to the head of the line for one reason: in all their years of practice, the surgeons in New York had never seen injuries as severe as mine in a living person. Their prior experience had involved only autopsy cases. They cut a deal — they would take on my case provided that they could use me as a teaching device for their students — a living cadaver.

I awoke from surgery and found myself lying immobile on my back, my appendages stretched by stainless steel cables attached to a device that looked like modern medicine's answer to the medieval torture rack. As the months went by, hospital therapists began to reintroduce my body to mobility by strapping me to a platform that they then levered into an upright position. Blood rushed into my legs, causing relentless, searing pain. The solution was to keep me on Demerol, to which I became addicted.

My darkest moment came when I was wheeled out of the hospital for a shopping spree to a medical supply store, where I was fitted with a leg brace and a massive, clunky platform shoe to make up for the slant of my reconstructed pelvis. Sitting there among wheelchairs, crutches, and all manner of geriatric and incontinence aids, I wondered, "Is this going to be the rest of my life?"

Until that night, I had always considered myself a chef. Even while working in the Howard Johnson's commissary, I knew that if I wanted to, I could join the brigade at any restaurant in the country and more than hold my own in the kitchen. I had the self-assurance of having mastered a trade and the brashness that comes from knowing that my skills would always be in demand. Fourteen-hour days on my feet were no problem. All my life I'd run the gauntlet of other busy cooks between the walk-in and my station, plating dish after dish and rushing them to the waiters. It had been easy. Now, at age thirty-nine, I realized that I could not take those fourteen-hour days behind the stove anymore. Hell, I couldn't even walk.

The reason I didn't sink into despair during my months in the hospital was the support I got from Gloria, who had moved into our small New York pied-à-terre, and friends such as Barbara Kafka. Food writer, teacher, restaurant consultant, and all-around dynamo, Barbara knew exactly how to buoy the spirits of a long-term convalescent.

She bustled into my room, took one look at the paint-by-numbers wall art, and exclaimed, "Ugh!" The next afternoon she returned with a couple of pieces from her own collection. The K-mart-quality prints came down and up went a work by the Italian painter and sculptor Marino Marini. I still dream of the spirited stylized stallions depicted in it.

Barbara also hauled in a small refrigerator and a case of Taittinger Champagne splits. The Taittinger was far better medicine than all the stuff the doctors were forcing down me. One cold split was just enough for Gloria and me to share before the meal she spoon-fed me at night.

Gradually, I regained both strength and confidence. I realized that I might never play tennis, ski, or be a line chef again, but there were other things I could do. Annoyance and impatience replaced meek acceptance. I wanted to get on with the rest of my life, whatever that might be. To my doctors' amazement, what they had predicted would be at least a six-month hospital convalescence was cut short. Three months after being wheeled into the Hospital for Special Surgery on a gurney, I left. I wasn't a pretty sight. But with the aid of canes and crutches, I could walk. And, contrary to the early prognosis, I still had both of my arms.

By Christmastime, I was back in our home in Hunter and pleased with my progress. My brother Roland made a trip to spend part of the holidays with us, and on New Year's Day I felt strong enough to take a walk with him around our snow-covered yard. But the fates had one more blow to strike against me: in my less-than-peak condition, I slipped on a patch of ice. My left leg crumpled beneath me and I heard a sickening snap. The ankle had been broken in three places. If I needed another wake-up call, I'd just received it.

Despite my new injuries, I attempted to resume my duties at La Potagerie, but things weren't working there for me anymore. Although I could order supplies and do a bit in the kitchen, I was no longer needed at the restaurant. The place was established. All the systems I had put in place were running efficiently without me.

Even though we were hugely profitable, bills went unpaid because of financial decisions with which I completely disagreed. But as the one on the scene, I had to deal with the repercussions. With an hour to prepare 150 gallons of soup, I often found myself confronted by a vegetable purveyor who refused to unload the day's order from his truck unless he first got a check. I knew that it was time for me to leave, but I had a family, a mortgage, and numerous barely healed injuries.

Then, thanks to a fortuitous phone call, I got a notion of a possible direction to take. My assistant at La Potagerie shoved the phone at me, saying, "Some guy named Burton Upjohn."

I tucked the handset under my chin and mumbled, "Hello," staying focused on the chicken soup bubbling in the kettle in front of me.

"Mr. Pépin," said a down-to-business voice, "I'm trying to arrange some cooking lessons as a gift to my wife. She's always wanted to go to Cordon Bleu in Paris, but I have a health condition and can't travel. I called Julia Child. She thought you might be interested. We live in Michigan. You'd have to come here for a few days, with your wife if you like. But I'd be willing to pay you."

I was only half listening.

"She just wants to learn a few French recipes," he went on. "Puff pastry, *demi-glace*, pâté, stuff like that."

Stirring the fifty-gallon pot, I said, "I don't usually do that sort of thing."

He either didn't hear or didn't care. "I'll pay you four hundred dollars," he said.

That sounded fine to me.

"You what?" said Gloria, when I told her about the conversation. "You were talking to Burton Upjohn, as in Upjohn Pharmaceuticals. Four hundred dollars is nothing. You could make more than that moonlighting for a few days at any restaurant in the city."

But I'd accepted, so we flew out to Kalamazoo, where Betty Upjohn and I fell into a daily routine. We went to the market each morning, bought whatever ingredients looked good, then decided on our menu. We spent the rest of the day cooking in her kitchen, and each night we fed six or eight people, most of them board members of the Upjohn company and close friends of the family. Each meal was served with a couple of wines, often Burgundies that Burton kept in his cellar. He wasn't much interested in wine, so he gave me a free hand to choose whatever I thought would go well with dinner. For someone from Kalamazoo, Michigan, who paid wine scant attention, he possessed a marvelous cellar, obviously built through consultations with leading connoisseurs and stored under perfect conditions. Each night we drank once-in-a-lifetime wines.

When the time came to settle the bill, I found out that Burton meant to pay four hundred dollars for *each* of my four days there. I had made nearly a month's salary in less than a week. In addition, Burton had taken a fancy to Gloria and given her a few hundred dollars for having come with me.

I knew from experience that not all teaching gigs would generate this sort of revenue. Earlier, I had done a few cooking demonstrations in New York area department stores at the insistence of Helen McCully, who told me that the exposure would be good for my career. My first was at Abraham and Strauss's flagship store in Brooklyn just before Thanksgiving. Working in a corner of the cookware department, I prepared a sweet potato dish and then demonstrated how to correctly carve a turkey. I enjoyed myself. Even in a department store crowded with holiday shoppers, a special rapport can develop between an instructor and a group of students. Abraham and Strauss was great fun, but unlike my experience with the Upjohns, it was far from financially rewarding. The pay was zero. It was hard to see how I could make a living out of that.

MY TRANSITION from salaried employee to independent operator was smoothed when my old friend, the restaurant impresario Joe Baum, who owned the Four Seasons, the Brasserie, and later the Rainbow Room, approached me to consult on a new project. A man of small stature, soft voice, and strong will, he was well respected and feared. His new restaurant was called Windows on the World and was located on the 107th floor of the newly built World Trade Center.

I was most involved with what was called the Big Kitchen, a commissary primarily designed to serve the complex of twenty-two restaurants on the main concourse of the North Tower — everything from a large American restaurant called the Market Bar and Dining Room to a soup place, a bread bakery, a delicatessen, a rotisserie, a seafood bar, a barbecue rib joint, and a takeout restaurant. The chef there, Arnold Sanger, had been a ski instructor with me at Hunter Mountain.

Joe had hired a San Francisco engineering firm to design the basement-level commissary. The West Coast company may have known a lot about structural engineering, but it was obvious to me that no one there had toiled in an institutional kitchen. One glance at the blueprints told me that we had a colossal problem — or, more accurately, several problems. My fifteen years at Howard Johnson's and La Potagerie convinced me that almost nothing about the design was right.

The two-hundred-gallon vats that were supposed to produce stocks, soups, stews, sauces, steamed vegetables, and any number of other products for the mini–restaurant empire within a skyscraper were to be placed in a part of the room where the ceiling was far too low. Any large institutional kitchen must have plenty of room above the kettles to accommodate an overhead rail and pulley system. Massive strainers run along this system; they are hoisted in and out of the kettles to quickly cook large quantities of vegetables in boiling water or stock. Nor was there enough space underneath the kettles for a container large enough to hold liquids emptied from the vats, and the pipes for draining the kettles were far too narrow and contorted into a series of right angles that guaranteed clogging. The walk-in icebox had a single door, sure to produce a constant mayhem of colliding bodies, flaring tempers, and spilled food. State-of-the-art mixers worth $7,500 each were perfect for dry ingredients but useless for the wet components of virtually every product the Big Kitchen was expected to make.

Fortunately, there was still time to make changes. I outlined the seriousness of the problems to Joe and suggested alterations to the blueprint that would make the commissary more efficient and a lot less expensive to operate.

"Forget it," he said. "I just got approval from the guys at the Port Authority for the original design. No way am I gonna open up that can of worms again. We'd be delayed for years. Make it work."

So I had to gerrymander a system that would somehow function despite the limitations of the facility. I finally decided that shovels were the best tools for emptying the kettles. The expensive mixers were wheeled off into a storeroom and forgotten. But the commissary operated more or less as intended, though at a far higher labor cost than it should have.

Windows on the World eventually opened more than a year later than planned, in April 1976. James Beard and Barbara Kafka also acted as consultants. The first chef at the restaurant was André René, a French chef from Alsace. The kitchen stood in the center, surrounded by many dining rooms that could be arranged to form small or large spaces, depending on the occasion.

Private rooms for large functions were located on the 106th floor. There was an Hors-d'oeuvrerie, a new kind of eatery shaped like a half-moon, which served hors d'oeuvres from all over the world, from saté to shrimp to caviar. Cellars in the Sky, a wine cellar with a dining area and a menu different from that of the main restaurant, was situated in the center of Kitchen on the World. Kevin Zraly, the wine master, compiled one of the most extraordinary wine lists in New York, including wines from practically all the winemaking areas of the world. There were other restaurants besides Windows, such as Sky-Dive, on the 44th floor, a modern restaurant for executive employees that turned into a bar at night.

~~~~~

FORTUNATELY, at about the time I began to create a career as a cooking instructor, a new retail phenomenon was taking root in California, birthplace for so many trends that eventually sweep this country. Kitchen stores, often combined with cooking schools, were opening up and down the West Coast. And the schools needed instructors. I became a charter member of this itinerant group all too familiar with red-eye flights to and from the West Coast, picking up teaching gigs of a few days here, maybe a week there. It was work, but I wasn't sure it would add up to a living.

The first time that I went to California, I had just put my crutches aside and was using a cane. I had been contacted by Michael James and Billy Cross, who ran the Great Chefs of France cooking school at the Robert Mondavi Winery. They wanted me to give hands-on classes in a cooking school they had set up in Rutherford, in the Napa Valley.

I was still feeble, so Gloria came along to help me. We went to California a few days early and stopped at San Francisco's Stanford Court Hotel, which at the time was directed by Jim Nassikas, one of the best hoteliers in the United States. The downstairs restaurant, called Fournou's Oven, was the site every year of cooking classes taught by Jim Beard. We had also planned to visit with Jean-Michel Jeudy, a young Frenchman who had just started as a maitre d' in a small restaurant in San Francisco. We had befriended him the year before in New York City, when he arrived unannounced, fresh off a French ship, at our apartment in Flushing. He stayed with us for a number of months until his permanent visa came through and then decided to move on to California.

Joining Jean-Michel, we went on a weekend getaway, first to the Napa Valley to have a quick look at the place where I would be giving classes, then up to Mendocino for some sightseeing in northern California. We arrived late in the morning at High Tree Farm, located in the middle of vineyards, vegetable gardens, and artichoke fields. Charlotte Combe, who was to be my assistant in the cooking classes, prepared a crisp puff pastry stuffed with Gorgonzola cheese, which we ate alfresco with some good California wines that were mostly new to my palate. After lunch, we continued on to Mendocino, where we had reservations in a small resort by the sea. It was cool, misty, and serene, and I was awed at how beautiful California was at that time of the year; it reminded me of the coasts of Brittany and Normandy.

After we settled into our bungalow overlooking the beach, I went for a stroll. To my surprise, I saw snails everywhere, sliding along the wet terraces and stairs of the resort. These were *petit-gris,* as we called the small gray escargots of Burgundy. My brothers and I had hunted many times for these small but excellent-tasting snails in France after a rain. We would go searching in the woods or in the grass along the country roads and — with luck — would bring back several dozen. Even though the Catskills provided many foraging opportunities for wild mushrooms, watercress, frogs, and wild leeks, I had never found any snails.

Exhilarated, I crashed into the bedroom of our bungalow and told Gloria of my find, grabbing a wastepaper basket, which I proceeded to fill with more than one thousand snails.

"Now what are you going to do with them?" Gloria demanded.

I put the wastepaper basket in the bathtub and covered the basket with a bath towel, tucking the edges underneath.

"They won't move from there," I said.

We spent an enjoyable evening out at dinner and a nightclub, reminiscing about old times with Jean-Michel, and returned to our cottage around midnight.

Gloria turned on the light and screamed.

The snails had escaped and covered not only the bathtub but the bathroom walls, ceiling, and mirror. Gloria was horrified; I found it funny. One by one I recaptured my snails and returned them to the wastepaper basket, this time securing the towel by placing a dresser drawer on top. Gloria wiped down the walls, ceiling, and mirror.

The following day I got some empty cardboard boxes from a liquor store, poked small holes in them, bought some lettuce, and placed it inside the boxes, with layers of snails in between. On Monday we returned to the Napa Valley to begin the classes and brought the snails, which I decided to incorporate into a menu. I noticed a field of ripe artichokes next door. We picked about two bushels of them, and I showed the students the proper turning and trimming techniques for artichoke hearts.

We soaked and washed the snails several times, then boiled them in big pots and extracted them from their shells with needles. This was tedious work, and most of my students were not crazy about handling the snails and removing their intestinal tracts. They eventually got it right, however, with the aid of a few bottles of wine. We cooked our snails in a barely simmering broth, consisting of white wine, chicken stock, and seasonings, for about three hours, until they were very tender. We sliced the artichoke bottoms and arranged them with the snails and a bit of the stock in enameled cast-iron *cocottes*. Then we puréed butter, parsley, garlic, shallots, a few almonds, and a dash of Pernod in a food processor, added generous amounts of this mixture to the snails, and baked them until they were bubbly and fragrant. It was the most wonderful snail concoction I had ever prepared. We greatly enjoyed our delicacies from Mendocino accompanied by crunchy bread and a mellow California Chenin Blanc.

AT THE BEGINNING of my teaching career, I had to overcome a few issues with communication. Most of them involved my overestimating my students' knowledge of cooking techniques that I thought were acquired as instinctually as breathing. One incident occurred while I was teaching a participation class in the test kitchen of the *New York Times*. As usual, some students wanted to do everything, while others preferred to sit and observe. In order to get her involved in the class, I asked one shy woman to strain the stock. She did — right down the drain — and came back with the bones in a colander.

"What do I do with these now?" she asked.

So much for the clarity of my teaching.

Some of my problems stemmed from my French view of certain raw ingredients. For example, the theme of a week-long session in my Hunter kitchen was how to prepare solid, substantial country fare from scratch. We smoked trout that Gloria caught, ate watercress from the creek, hunted frogs in a nearby swamp, picked wild mushrooms and leeks, and collected eggs from the chickens at the farm next door. We made fresh farmer cheese with unpasteurized milk and snacked on homemade prosciutto, salami, and apricot preserves from the previous summer.

I planned to make a rabbit terrine for our last meal. The preparation of my terrine takes five to six days. The first day of classes I asked for volunteers to work on the pâté. Everyone wanted to take on the challenge until I pointed to a cardboard box in the corner, where four rabbits munched on salad greens and carrot trimmings. Not one of the students felt disposed to participate in the first step in my terrine recipe, although everyone devoured the final product.

Although I hardly chose it myself, my timing in turning my professional energies toward teaching couldn't have been better. As Americans began to take more of an interest in food, the cooking-school phenomenon that had originated in California spread across the country, and soon the schools far outnumbered the qualified teachers. I had no sooner finished a week's teaching at one school than the owner would pull out her datebook and say, "So, can you do the same week next year?"

My schedule was filled for a year in advance with repeat customers. I began crisscrossing the United States, sometimes spending forty weeks a year on the road. The days flew by. My schedule typically included morning and afternoon or even evening classes, ten to twelve hours each day, five days a week, with weekends often dedicated to cooking demonstrations in kitchenware shops or department stores. When I saw everyone in a class listening attentively and nodding their heads in understanding, I loved it. The pace was grueling, but it was far easier than the shifts in restaurant kitchens.

During the periods that I was at home, my various work projects — planning classes, testing and writing recipes — monopolized the kitchen and much of the rest of the house, so after I had been home for a couple of weeks, Gloria was quite happy to have me out of the way for a few days.

In my travels, I was also discovering the foods of America. During a break from teaching, my trusty assistant Charlotte suggested we duck into a storefront Chinese joint in Redwood City, California. Typical of such places, a large glass aquarium took up much of one wall of the dining room. In it, the *spécialités de la maison* finned listlessly by until they were scooped out and taken to the kitchen. I was fascinated by a half-dozen enormous crabs on the bottom of the tank.

"Dungeness," said Charlotte. "You ever have them?"

I had never even seen one.

"We'll have two crabs," she said to the owner. "Just steamed, with nothing else on them."

What ensued was a crab fest beyond compare. In lieu of the little nibbles and bites of crab I was used to, I engorged lumps of the sweetest crabmeat I'd ever tasted and joined the ranks of the West Coast's Dungeness devotees, who prefer the crabs cooked the American way, steamed with as little adornment as possible.

I began to coopt traditional American foodstuffs into my French repertoire. During a teaching stint in Virginia, I had my first encounter with a Smithfield ham and was appalled when my hostess proceeded to cook it. I saw that beautiful piece of meat as a possible replacement for the proscuitto-like cured hams of southern France and confirmed my intuition by slicing a thin piece off another "raw" ham and eating it, much to the horror of my American companions. As a teacher I first tasted Boston baked beans, corn on the cob, Cajun seafood gumbo, and tamales. I ate fried chicken, mashed potatoes, black-eyed peas, okra fritters, and pumpkin pie. I became addicted to corn bread, club sandwiches, brownies, cheesecake, and ice cream with chocolate fudge.

In the process of my travels and tastings, I was unconsciously moving away from a purely French style of cooking. The rigid culinary constraints that my classical French training had instilled in me were dissolving but provided just enough structure so that I could assimilate new ideas without creating silly or absurd recipes. I no longer attempted to label my food as one style or another. I simply cooked the way I felt, based on the ingredients at my disposal. That became my definition of American cuisine.

～

TEACHING also gave me an opportunity to experience foreign cuisines firsthand. Gloria and I were invited to go on an official visit to China with twelve other food lovers. The trip had been organized as an exchange of culinary culture between East and West — the chefs' answer to Ping-Pong diplomacy. The three professional cooks in our group — Bo Friberg, a pastry chef who was teaching at the California Culinary Academy; a young American chef named Cindy Pawlcyn, who owned a restaurant in California; and I — worked together, demonstrating our dishes to Chinese chefs and onlookers. The Chinese chefs, in turn, demonstrated their techniques to us.

We flew to Shanghai and then traveled by train and bus throughout China, finishing up in Beijing two weeks later. Much of what we witnessed was banquet cooking, the haute cuisine of China. Unfortunately, so many cooks were involved in each preparation that, language problems aside, it was difficult to speak with someone who could articulate a general philosophy of the dish. For each recipe demonstrated, at least three chefs participated. One gathered and prepared the main raw ingredients. He gutted and filleted a fish, then bowed and disappeared. A second chef arrived to prepare the garnishes, peeling vegetables, mincing scallions, chopping ginger or garlic. He bowed and vanished, and a third chef finished the dish, stir-frying everything and presenting it on a plate. A fourth chef, who specialized in carving flowers and animals out of vegetables, then appeared to demonstrate his specialty.

At Chu Fu, the birthplace of Confucius, we had the chance of working alongside the monks in Confucius's own mansion. The kitchen had an adobe floor and a big stove fueled by wood and coal, just like the one I had used as an apprentice. It was winter, and with the wood and coal, everything seemed to be covered with a coating of black dust. I was excited to work in that rustic kitchen. The food was straightforward, consisting of stews, soups, soybeans, rice and noodle dishes, very different from the many-steps cooking we had been exposed to in Shanghai. Meat and fish were used minimally.

One dish we encountered gave new meaning to the word *freshness*. En route by bus from Shanghai to Beijing, we stopped for lunch at a little restaurant at the base of a mountain. The chef decided to prepare a few large bass in his special manner for our group. He grabbed a four-pounder from the tank and within seconds had scaled it alive, gutted it, cut slits into the skin, rolled the fish in egg white and cornstarch, and wrapped the head in a water-soaked cold towel. He then inserted a wooden skewer through the gills and lowered the fish into the hot oil of a deep-fryer. The skewer, extending horizontally beyond the fish on either side, rested on the rim of the fryer, holding the head of the fish above the oil. The whole operation took a couple of minutes, at the most. The chef hurriedly placed the fish on a platter, rushed it to our table, and removed the towel from around the head. Uncooked and cold, it was still moving, the mouth opening and closing gruesomely. The presentation was not received in the spirit in which it was presented. Members of our group started screaming.

"Do something," said Gloria.

I cut off the head of the fish and placed it on the side, so that people could enjoy the fish, which was quite good. Most of my fellow travelers, however, had lost their appetites.

I WAS WITH Helen McCully, teaching cooking classes in San Diego and San Francisco, when we learned that Jim Beard, who had also been teaching in San Francisco, had taken ill and was hospitalized, so we went to visit him. That morning I had demonstrated how to prepare a braised salmon with a wonderfully rich butter sauce. I took a hefty slab to Jim at the hospital. When I walked into the room carrying a covered plate, Jim's big round mug broke into a grin.

"You allowed to eat this?" I asked.

Jim's eyes widened and he reached up from the bed for the plate. His reply got lost in mumbles and smackings as he stuffed salmon into his mouth, pausing only occasionally to close his eyes and moan with pleasure. Within a couple of minutes, he had all but finished his buttery treat.

At that point, a nurse erupted into the room and grabbed the dish from under his nose.

"Your doctor has you on a restricted diet!" she said. "Do you want to kill yourself?"

Everyone shrank back.

Jim, in a piping child's voice, said, "I was just tasting."

JIM WAS SOON well and back to his regular teaching sessions at the Stanford Court Hotel and had a chance to return my favor.

"Marion Cunningham and I are going to have dinner at this swell place a young friend of mine runs over in Berkeley," he said to me over the phone. "Want to join us?"

Which is how I found myself walking through the front door of a cute little establishment called Chez Panisse. When you entered a restaurant with Jim, whether it was a three-star bastion in Manhattan or some unheard-of boîte in the hills above downtown Berkeley, you almost always proceeded past the tables and the smiling maitre d' directly into the kitchen, where Jim would greet the chef — as often as not a dear friend — while maintaining a weather eye for any succulent tidbits that might be on hand for the scarfing.

This time a petite woman, clad chin to toe in a white apron, came running from the back of the kitchen and buried herself in one of Jim's legendary bear hugs.

"Jacques," said Jim, "I'd like you to meet Alice Waters."

With her small size and her almost hyperactive intensity and enthusiasm, Alice reminded me of the restaurant women in my own family — my mother and aunts, all hardworking, serious about their craft, all clever businesswomen, yet hospitable and friendly at the same time.

We took a table in the small dining room, and Alice launched into a detailed life history of every morsel of food we were about to eat — the exact bay the oysters had been pulled from, a full CV of the shepherd who'd raised the lamb, the provenance of every potato, beet, carrot, and leaf of baby lettuce — all of it local, seasonal, and, when possible, organic.

The philosophy she was promulgating with such zeal was so commonplace in France that I took it for granted. Fresh, local, seasonal, know your sources: Maman had settled for no less from the moment she first opened the humble door of Hôtel L'Amour in Neyron. It was a given, not a religious mantra.

In any case, I was of the opinion that a chef could say whatever he or she wanted. The proof was in what came out of the kitchen and was placed on the table. I was impressed by Alice's simple salad of unfashionably small greens and remembered how I had been scolded when Roland and I had picked such a salad from our family patch. Alice used oil and vinegar of the best quality and garnished the salad with buttery croutons made with country bread and wedges of perfect hard-cooked eggs. It was rare in the United States, and anywhere else for that matter, to be served hard-cooked eggs that did not have green-tinged yolks, rubbery whites, and a sulfur smell, all indications of improper cooking.

The quality and simplicity of all the food at Chez Panisse impressed me. More often than not, talent is revealed in the execution of simple dishes. I loved the small, juicy, flavorful grilled leg of lamb that Jeremiah Tower, the chef at Chez Panisse with Alice, served us after a starter of oysters and spicy sausage. The combination was new to me, and I thought it represented a great pairing.

～～～

CRAIG CLAIBORNE and I traveled together to St. Louis to conduct cooking demonstrations. In theory, we did so to raise money for a charity. But I knew that Craig, who was still restaurant critic for the *New York Times,* was going to use the opportunity for some serious scouting. Far from being a Manhattan food snob, Craig was surprisingly democratic in his never-ending quest for new, interesting places to introduce to his readership, driven, I suspect, by his conviction that the country's finest restaurant was out there somewhere, waiting to be discovered, preferably by him.

Nowhere was this as apparent as it was in his approach to Chinese food, which at that time ranked at the very bottom of the eating chain for food snobs. Craig, who had trained as a classical French chef, viewed the Chinese cooking tradition as an equal of French cuisine. He not only discovered New York restaurants such as the renowned Uncle Tai's but reviewed them with the same vocabulary and rated them on the same scale as Lutèce, Le Pavillon, or any other three-star French place in New York.

But after a few days it became apparent that Craig was not going to find the country's greatest undiscovered chef in St. Louis. In my opinion, we had already visited every restaurant in the city worth reviewing, and then some. But Craig wanted to try an obscure Chinese dive. To me, it sounded like your standard strip-mall egg roll palace. But Craig was a diligent reporter, and when it came to ferreting out something new and truly good, nothing stood in his way, including the national pastime.

The St. Louis Cardinals had won the pennant, and one of the World Series games was to be played at home that night. A representative from the mayor's office came to our hotel and ceremoniously presented us with two tickets to the game, along with an invitation to join the mayor and other dignitaries in his box. Craig immediately declined, stating that we had to go to a Chinese restaurant. He may as well have slapped the face of the mayoral emissary. A Chinese restaurant? And a lousy one, as it turned out.

As much as I enjoyed the experiences of traveling around the country to teach at cooking schools, part of me still yearned for the heat and bustle of a commercial kitchen. The days of the traditional French apprenticeship were now long gone even in France, but I felt the urge to pass the craft along to a new generation of aspiring professional cooks. I felt I owed a debt to the trade.

Which is why I was very interested when a New Yorker named Dorothy Cann Hamilton approached me with what at first seemed like a long shot of an idea. During a trip to France in the early 1980s, Dorothy visited a cooking school called le Centre de formation technologique d'alimentation de la chambre de commerce et d'industrie de Paris, called le Ferrandi for short, after the Parisian street on which the school was located. Being a Francophile at heart, Dorothy decided to replicate le Ferrandi in the United States. She thought that this school, which she named the French Culinary Institute, should be staffed with French chefs who had lived here and were as familiar with the American way of life as they were with French culinary techniques. At her invitation, I became a dean at the school. Alain Sailhac, a dear friend and the chef at Le Cirque for close to ten years, was also made a dean, as were André Soltner, chef-owner of Lutèce, and Jacques Torres, the pastry and chocolate genius.

The typical age of my FCI students fell between twenty-five and thirty-five, though some were well over sixty. Most were preparing for their second career, and many were fascinating people: doctors, lawyers, physicists, producers, accountants, stockbrokers, you name it. They brought excitement to classes. One student had been head of surgery in a large hospital in Philadelphia. He decided to change careers in his late forties and move on to cooking, which he had wanted to do all his life. He finished the program and went on to work a ten-dollar-an-hour job on the line at Philadelphia's renowned Le Bec Fin. He was happier behind the stove than he had ever been in an operating room.

Because of Dorothy, a future chef can learn in a matter of months, without leaving Manhattan, much of what I had to absorb over the course of a three-year apprenticeship. In one way, though, we have failed in our mission at FCI — or perhaps American society as a whole has failed. All of us at the institute would like to see more African American students in our classes. I think back to my first days at Howard Johnson's. At that time, the vast majority of faces in kitchens throughout America were black. These chefs were as smart and talented as anyone I'd worked beside. It baffles me that African Americans have been largely absent from the culinary revolution of the past four decades. With notable exceptions, such as the late Patrick Clark of New York's Tavern on the Green, few African American chefs have been accorded the star status that has gone to white kids from the suburbs who grew up on TV dinners. There is a lost generation of African American chefs, and the nation's cuisine is the poorer for it.

When I began teaching at the FCI, I could not help but com-

With Helen McCully
and James Beard.
(Courtesy of *House
Beautiful*)

With Claudine in
Helen McCully's
kitchen, early 1970s.

Judging the cooking segment of a beauty pageant, 1960s.

With Jean Nidetch, founder and president of Weight Watchers, on a pilot television show in the late 1960s. The show was never aired.

In my garden in
Hunter, New York,
1970s.

Craig Claiborne
and I at the
Tastemaker awards
ceremony, 1978.

Shooting the photographs for *Everyday Cooking with Jacques Pépin* in my
Madison, Connecticut, kitchen with (*left to right*) Ann Bramson, my editor
at Harper & Row; Gloria; and Gloria ("Zim") Zimmerman, 1982.

One of my chefs prepares for the opening of La Potagerie, 1970.

At the R. T. French Tastemaker cookbook awards ceremony with Gloria, James Beard, and Julia Child.

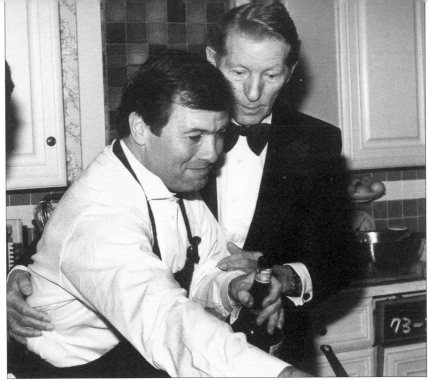

Cooking for a benefit for the March of Dimes with Danny Kaye, 1980s.

With the artist Ed Giobbi, who created pasta primavera.

With Claudine at a KQED book signing for *Jacques Pépin Celebrates* in Mill Valley, California, 2002.

With Jean-Claude Szurdak on Windham Mountain near Hunter, New York, 1995.

With Julia Child, circa 1998.

pare the training my students got during their six-month crash course, designed to impart 250 basic culinary competencies (how to poach an egg, "turn" a potato into a perfect football shape, fillet a fish), with the long years I spent learning many of the same techniques as an apprentice and as *commis*. I don't want to romanticize my training. It was an artifact of a different era, and although it worked then, it is unacceptable in today's fast-paced world. But there is something to be said for carefully learning techniques and absorbing long-established culinary traditions. If nothing else, it gives a young cook perspective that can help in avoiding some of the mistakes common in kitchens run by chefs who rely on gone-wild notions of "creativity" instead of common sense.

In succumbing to the temptations of overexperimenting, many novice chefs felt they were applying the tenets of nouvelle cuisine. But these very excesses caused nouvelle cuisine to become misunderstood as a cuisine of small portions and high prices, pretentious overdecoration, weird mixtures, and miniature vegetables. Although invention and creativity were among its dogmas, it was never intended to shock the diner with esoteric ingredients or strange presentations.

Imagination, the "mistress of error" in the words of Pascal, can be truly dangerous in a kitchen if the cook has little knowledge of technique and poor taste buds. Adding more and more ingredients — several types of oil and herbs, such as sesame seed, olive, and walnut oils, and tarragon, chives, and the like — does not produce a coherent dish. As I get older, I tend to take away from the plate rather than add to it. For the sake of personal expression and originality, many chefs fell into a style of cuisine that they had fought against fiercely: standardized food. What used to be called, ironically, *cuisine de palace* (hotel food) in France and "Continental" food in the United States — boring, repetitive dishes, often involving thick sauces, pale and overcooked vegetables, and potatoes piped around the periphery of the plate — was replaced by bad nouvelle cuisine: paper-thin slices of meat fanned out in the middle of an oversized plate and surrounded by eight types of undercooked baby vegetables and three different overreduced sauces, finished with butter, with a slice of exotic fruit or a few raspberries on top. That is not simplification; it is complication.

Yet when nouvelle cuisine is properly understood and controlled by a thorough knowledge of basic techniques and, more than anything else, by a healthy dose of good common sense, its standards still apply: use the freshest possible food, be innovative, use new ingredients, seek variety in the kitchen, and insist on lightness in sauces.

Nouvelle cuisine left other marks on today's cooking. Chefs became aware of what constitutes quality ingredients and demanded them. Supermarkets responded to the requests of an increasingly sophisticated clientele by regularly providing ingredients that had been practically unknown twenty years earlier: extra-virgin olive oil, aged wine vinegar, fresh herbs, various species of fresh and dried mushrooms, dried tomatoes, new types of vegetables, and esoteric fruits, to name but a few. With its emphasis on the best possible ingredients, smaller portion sizes, more vegetables and less fat and meat, and cooking techniques such as steaming or microwaving, nouvelle cuisine also helped make health concerns a more integral part of serious cooking. The movement's revolutionary dictum that restaurants should be mindful of the health of their customers — something an older generation of chefs had virtually ignored — had mushroomed into a real health food movement by the 1980s.

~

DESPITE MY SUCCESS as a cooking instructor, I still felt frustration because culinary issues were not recognized as academically important. They were still considered trade school stuff. Julia Child and I approached Dr. John Silber, the president of Boston University, and explained that we were interested in establishing a program that would deal with food in the context of social studies. I outlined the arguments that had been dismissed by my doctoral adviser at Columbia. What was needed, I argued, was a program in which students would learn about social and historical phenomena through food — food production, food habits, beliefs about food. Such a program would address the core concerns of human existence. In Homer's *Iliad,* I pointed out, Agamemnon cooks for his guest. In Baudelaire's "Artificial Paradise," wine is the poet's inspiration. In Colette's *Chéri,* breakfast becomes an important ritual with sexual overtones. In Flaubert's *Madame Bovary,* the wedding feast is meticulously depicted. I reminded Dr. Silber that modern anthropologists such as Claude Lévi-Strauss and Peter Farb, philosophers and physicians such as Aristotle, historians such as Fernand Braudel, and psycho-sociologists such as Jean Soler have all discussed eating patterns and food within the context of civilizations.

In 1992 Boston University launched a master of liberal arts program with a concentration in gastronomy under the directorship of Rebecca Alssid, and I was made an instructor in the program.

ONE OF THE MOST important things my students have taught me is the difference between a home cook and a professional. It's a distinction many chefs fail to make, which accounts for the large number of beautiful cookbooks that are impossible to use. For years, because of my training, I was used to thinking and cooking only as a professional, and as I continued to teach and demonstrate, I gradually began to change my philosophy of cooking. All good cooks — whether home cooks or professionals — are aware of the dissimilarities between these two styles and shape their cooking accordingly.

The home cook wants to please a family and is usually attached to a few recipes. The professional cook learns in a more structured way to prepare food from recipes that are altered according to the whims of the customers and the habits of the restaurants.

There are obvious differences in equipment. A professional

kitchen has machines that slice, chop, and purée ingredients with a speed and proficiency not attainable with conventional food processors, and restaurant stoves kick out several times more heat than home stoves do. Constant repetition of techniques and recipes enables the professional to find faster and better ways to prepare a dish than is possible for a person who makes it only occasionally.

Yet because of the time and attention a home cook can devote to one dish, some recipes are always prepared more successfully at home. Cooking meat slowly in a cast-iron Dutch oven, where a dish can be gently braised, basted, then served in its natural juices, is extremely difficult to do in a restaurant kitchen. Casserole dishes and small roasts are also much better at home, where they can get more attention than in a restaurant. Many vegetables that have to be served immediately after cooking fare better, too, in the home kitchen. A simple boiled potato, which should be drained, dried for a few seconds over high heat, and served right away, often sits for hours in water in the restaurant kitchen. Cheeses and fruits are at their fullest flavor in the home, where they can be handled at room temperature rather than refrigerated for long periods beforehand.

From my first days as a cooking instructor, I noticed the same issues cropping up again and again. Most students had trouble with the same basic techniques, regardless of whether the class was made up of aspiring chefs or businesspeople wanting to add new flourishes to their cooking hobby. I began jotting down these recurring areas of difficulty, first just as notes to myself, reminders of what not to take for granted during my classes. Over time, this random collection of jottings on assorted scraps of paper and scribbles in the margins of typed recipes expanded until it filled a dog-eared file folder. The contents of that folder would soon prove to be unexpectedly useful.

Braised Rabbit en Cocotte with Mustard Sauce

YIELD: 6 SERVINGS

RABBIT WAS A POPULAR MEAT of my childhood and still is one of my favorites. My mother used to cook it in a creamy fricassee, and my aunt Hélène roasted it. I have made rabbit into terrines and stews. I have grilled it and roasted it with a finishing crust made of mustard and bread crumbs. This recipe is inspired by La Marraine, my aunt from Valence, who made the best roast rabbit imaginable in her enameled cast-iron *cocotte* (a lidded casserole) on top of the stove. Rabbit usually comes with a liver and kidneys. If they are not part of the package, substitute 2 to 3 chicken livers.

- 1 rabbit (about 2½ pounds), cleaned

STUFFING

- ½ cup chopped onion
- 2 teaspoons chopped garlic
- 2 tablespoons chopped fresh chives
- 2 tablespoons chopped fresh parsley
- 1½ cups diced (½-inch pieces) leftover bread, preferably from a baguette or country loaf
- 1 large egg
- 1 tablespoon Armagnac
- ½ teaspoon salt
- ½ teaspoon freshly ground black pepper

- 3 tablespoons good olive oil
- ½ teaspoon salt
- ½ teaspoon freshly ground black pepper
- 2 onions (about 10 ounces), quartered

1 head garlic (12 to 15 cloves), cloves separated but not
   peeled
8 ounces regular mushrooms, left whole
1 teaspoon dried *herbes de Provence,* or 1 teaspoon chopped
   fresh thyme
1 cup dry, fruity white wine
2 teaspoons Worcestershire sauce
1/2 cup heavy cream
3 tablespoons Dijon-style French mustard

1 tablespoon coarsely chopped fresh parsley, for garnishing

FOR THE STUFFING: Remove the liver and kidneys from the rabbit, chop them coarsely, and put them in a bowl. Add the onion, garlic, chives, parsley, bread cubes, egg, Armagnac, and the salt and pepper. Mash with your hands until the mixture is well combined, then push the stuffing into the cavity of the rabbit. Cover the opening with a piece of parchment paper, and tie it in place with kitchen string to hold the stuffing inside.

FOR THE RABBIT: Heat the oil in a large round or oval baking dish with a lid, preferably an enameled cast-iron *cocotte,* or use a large saucepan with a lid. Sprinkle the 1/2 teaspoon each of salt and pepper on the rabbit. When the oil is hot, add the rabbit, and sauté over medium heat for about 5 minutes on each side, or until it is nicely browned. Add the quartered onions, unpeeled garlic cloves, mushrooms, *herbes de Provence* or thyme, white wine, and Worcestershire sauce. Bring to a boil, cover, and boil over high heat for 1 to 2 minutes, then reduce the heat to very low, and cook for 1 hour. At the end of the hour, increase the heat to medium, and cook, partially covered, for 30 minutes longer, or until the rabbit is fork-tender and the juices are reduced to about 3/4 cup. Add the cream and bring to a boil. Remove from the heat and add the mustard. Do not boil after you add the mustard.

To serve, remove the rabbit from the *cocotte,* and place it on a platter. Remove and discard the string and paper from around the rabbit, and cut the meat into pieces. Surround with the mushrooms, garlic, onions, and pan juices, sprinkle on the parsley, and serve immediately.

16

Writing

I SERVED my food-writing apprenticeship at a stove in Time/ Life's test kitchen. Craig Claiborne had agreed to write the text for the volume on *Classical French Cooking* for the company's well-respected Food of the World series. He asked Pierre Franey and me to choose the dishes for the book. Although coming up with a list was no problem, neither Pierre nor I had ever worked with actual written recipes for classic French dishes. We'd learned to prepare them as apprentices through observation and imitation.

Time/Life solved the twin problems of acquiring the text for the recipes and the color photographs that were to illustrate them by hiring me to go into their kitchen studio and cook. While the photographers set up their cameras and lights, I cooked with a bevy of editorial assistants peering over my shoulders, recording every move and measurement on steno pads. There was none of the fakery or shortcuts that food stylists frequently used at the time to get appetizing-looking photographs. Everything had to be real because it was going to find its way into the text of the book, and it wouldn't do to have our readers deploying blowtorches to get the skin of a turkey that perfect hue of brown, using shaving cream instead of whipped cream, or brushing everything with oil to make it shine.

Occasionally, I felt as if I were cooking in a time warp. For the cover shot, we decided to do a *chaud-froid* of chicken, a complex, highly stylized buffet dish made famous by the great French chef Carême. The last person I had prepared a *chaud-froid* of chicken for was M. Aicardi under the Félix Gaillard government.

But I dutifully set to work, first poaching two capons slowly in a stock of vegetables and herbs. After they cooked, I removed the skin, carved the four breasts from the carcasses, and sliced them into medallions. I made a mousse of goose liver, whipped cream, cognac, and seasonings and placed it on each side of the breastbone of one capon to re-create its original shape. I spread the remainder of the mousse on the reserved medallions. I clarified some of the stock to create a clear aspic, and I reduced the rest of the cooking stock, transforming it into a velouté with a bit of thickening. A little of the aspic was added to the velouté to make a *chaud-froid* sauce, so named because although the sauce is prepared hot *(chaud)*, it is served cold *(froid)*. I coated the medallions of chicken and the whole re-formed chicken with the sauce and decorated the surface of the medallions with little daisies made of blanched leek greens and truffle pieces. The next step was to coat the medallions and the chicken with aspic. Finally, the medallions were layered on top of the chicken, and the extra aspic, by then set, was cut into small, diamond-shaped dice and arranged around the capon on a silver platter. From beginning to end, it took two days to prepare my *chaud-froid*.

The photographer stood over the dish and shot it from above. Everyone oohed and aahed about how beautiful the photograph was.

"What the hell is *that?*" said the editor-in-chief when he saw the photo. They sent me back to the kitchen for two more days to replicate the dish for another photo shoot.

That time the photographer shot the chicken with a silver bucket and a bottle of Champagne next to it. "For balance," he said.

"Champagne makes the book look too upscale for our intended audience," said the editor-in-chief.

I had to create the dish for the third time, which was fine with me. I was getting a per diem fee.

MY METAMORPHOSIS from chef to writer had its roots in one of the many small arguments I had with Helen McCully. It involved, of all things, poaching an egg.

"Americans have no idea how to do it right," Helen announced in her kitchen. "You should show people how to poach eggs, to turn carrots, peel asparagus, wrap a fillet of fish in dough . . . and many other of your techniques that you just take for granted."

She devised a format that was tailor-made for a young man who was well versed in cooking technique but deficient in many of the fine points of English composition. The series of articles she proposed for *House Beautiful* was going to feature short pieces that relied heavily on step-by-step how-to photographs. The writing that accompanied them would take the form of expanded captions. At first Helen corrected most of what I wrote, but as time went by she gave me pointers and I pecked out my columns on the same clackety manual typewriter that had produced my essays at Columbia. Eventually my name appeared at the top of the page. I was a magazine columnist.

One lunch hour when I was behind the counter at La Potagerie, Diane Harris, an editor at Simon and Schuster who had seen me on *What's My Line?*, approached me and asked if I wanted to write a cookbook.

"A soup book, of course," she said. "Everyone's dying to get your recipes."

Because of the success of La Potagerie, I worried that I was getting a reputation as "the Soup Chef" and didn't want to pigeon-hole myself.

"I'd love to write a cookbook," I said, "on any other topic."

"Well, on what, then?" she said.

"How about a book about the type of food I cook at home for my friends and family?" I said. "Simple, familiar French dishes."

In a few weeks, she sent me a contract, which I signed and returned.

I finished the manuscript in six months. It was a tough schedule, but I was determined to meet the deadline, and I did. After a couple of months, I dropped Diane a short letter inquiring about the manuscript's status. She replied neither to that letter, nor the next, nor did she return any of my phone calls. Six months later, I still had no news from Simon and Schuster, which was frustrating, to say the least.

At Craig's house in East Hampton I met Herb Nagourney, president of Quadrangle Books, the *New York Times* book company. He was spending the weekend at Craig's with Ann Bramson, a freelance editor who would later become his wife. I suggested to Herb that the technique columns and accompanying photographs that I was doing for Helen in *House Beautiful* could be turned into an interesting new type of cookbook.

There was a complication, however: my contract with Simon and Schuster gave them the right of first refusal on my next book project. Herb suggested that I write a letter demanding that they revert the rights to me, but instead of doing so, they printed the book I had written earlier. *A French Chef Cooks at Home* reached the bookstores in the spring of 1975.

There was still the issue of their claim to my next book.

"Just send them the proposal. Give them sixty days to respond yes or no," said Herb.

I followed his advice and got a prompt response from Simon and Schuster. They had absolutely no interest in the technique book.

I had not planned to include recipes in *La Technique,* as it would be called, although I ended up with about one hundred. The book was dedicated to showing each exact step involved in more than 150 basic cooking techniques, and it grew from the battered folder containing my teaching notes. Initially, I had anticipated needing four hundred to five hundred photos, but as I got into the book, the number of pictures grew to one thousand and eventually to fifteen hundred. After I had worked on the manuscript for a good year, Ann Bramson came on board as my editor, and the book was finally published in the fall of 1976. When the time came to sell paperback rights to *La Technique,* Simon and Schuster, who had so resoundingly turned down the project originally, led the list of bidders. They issued the book in paperback, and it stayed in print for the next twenty-two years.

~~~~~

MY PROFESSIONAL LIFE was moving into high gear, and I found myself buried under a growing mountain of detail: editing and recording recipes, making travel arrangements and managing my teaching schedule, and bookkeeping.

"This has to change," Gloria said. "You need an assistant."

We placed an ad in the local paper and received two promising applications. One came from a woman who had just sent her children off to college and was eager to reenter the workforce. She lacked clerical experience but was pleasant, cheerful, and eager, and had the ever-ready sense of humor that is a prerequisite for anyone who is going to spend much time in my company, professional or otherwise.

The other candidate was a woman named Norma Galehouse. She was extremely well qualified in every way. She was interested in food, and her lengthy résumé even included a job as the editor of a company magazine. Gloria and I weighed the two candidates. In the end we decided that Norma Galehouse was just a little too professional to fit into the shoot-from-the-hip atmosphere of our business. Her obvious efficiency was a little frightening. Better to take on someone less set in her ways. We hired the other candidate.

By the middle of the first day, we realized the woman would have to go.

But neither Gloria nor I had ever fired anyone. And this employee was as hardworking and pleasant as she could be. It wasn't her fault she couldn't type, spell, or keep accounts.

"I guess you're going to have to tell her it's not working," I said to Gloria.

"Me? Whose assistant is she?"

A week went by with no improvement in the woman's performance, except that she was getting more friendly and cheerful every day. Her delight in having that job was exceeded only by her incompetence. On Friday afternoon, I handed her some handwritten recipes to be typed for an upcoming class. She took one look at me and burst out in sobs.

Gloria had found the nerve to dismiss her on the spur of the moment, obviously without mentioning it to me.

I put in a call to Norma, and she agreed to come aboard. We clicked from the first day. Without a competent assistant, I could never have undertaken my grandest and most adventurous book project, *The Art of Cooking*, in two volumes, acquired by Judith Jones, a well-known editor at Knopf, and serialized in *Gourmet* magazine.

I wanted each section of the book to feature a beautiful dish first, and through the making of the dish, explain the techniques involved. It was a huge undertaking, and from 1985 to 1988 Norma and I worked flat-out on the book. I cooked everything from roasted woodcock to *pommes soufflées* (souffléed potatoes), and rarely seen charcuterie dishes such as blood sausage, sweetbread pâté, and cured and breaded pig's feet. I hired and befriended a local photographer, Tom Hopkins, who came to each of the cooking sessions we scheduled, and he photographed me as I worked, taking hundreds of photographs as I cooked through fifteen to twenty dishes a day. I wrote and rewrote the recipes with introductions; Norma made sense out of my scribblings and sent a typewritten mini-manuscript after each session to Judith, who started on the editing.

MY WRITING CAREER might have been taking off, but sadly, that of Craig, who had done so much to help me get my start in the United States, was in rapid decline. As a restaurant reviewer, Craig was not only tireless but scrupulously fair-minded, a disciplined professional who was respected by his readers and restaurateurs alike, and rightly so. Craig was the first American to take restaurant reviewing seriously. He invented the vocabulary of restaurant criticism still used in this country. Before Craig, there had been none. It is his legacy to America.

So it's unfortunate that Craig is often remembered as the person he became toward the end of his life, bitter and struggling with a host of mental and physical afflictions, fighting a losing battle against alcohol and innumerable demons of his own making. Craig had one sworn enemy — himself.

I first noticed the change in Craig one night when he, Pierre, and I joined another friend, Ann Seranne, a cookbook author and food consultant for whom Craig had worked, for a car journey out to New Jersey to see about finding a kennel to house the championship Yorkshire terriers Ann owned. Ann was a beautiful, sensitive woman, and for no reason at all, Craig began ranting at her, somehow interpreting her perfectly natural desire to have a first-class home for her dogs as a severe character flaw.

"You're a consummate control freak, Ann," he said. "Everything has to be just perfect for you, doesn't it. You have to be right all the time. Well, people are getting tired of you . . ."

Several times, I tried to interrupt, but Craig raised his voice and continued his tirade. By then, Ann was crying. If anything, that spurred Craig to greater heights of insult.

This turned out not to be an isolated incident. Everywhere I went in New York, I heard stories of Craig's erratic behavior when drunk. He got mad at the *Times* and walked out in a snit, under the mistaken belief that his name was more powerful than the newspaper's.

To prove his point, he spent a great deal of his own money to launch a food newsletter. But the fans failed to materialize, and Craig, with a bigger chip on his shoulder than ever, was forced to retreat to the *Times*, only to stomp out the door a second time.

His lengthy and mutually profitable writing partnership with Pierre also ended badly. Craig expected Pierre to maintain the same workaholic schedule that he did. As book and article projects piled up, Craig and Pierre were spending so much time together that rumormongers began to suggest that their relationship was more than just professional — which, as any attractive woman who had ever spent more than a few moments with Pierre would testify, was totally off the mark.

By that time, Pierre's column in the *New York Times*, "60-Minute Gourmet," had become a popular fixture; he was writing books with other collaborators such as Bryan Miller; and he was branching out into television, working for PBS. Essentially, he was becoming more successful than Craig, and that created a serious strain on their friendship. Eventually, their collaboration of several decades fell apart, and each went his own way. It surely couldn't have helped Craig's self-image when I started writing a monthly column of my own, "The Purposeful Cook," for the *Times*.

Craig's life was falling apart in other ways as well. His jovial, long-time companion Harry Creel was struck by a car and killed, a devastating loss. Craig and Harry had met when they served in the navy and had been together ever since. Harry was just the sort of stabilizing force Craig needed in his life. He was a well-padded, Southern good old boy, and about the only person Craig knew who wasn't an accomplished cook. But that didn't stop Harry from lending his particular talents to Craig's dinner parties, scrubbing pots, pans, dishware, and crystal, in his role of "the Dishwasher King."

In an era when being out of the closet was both rare and not without risk, Craig was always open and casual about his sexual orientation. His memoir, *A Feast Made for Laughter,* detailing the sexual abuses he'd suffered from his father as a child, was intended as a catharsis, but it failed to enthrall readers and got a mostly negative critical reception, which pushed Craig deeper into his black mood.

All of us were worried about our old friend.

~

WRITING was an extension of my teaching career, in many cases a natural outgrowth of classes that I was presenting at cooking schools on my travels around the country, a productive way to fill the days when I was at home. As the sales figures for my books climbed, I saw that writing was a way of reaching a vastly larger audience than teaching could provide. In a good week, a few dozen students would attend my classes, but a single printing of one of my books would reach tens of thousands of readers. Also, being a published author made me more in demand as a teacher, and face-to-face sessions with cooking students resulted in fresh ideas and increased book sales. Writing and teaching were symbiotic.

But this dynamic pattern of work was nothing compared to what happened after Marjorie Poore, the executive producer at the PBS station KQED in San Francisco, approached me one spring evening in 1988 following a guest appearance I'd made on Martin Yan's show.

"I'd like you to tape a series for us," she said.

Chicken Salad
à la Danny Kaye

YIELD: 4 SERVINGS

To MOST AMERICANS, Danny Kaye is remembered as a splendid comedian and actor. I think of him as a friend and one of the finest cooks I have ever known. In every way, Danny was equal to or better than any trained chef. His technique was flawless. The speed at which he worked was on par with what you'd find in a Parisian *brigade de cuisine*. Danny taught me a great deal, mostly about Chinese cuisine, his specialty.

Whenever I traveled to Los Angeles, Danny picked me up at the airport and took me to his house, where we cooked Chinese or French food. His poached chicken was the best I have ever had. His method was to put the chicken in a small stockpot, cover it with tepid water seasoned with salt, peppercorns, and vegetables, and cook it at a gentle boil for only 10 minutes, then set it aside off the heat for 45 minutes. As an added touch, he always stuck a handful of knives, forks, and spoons into the cavity of the chicken, to keep it submerged. The result is so moist, tender, and flavorful that I have used the recipe — minus the flatware — ever since.

CHICKEN

  1 chicken, about 3¹/₂ pounds
¹/₂ cup sliced carrot
  1 cup sliced onion
  1 small leek, washed and left whole
  1 rib celery, washed and left whole
  1 teaspoon salt

¼ teaspoon black peppercorns

2 sprigs thyme

2 bay leaves

About 7 cups tepid water, or more if needed

DRESSING

2 tablespoons Dijon-style mustard

1 tablespoon white wine vinegar

1 teaspoon finely chopped garlic

¼ teaspoon salt

¼ teaspoon freshly ground black pepper

½ teaspoon Tabasco hot pepper sauce

5 tablespoons extra-virgin olive oil

GARNISHES

1 dozen Boston lettuce leaves, cleaned

2 dozen fresh tarragon leaves

FOR THE CHICKEN: Place the chicken breast side down in a tall, narrow pot, so it fits snugly at the bottom. Add the remaining poaching ingredients. The chicken should be submerged, and the water should extend about 1 inch above it. Bring to a gentle boil, cover, and let boil gently for 10 minutes. Remove the pot from the heat, and set it aside to steep in the hot broth for 45 minutes.

Remove the chicken from the pot, and set it aside on a platter to cool for a few minutes. (The stock can be strained and frozen for up to 6 months for use in soup.) Pick the meat from the chicken bones, discarding the skin, bones, and fat. Shred the meat with your fingers, following the grain and pulling it into strips. (The meat tastes better shredded than diced with a knife.)

FOR THE DRESSING: Mix together all the dressing ingredients in a bowl large enough to hold the chicken salad.

Add the chicken shreds to the dressing and toss well. Arrange the Boston lettuce leaves in a "nest" around the periphery of a platter, and spoon the room-temperature chicken salad into the center. Sprinkle with the tarragon leaves and serve.

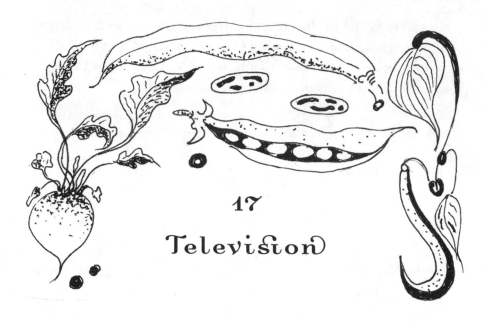

17

Television

I AGREED TO COOPERATE with Marjorie, but had no reason to feel our efforts would result in anything but another stillborn TV program. Aside from providing me with a few good laughs and exposing me to an interesting culture, my television career had up until that point consisted of a string of false starts and minor disappointments that began in the late 1960s, when I had my first audition. Gloria, who managed a recording studio that booked talent for commercials, had become friendly with Don Morrow, a famous commercial actor of that time. Don telephoned Gloria to say that he had recommended me to a producer, who was looking for someone to do a cooking show that they were proposing for television. A few days later, his producer-friend called me and said that I should report to an address in New York for what I assumed would be a screen-test interview.

It was after 5:00 P.M. when they finally put me on. Most of the studio technicians were far more interested in catching their trains home than watching me. And by then, it was obvious to all why I was scheduled last. Everyone else was professional talent — actors who did commercials. I'd seen them on television, pitching everything from coffee to breakfast sausages.

"So what are you going to cook?" said the producer, without looking at me as I came onto the kitchen set.

Cook? There must have been a misunderstanding. No one had mentioned anything about having to cook. But it did explain why the other candidates had all carried shopping bags that bulged with breads, meats, and vegetables.

Figuring that I didn't have anything to lose by winging it, I rummaged through the garbage can next to the prep table and found a tomato, half an onion, a piece of celery, and some parsley, all discarded by my predecessors. Opening the refrigerator, I saw a little butter and some eggs and realized that I had the makings of an omelet. Not much, but better than nothing. I arranged my ingredients on the set and was ready to go in a few minutes. I sliced the onions and celery and began to sauté them in butter while I chopped the parsley, cut the tomatoes, and beat my eggs, chattering the whole time.

In the end, my knife skills got me the job.

A month later, Gloria and I went to Baltimore to tape three pilots for the proposed show. The program was to air weekly and was to be hosted by Jean Carpenter, the wife of the astronaut Scott Carpenter. It was to be a live show for women, with interviews and a cooking segment. I would appear with Jean Nidetch, the founder and president of Weight Watchers, and I was to prepare a low-calorie recipe for each show.

We filmed three pilots that afternoon. Gloria had brought several shirts for me, so I could change between segments and make it appear that the various shows were filmed on different days. After the first segment, the producer approached Gloria.

"Is everything okay?" she asked.

"Perfect," he said. "Love the accent."

I was flabbergasted. So was Gloria. Me? An accent?

My TV career was launched. Or so I thought. But despite everyone's enthusiasm, the series was never aired, and my life as a television personality went into a two-decade hiatus.

Things didn't pick up until the early 1980s when I taped a series of thirteen cooking shows at WJCT-TV, the PBS station in Jacksonville, Florida. We planned to film the thirteen shows in five shooting days. For this show, I made comfort food that everyone could relate to: vegetable soup, corn dumplings, mussels Provençal, chicken in mustard sauce, sausage and potato stew, potato ragoût, fried eggplant, apple brown betty, and chocolate cream. I learned a great deal about cooking on TV and felt more comfortable with the medium, but I wasn't any closer to stardom. The Jacksonville effort went nowhere.

After that, hardly a year passed without my being approached by one TV producer or another. Representing stations such as WGBH in Boston and WNET in New York, they seemed genuinely interested in making a show with me. They were certainly respected professionals with numerous successes among their credits — far from fly-by-nights. But after a flurry of assurances, the phone calls became less frequent, then dwindled to silence. Nothing ever materialized for one simple reason: lack of money. I became convinced that the only requirement for getting my own PBS show was raising half a million dollars, an undertaking that I knew nothing about.

At KQED, Peter Stein, a talented producer, was assigned to my project, and Susie Heller, a friend from my China trip, was the culinary producer. We decided to tape in July 1989 to fit within my schedule of cooking classes. Marjorie had assured me that the necessary money would be secured by Christmas 1988.

A few months went by, and I assumed the deal had gone dead like so many others. But Marjorie called, insisting that the show was still very much alive, that it was only a matter of time before she lined up the necessary sponsors. Many companies were interested.

I'd heard it all before.

Her Christmas deadline passed. By April, we still hadn't found sponsors. On the fifteenth of the month, Norma came into my office. "Marjorie's on the line," she said.

I picked up the phone.

"We're funded," said Marjorie. "It's a go."

I should have been delighted. But my first thought was that with less than three months to test the recipes and organize them into a companion book for the series, I could never be ready in time.

On television, I wanted to teach viewers essential techniques of cooking, as I had done in my classes and books. The dishes would be easy to make, nutritionally sound within the bounds of common sense, and quick to prepare. They would also be original and interesting, and within the budget of the average home cook. Norma and I went into high gear and finished the manuscript just in time for me to tape the shows in July. The shows began to air in September 1989 and continued for the next twenty-six weeks. We had terrific ratings and enough viewers to warrant the sponsors' continued support.

THANKS TO MY TV connections and my friendship with Julia, I was able to play a supporting role in the creation of one of America's classic comic routines. I was in Boston promoting *La Méthode* and was scheduled to fly from there to Los Angeles to appear with Julia on Tom Snyder's *Tomorrow Show.* In Los Angeles, I was met by a limousine, a bodyguard, and someone who stayed behind to collect my luggage. I was rushed to the studio, went through makeup in a few minutes, and arrived on the set, where Julia was arranging ingredients. She was in California, visiting friends in Pasadena for a few weeks, so she had been in charge of procuring the food we would cook. In true Julia style, she bought enough to feed the whole studio audience: veal, scallops, salmon, leeks, tomatoes, artichokes, and an assortment of herbs.

We had only five minutes before airtime, and Julia grabbed the trusty — and extremely sharp — seven-inch-long chef's knife that I always carried with me when I traveled, and she began slicing a shallot. Midway through, she cut herself, almost severing the end of her index finger.

With the director counting down the seconds till we were on air, we pushed the loose piece of flesh back over the cut. Julia hastily wrapped her bloody hand in a towel and proclaimed herself fine. Then she calmed Tom down and told him not to worry, that we would be cooking together and she'd just use one hand. Nobody would know, she assured him, so it would be best not to mention the injury at all.

Suddenly we were live! Julia, six feet two or three inches, in the center, Tom, nearly six feet seven inches, on one side, and me, looking like a hobbit, on the other. Tom immediately said to the audience, "Julia, would you mind if I told people that you just cut your finger?" Well, there was no hiding it anymore. We had a great show; we cooked, tasted, kidded around. Paul Child came on stage and made two batches of one of his famous drinks, which he called, whimsically, *à la recherche de l'orange perdue*. It was delicious, and we consumed both batches. The ingredients give a fair idea of our mental condition afterward:

> 6 tablespoons dark Jamaican rum
> 9 tablespoons dry white vermouth
> 2 teaspoons bottled sweetened lime juice
>   Juice of 1 lime
> 1 tablespoon orange marmalade
> 1 whole seedless orange, quartered
> 5 shakes orange bitters
> 1 cup ice cubes

Following the show, we went to the hospital, where eight stitches were required to reattach the tip of Julia's finger. Then we proceeded on to L'Ermitage, owned and operated by Jean Bertranou, the best French chef on the West Coast, where Julia and Paul had been eager to eat.

A few days later, Julia appeared on Johnny Carson's television show, and what they talked about was her finger. I met her later that week in San Francisco, where together we were going to prepare omelets on the *Kathryn Crosby Show*. We made the omelets, but mostly we talked about Julia's finger.

That was the inspiration for Dan Aykroyd's famous spoof on *Saturday Night Live*. Dressed as Julia, he merrily cuts up a chicken, with blood spurting all over the place. As he collapses, he screams heroically, "Save the liver!"

CLAUDINE WAS at Boston University, where she was doing graduate work, and she had a small apartment there. She decided to make dinner for me one evening. She knew what I liked and wisely kept the food simple: roast chicken, sautéed potatoes, a green salad, and fruit for dessert. Unfortunately, she started cooking too early and I came late — not a good combination. She anxiously looked at my face and, reacting to my muteness, asked, "So, how is it?"

I answered, "As a father . . . or as a chef?"

As a father, I found it exceptionally good. But the incident gave me an idea. It would be great, I thought, to do a father-daughter series. The producers, however, objected. *Cooking with Claudine* would take away from the rapport that I had established with my regular audience, they argued.

I disagreed, saying that Claudine would act as a friendly, nonprofessional foil whom the audience could relate to. She would ask the questions on their minds, even make the same sort of errors they would make. Eventually, the KQED brass relented, although Claudine was not allowed to look into the camera and could only react to what I did and said. *Cooking with Claudine* boasted ratings higher than my shows had ever achieved, and from then on Claudine was allowed to act as she pleased on the set.

Claudine has a great palate, and she eventually chose a career in the wine business. I maintain a fairly casual attitude toward wine and food, one that still reflects my father's teaching. I have my preferences, of course, but a wine has to be downright bad for me to refuse it and drink water with a meal. I even like to mix leftover wines, an exercise that makes Claudine crazy. Although I usually mix red with red and white with white, I have been known to add a little leftover white wine to leftover red. And I know all too well how Claudine reacts to that — as a daughter . . . and as a wine expert.

Claudine accompanied me to France when CBS asked me to tape a few segments about the foods, wines, and cheeses of the Savoie region as a part of their coverage of the 1992 Winter Olympics in Albertville. My brother Roland, who had moved back to the Lyon area, joined us. We took an afternoon off to find the two mountain villages where we had stayed that summer during the war. The hamlets lay in ruins, destroyed by the Germans, and the big, beautiful communal bread oven that had been the center of the communities was nothing more than a mound of rubble.

Among the few houses left, however, was the one where Roland had boarded. The son of the family who took Roland in, now an old bachelor living alone in a space he shared with the few cows, invited us in to share some chestnuts that he was roasting and to drink a glass of his homemade wine.

Bichon was also back in Lyon, owner of his own restaurant after stints behind the stove in Paris and aboard the ships of the French line. An impromptu party was in order. The café Bichon ran was a lively, noisy place that served as a neighborhood hangout. The food was simple regional fare but of unsurpassed quality.

It was almost eerie how much my little brother, then in his early fifties, resembled Papa, not only physically but in temperament. When it came time to serve dessert, he told Claudine that he was going to demonstrate a new form of service. He stood at the head of the long table and dealt out the plates — literally — flipping them toward us with the finesse of a Monte Carlo baccarat dealer, breaking only a few. It took a good five minutes before anyone could eat, we were laughing so hard. I thought of that happy gathering a few years later when word reached me that my little bother had succumbed to lung cancer.

Semi-Dry Tomatoes and Mozzarella Salad

YIELD: 4 SERVINGS

*I*N THE *Today's Gourmet* series, I wanted to create dishes that were elegant, modern, original, light, and reasonably quick to prepare. TV demanded that the dishes be visually attractive, too. It was fun to dream up new recipes with that focus in mind. This one is a good example.

Partially drying the tomatoes in the oven concentrates their taste, giving them a wonderfully deep flavor and great chewiness. The red of the tomatoes, the white of the cheese, and the green of the basil make this dramatically colorful salad especially enticing. Serve with good crunchy bread.

1½ pounds plum tomatoes (about 6), cut lengthwise into halves (12 pieces)

¾ teaspoon salt

10 ounces fresh mozzarella cheese, cut into ½-inch slices

2 tablespoons drained and rinsed capers

½ teaspoon freshly ground black pepper

1 teaspoon chopped garlic

3 tablespoons extra-virgin olive oil

½ teaspoon grated lemon rind

About 1 cup (loose) basil leaves

Preheat the oven to 250 degrees. Line a cookie sheet with aluminum foil. Arrange the tomato halves cut side up on the sheet, and sprinkle ½ teaspoon of the salt on top. Bake for 4 hours.

Remove the tomatoes from the oven (they will still be soft), and put them in a serving bowl. Let them cool, then add the mozzarella, capers, remaining ¼ teaspoon salt, pepper, garlic, olive oil, and lemon rind, and mix to combine.

Drop the basil leaves into 2 cups of boiling water, and cook for about 10 seconds. Drain, and cool under cold running water. Press the basil between your palms to extrude most of the water, then chop finely. Add to the salad, toss well, and serve.

18
Gloria's Restaurant

AFTER NEARLY A DECADE of working to establish myself as a teacher and writer — a career that allowed me to earn a comfortable living without having to toil in a restaurant kitchen — I went back into the kitchen. This one was located in Madison, Connecticut, and was called Gloria's French Café. The owner-manager was my wife.

Most avid home cooks dream of owning a restaurant someday. Wouldn't it be great to have friends stop by anytime for dinner, to create great food, to please people, and even to make money from it? This romantic vision partly explains the high failure rate of restaurants.

The creation of Gloria's French Café had a lot more to do with happenstance than long-range planning. Following my accident, I could no longer ski, and winters in Hunter became unbearably depressing. They reminded me of what I had lost and presented a constant hassle: thawing pipes, shoveling snow, digging out stuck cars, all chores I performed with difficulty because of my injuries. It was time to leave the Catskills.

Gloria and I took a road map of the Northeast and drew a line north and south of New York City. Our new home had to be within a couple hours' drive of the city so I could easily get to work. The allure of a milder climate made us decide to limit our search to coastal areas. That still left a considerable corridor running from Connecticut down to the Jersey shore.

The place we finally bought in Madison had all the trappings of a new Pépin house, which is to say that it was barely habitable, having sat vacant for a year after the three elderly sisters who owned it moved into a nursing home. If we'd done the intelligent thing, we would have called in a bulldozer, knocked down the structure, and started from scratch. But we saw its potential. Four acres of land offered enough space for gardens and a big yard. On one side was a synagogue, on the other an Episcopal church, ensuring both privacy and, I felt, a double layer of supernatural protection. The scrubby, mosquito-infested swamp in the backyard could be dredged and dammed, creating a pond full of trout and frogs. Where others saw a warren of small rooms and low ceilings, I saw a vast, open-concept kitchen–dining room–living room, with a cathedral ceiling. We moved in on a snowy December day and began a program of renovations and reparations. A quarter-century later, our home is still a work-in-progress.

From the time when Jean-Claude and I fixed up our first apartment in New York, nailing up new shelves and moving countertops to create a functional and pleasant workspace, I have always tried to make my kitchen the site for special family occasions, the heart of our lifestyle, and the setting for celebrations. I had always hoped for a dwelling built around a kitchen open to all the other living spaces. The Madison house allowed me to realize that dream.

I felt no need to kowtow to convention or conform to the design of a standard kitchen. Mine had to be functional, easy, and friendly. The first rule for me is to feel good in my kitchen. The worktable should be the proper height; pots, pans, and lids accessible; outside light plentiful. There should be wood-textured cabinetry with smooth, nonporous counters, a stove with a lot of BTUs, a large refrigerator, an ice machine, and plenty of sharp knives and rubber spatulas.

Our kitchen is wide open; I do not mind when the smells of cooking drift through a house. Many of our pots, pans, and skillets hang on a wall of natural gray barn wood. I find my displayed kitchen utensils aesthetically pleasing. I like the view of the pond and the woods from my kitchen window. We have two dishwashers, a six-burner gas stove against the outside wall, and a two-burner gas stove in the center island countertop, which is particularly useful when television shows are shot at my home. Our large refrigerator has a freezer at the bottom. The grill is outside the kitchen door in the yard, between a gas stove used to deep-fry fish, meat, or vegetables, and a wood-burning bread oven that makes for great summer parties.

The large center island in our kitchen has a granite top. The walls behind the stove are tiled in blue and white, our favorite colors. My own hand-painted tiles, as well as ceramic paintings, decorate the walls. The knives and electric appliances, from toaster to food processor, are within easy reach. I designed a rolling garbage bin that fits into a tiled area under the counter. Above it is a wide drawer that holds dispensers of plastic wrap and aluminum foil. A roll of paper towels on a dowel is secured to the face of the same drawer. There are no gimmicky pieces of equipment in our kitchen. Utensils are used daily and also serve as decorative elements. The space feels comfortable when I am cooking alone and just as comfortable when I am cooking with Gloria or Jean-Claude. It is a convivial space. Most of our conversations and discussions take place in the kitchen. In the kitchen we meet first in the morning, and it is here that we do our chores and conduct our daily lives. We always — and I do mean always — set the table for dinner for the two of us, in the dining room in cold weather and on the porch adjacent to the kitchen as soon as the sun warms it to a comfortable temperature. For lunch, as a concession to my American-ization, we usually eat at the counter in the kitchen.

~~~~~

I HAD LOVED to forage for food in the forests of the Catskills, and I feared that moving to densely populated coastal Connecticut would curtail my life as a hunter and gatherer. As soon as the snow melted that first summer in Madison, I began to prowl the country-side. Used to a landscape of rolling forests and small fields, I found the salt marshes and rocky shoreline foreign terrain.

But slowly, the coast began to reveal its culinary riches. A new friend complained about a shallow channel where his outboard of-ten scraped something hard and grating. I went to the area at low tide and discovered a shoal of mussels easily a foot thick. I could gather a feast in a matter of minutes and usually cooked the mus-sels simply, with onions, white wine, and leeks. On the beaches of Madison, Guilford, and Clinton, I learned how to feel for the large quahog clams — some weighing nearly a pound — in the muck with my foot, and with them Gloria made the best spaghetti and clam sauce ever. Using a piece of string and a chicken leg or car-cass, I soon got the hang of lifting ferocious blue crabs from the marshes around Long Island Sound. These I transformed into a hot crab boil, with potatoes, corn, onions, and sausage. I drained them and piled them directly on the big wooden table on the porch, and we split them down the middle and ate them with the fingers. Lobsters, plentiful in summer, turned out to be even better — more hard-shelled and flavorful — in winter.

I immediately noticed a great variety of *Boletus* mushrooms, or cèpes, near our house, though not as many chanterelles as in up-state New York. But after I started walking the woods with Gerry Miller, an artist, shaman, and bona fide mycologist, I learned to recognize some thirty kinds of edible mushrooms that grow around Madison.

In the pond behind the house, I occasionally caught frogs, just as I had in Hunter, skinning and sautéing them, usually with garlic and parsley. One of the great treats of the summer was *la petite friture,* or fried whitebait. Especially in late August, Claudine and I went to the sound when the tide was coming in and dragged a net through shallow water to catch these wonderful, pencil-thin fish, each about three or four inches long. We enjoyed them, head and all, almost like French fries, with a cold glass of white wine or cider.

Jean-Claude came down from Hunter to visit me that first winter. With a bottle of icy Sancerre, we went down to the Madison wharf and sat together on a rock, popping open the oysters that clung within reach just below the tide line. The oysters were plump and briny; the wine as icy as the wind that blew in our faces. Madison had started to feel a bit like home.

IN THE WINTER of 1982, I was approached by the owner of the Dolley Madison, a traditional New England restaurant and inn in Madison. Business was bad, and despite the place's great location, it had been closed since the previous summer. He wanted me to take it over. I was quite busy at the time with cooking classes, yet the challenge of trying to open a successful restaurant where so many others had failed was tempting, and Gloria wanted to give it a go. Fifteen years after her first visit with me to France, Gloria had thoroughly adapted to the French approach to dining. When we traveled there (or anywhere else, for that matter), the first thing she determined each morning was where we would have lunch, where we would have dinner, and, eventually, where we would stay that night. Finally, she had her priorities straight.

So we signed a lease for a trial period of six months, spanning the summer and early fall. I took a leave of absence from my other obligations and worked with Gloria to create the ambience and menu for the restaurant and to train the staff. If the business worked, Gloria planned to renew the lease in the fall and continue on her own.

My idea was to create a dining experience that was rarely

offered in the United States. Even today, many Americans have a limited view of what constitutes French cooking. Their experience is largely confined to France's haute cuisine, the food that is prepared in Michelin-starred restaurants. This complex cuisine is structured and recorded in books, makes use of esoteric and expensive ingredients, and is composed of separate preparations that eventually end up in one finished dish. This is not a cuisine to be partaken of every day, and it is only one of several styles of French cooking.

Cuisine bourgeoise is based on the freshest local products of the earth. Its regional emphasis brings to light how different the cuisines of France can be. *Cuisine bourgeoise* is often prepared by women chefs who have great respect for tradition, culture, and the integrity of the ingredients. At its best, it is perhaps the most satisfying cuisine of France.

Cuisine ménagère, or home cooking, is the cuisine of every day. Mostly done by women who have to cook after work under constraints of time and budget, it has to be filling, inexpensive, and fast — a daily dinner for a working family. Finally, there is farm cooking, a humble cooking of the *terroir* that is difficult to sample unless one arrives unannounced. If guests are coming, the farmer or his wife will *mettre les petits plats dans les grands,* "place the little dishes into the big ones," meaning "get fancier." Farm cooking depends on a few ingredients that grow locally, and the recipes are passed verbally from mother to daughter. While the ingredients are few, they are of high quality, ranging from homemade bread, cheese, and wine to home-grown potatoes and farm-raised calf or rabbit.

Gloria's French Café was going to draw from the *cuisine bourgeoise* and *cuisine ménagère* traditions. It would be the type of restaurant my mother ran when I was a child, straightforward and inexpensive, with a set menu. A place for neighbors to gather and enjoy good food. And who better to take on as an adviser than a woman who had opened and operated several such restaurants herself?

By then in her late sixties, Maman still maintained the same frenetic pace that she always had. Age might have sprinkled some gray into her thick, dark hair, but it had done nothing to her energy level except increase it, if that was possible.

As owners of a small business, she and my father were not eligible for the government health plan, so all of their savings had to be spent on my father's medical care. Upon his death, Maman found herself broke. But by the time she came to help open Gloria's French Café, my mother had rebuilt her fortune and then some. She worked for a catering company and shrewdly invested in a series of rental units, eventually owning two apartments and a rooming house in addition to the family home in Neyron.

As I planned the menu for the café, I realized that although I had worked mostly with men in the great restaurants of Paris and New York, the sort of cooking I was now turning to had been shown to me by women. It was the type of cooking I most loved to do.

We set our menu and priced our dinners at sixteen dollars, all-inclusive, including tips but not wine from our limited and inexpensive list. We spent two months cleaning, repairing, and decorating the kitchen and dining room, and we removed the swinging kitchen door so patrons would feel welcome to come and speak with us and see how clean the kitchen was. For the first time in three decades, Maman and I were working in the same kitchen. Gloria oversaw waitresses in the dining room. Gloria's mother, Grandma Julia, was the official laundress, washing the red and blue tablecloths and napkins every night. Our friend Gloria Zimmerman, a.k.a. "Zim," came early in the mornings to help prepare the day's dessert and make the bread from the dough that had risen slowly overnight in the walk-in icebox.

As guests sat down, they were given a basket of fresh bread and a treat, usually a small crock of chicken liver mousse, cold ratatouille, or fresh herb cheese. Maman was in charge of the hors d'oeuvres. Composed of six different items, they arrived automatically at each table. Two were standard: a slice of homemade veal and pork terrine and a stuffed egg Jeannette. The remaining four changed according to market and seasonal considerations, but could include melon slices, radishes, salads of tomatoes or lentils, grated carrots and walnuts, a tangy cucumber and dill salad, or stuffed zucchini.

Our soups were usually made from vegetables, and there were usually four main courses — a roast meat, a stew, a fish, and a standard pan-fried sirloin steak — with three vegetable dishes as accompaniments. We offered four or five desserts, including two standards: a rich chocolate cake served with a rum sauce, and a big slice of a thin-crusted fruit *galette,* or tart, made with whatever was at the peak of ripeness.

All this for sixteen dollars.

We sucked in a collective deep breath and opened the doors for business.

〜

FROM THE FIRST night, Gloria's French Café was profitable, thanks to lessons of economy I had learned in my early culinary career. I actually feel ill when I see food wasted. At Gloria's French Café, nothing edible was ever discarded or allowed to go bad. Everything was portioned, organized, and controlled. When we peeled tomatoes, the skins and seeds went into stock, and the strained juices were added to soups and sauces. The cubed flesh of the tomatoes was kept to be sautéed with shrimp or chicken. The stems of parsley, tarragon, and other herbs went into stock. The fat from a veal shoulder was used in our homemade pâté, just as the fat from our chicken bones added to stock was used to make our chicken liver mousse.

It has always been my habit when I arrive at a restaurant kitchen to check the garbage bin to see if anything usable has been discarded and to inspect the walk-in refrigerator to see if there are leftovers that can be recycled in one way or another. Poor Zim: she had burned a few of her cakes, tarts, and breads the first week and had tossed them in the garbage. She took to hiding damaged pastries and breads in the trunk of her car, so she could take them home and dispose of them herself, away from my judgmental eyes.

Gloria ran a similarly tight ship in the front of the house, where fresh flowers, crisp tablecloths, shining floors, and pleasant aromas greeted our first customers at 6:30 P.M. We usually served two full sittings each night during the week and two and a half to three sittings on weekends.

So it was with some amazement that our regulars read the notice in the window at the beginning of October, saying that we were closing the restaurant for good. The initial six-month lease had run out, and Gloria had no intention of renewing.

"It's slave work," she said. "I have it out of my system for good, thank you!"

Another reason for her decision to close was an August 1982 review of the restaurant that appeared in the *Hartford Courant*. We had had a few reviews before, all of them complimentary about the food and the service. This one, however, written by Bryan Miller, the *Courant*'s restaurant critic who later moved to the *New York Times,* was different. He praised the food, but he criticized Gloria's service as being rude and plainly inept. Lacking the thick skin you have to develop to make it in the restaurant business, Gloria was devastated, and also puzzled. She did not remember the negative incidents described so vividly in the paper. It turned out that another woman was taking care of the front of the house on the nights Miller dined at the café. Although Miller's criticism was warranted, the culprit was not Gloria.

Giobbi's Primavera Pasta

YIELD: 4 SERVINGS

I SHOULD BE JEALOUS of Ed Giobbi. My wife turns to his cookbooks more often than to mine, and the guy isn't even a professional cook or writer. He's a highly successful artist. Cooking is his hobby.

One of Ed's claims to fame is that he invented the now well-known dish called pasta primavera. When Sirio Maccioni opened the first Le Cirque restaurant in 1976, he asked Ed if he knew of a recipe for pasta that would be a bit different and new. Ed boasted about a dish his grandmother had made, which consisted of room-temperature raw tomato pieces combined with hot pasta. Ed halved, seeded, then diced ripe tomatoes, and mixed them with black pepper, extra-virgin olive oil, salt, shredded basil, and finely chopped onion and garlic. As soon as the pasta cooked, he drained it and tossed it with the tomato mixture. He served the dish immediately, with grated Parmesan cheese. It is one of my favorite meals in the summer when the vines in my garden sag under the weight of ripe tomatoes. The tomato salad is also great on top of *crostini* toasts.

TOMATO SALAD/SAUCE
- 1 pound ripe tomatoes (2 or 3 tomatoes)
- 1 teaspoon finely chopped garlic
- $^3/_4$ teaspoon salt
- $^1/_2$ teaspoon freshly ground black pepper
- $^1/_3$ cup extra-virgin olive oil
- 1 cup shredded basil leaves

Salt to taste

8 cups water

1 pound penne or bow-tie pasta

⅓ cup freshly grated Parmesan cheese (preferably Parmigiano-Reggiano)

FOR THE TOMATO SALAD/SAUCE: Cut the tomatoes in half crosswise, parallel to the stems, and gently press the seeds out. Cut the flesh into ½-inch pieces, and put them in a bowl large enough to hold the finished dish. Add the remaining salad ingredients, and toss well.

FOR THE PASTA: Salt the water and bring to a boil. Add the pasta, stir well, bring back to a boil, and boil, uncovered, stirring occasionally, for about 10 minutes, more or less, depending on how firm you like your pasta. Add a 6-ounce ladle of the hot pasta water to the tomato salad. Drain the pasta in a colander, and add it immediately to the tomato salad. Toss thoroughly, and divide the pasta among four soup plates. Sprinkle generously with the Parmesan cheese, and serve immediately.

Pissenlit

(DANDELION SALAD)

YIELD: 4 SERVINGS

*P*ISSENLIT, as the common dandelion is often called in France, is considered a great early-spring treat in our family. Gloria loves to pick the greens at the end of March and the beginning of April, especially the small white specimens hidden in the fallen leaves behind our guesthouse. This family tradition started for me with my father and my two brothers, and now my wife and daughter, Claudine, are great lovers of *pissenlit* salad. The leaves should be picked before the flowers start forming, while they are small, white, and tender. There is no comparison between the tender wild dandelion greens you pick yourself and the ones that are found in markets.

With a small paring knife, cut about an inch below the ground to get the dandelion plant in one piece. Cut the leaves away from the root, and discard any that are damaged or darkened. Our version always includes pieces of pancetta as well as croutons, boiled eggs with soft yolks, and a dressing made of garlic, anchovies, and olive oil.

4 large eggs
5 ounces pancetta, cut into pieces about 1 inch long, $\frac{1}{2}$ inch wide, and $\frac{1}{2}$ inch thick (about 2 dozen)
2 cups water
6 tablespoons extra-virgin olive oil
2 teaspoons chopped garlic
4 anchovy fillets in oil, finely chopped
1 tablespoon red wine vinegar
$\frac{1}{2}$ teaspoon salt
$\frac{1}{2}$ teaspoon freshly ground black pepper
A piece of baguette (about 3 ounces), cut into sixteen $\frac{1}{4}$-inch slices
About 8 ounces (8 cups packed) dandelion greens, washed two or three times and spun dry

Lower the eggs carefully into boiling water, and boil them at a simmer for 7 minutes. Pour out the water, shake the pan to crack the shells, then fill the pan with ice, and let the eggs cool in the pan for at least 15 minutes. Peel the eggs under cold running water, and cut them into quarters.

Meanwhile, put the pancetta pieces in a saucepan, and cover them with the water. Bring the water to a boil, and boil gently for 10 minutes. Drain, then put the pancetta in a saucepan with 1 tablespoon of the olive oil. Cook gently for 5 minutes, or until crisp and lightly browned. Transfer the pancetta along with the rendered fat to a salad bowl, and add the garlic, anchovies, vinegar, salt, pepper, and 4 tablespoons of the olive oil. Mix well.

Preheat the oven to 400 degrees. Spread the remaining 1 tablespoon oil on a cookie sheet, press the slices of bread into the oil, and then turn them over, so they are oiled on the second side. Bake for 8 to 10 minutes, until nicely browned.

At serving time, add the greens to the salad bowl, and toss them with the dressing. Divide among four plates, and top with the bread and quartered eggs. Serve.

Locust Flower (Acacia) Fritters

YIELD: 6 SERVINGS, 12 TO 15 FRITTERS

THIS IS A TASTE from my youth that we still enjoy a few times each early summer. Two large locust trees next to our garden supply more fragrant flowers than we can use during the few weeks a year that these blossoms are available. The tiny white flowers have the sweet flavor of honey and a powerful spicy and musky aroma.

     4 cups locust flowers, stems removed
     4 tablespoons Grand Marnier
    ¼ cup sugar
  1½ cups all-purpose flour
     1 can (12 ounces) beer
     1 teaspoon pure vanilla extract
     2 large egg whites

  2½ cups canola oil, for cooking the fritters
         Confectioners' sugar, to dust the finished fritters

Mix the flowers, Grand Marnier, and sugar together in a bowl, cover, and refrigerate for 1 hour.

When ready to cook the fritters, place the flour, about two

thirds of the beer, and the vanilla in a bowl. Mix well with a whisk until the batter is smooth, then add the remainder of the beer, and mix well.

In a separate bowl beat the egg whites until they form peaks but are not too firm. Using the whisk, combine them with the beer batter. Fold in the locust flower mixture.

At serving time, preferably, put enough of the oil in a large saucepan so that it is about 1 inch deep in the pan. Heat to 375 degrees. Using a large spoon or a small measuring cup, pour about ⅓ cup of the batter into the hot oil. Repeat, cooking 4 or 5 fritters at a time in the oil. Cook the fritters for about 4 minutes on one side, then turn with tongs, and cook for 4 minutes on the other side. They should be crisp and nicely browned on both sides.

Lift the fritters from the oil with a slotted spoon, and place them on a wire rack. Repeat, making additional fritters with the remaining batter. Dust with confectioners' sugar before serving.

NOTE: If cooking the fritters ahead, recrisp in a 425-degree oven for 5 to 6 minutes, or until crisp and hot, then dust with the confectioners' sugar just before serving.

19

A New Way to Cook

THE NEW MILLENNIUM began on a dark note. My old friend Ed Giobbi and I visited Craig Claiborne at his apartment on West 57th Street one evening in 2000 and were shocked at what we saw. The man I will forever associate with sunny, friend-packed afternoons on the beaches of Long Island had become a recluse, spending his days and nights alone in a dark hole of a studio apartment in the Osbourne House, an imposing old rococo building next to the Art Students League on West 57th Street, while he clung to the enormous million-dollar Hamptons home, which he did not want to visit because of his poor health.

We pushed him in a wheelchair to Osteria del Circo, a restaurant a couple of blocks away that was owned by the Maccioni family of Le Cirque fame. It is a fine, lively place with great Tuscan food, but Craig had little interest in the restaurant or the meal. He wrapped his shaky hands around his usual tumbler of scotch and responded to our efforts at conversation with monosyllabic replies or incoherent mumblings. When the food came, he mouthed it with a distant look in his eyes, rejected it, ate a bit more of a new dish, rejected that. Halfway through the meal, he said he wanted to leave. We called for the bill.

A few weeks later, Craig died.

I had reached the age where many of those dearest to me were gone: Papa, Helen, Bichon, Pierre, and now Craig. But I have never been one to focus on the past. As time goes by, I concentrate on doing the things I love the most with the people I care about most.

THE WORLD is divided into two types of fishermen: those who catch fish and those who do not. Gloria is of the first group. She barely wets her hook before she's pulling in a flopping trout or bass. I can sit next to her, use the same bait, the same gear, and fish all day without a nibble.

So naturally there was some wifely derision when Jean-Claude and I set out one morning a few months ago on a fishing trip in Long Island Sound. "We'll be supplying dinner," I said.

Gloria muttered something about my picking up a pork loin at the market on the way home.

Her skepticism was reinforced when Jean-Claude began to assemble our provisions. Jean-Claude has retired to Hunter after owning a successful string of pastry shops in New York City. Now he dedicates his days to doing exactly what he pleases, most of which centers on some aspect of eating or drinking. He doesn't understand the point of spending an invigorating day on the water without refreshments. That morning, we selected a couple of bottles of vintage Champagne from my cellar. From his home, Jean-Claude had brought an assortment of artisanal cheeses, some proscuitto, and several duck breasts he had smoked.

With two friends, we set out from the harbor in Old Saybrook, Connecticut. For early November, it was an exceptional day. Temperatures were in the mid-6os. We could see the sun through thin, high clouds. And the sea was flat calm. Still, as anyone who knows will attest, mid-November is far from the best time for a fishing expedition on Long Island Sound.

For the first hour or so, it looked as if we would indeed be dining on pork loin that evening. We caught plenty of fish, beautiful striped bass, but all of them too small to keep. In those waters, striped bass have to be a minimum of twenty-nine inches in length to catch legally — fish that are as long as my legs and weigh upwards of ten pounds each. The captain suggested a change of tactics, and bluefish started hitting. In another spot, we discovered the home for the parents of the undersize stripers that had teased us earlier. Soon we all had our limit of keepers. We had the same result when we tried for blackfish.

We began to fillet our catch on the wharf. After I sliced the meat off the bones of a big striper, the captain, in an effort to help, grabbed the carcass and went to toss it into the harbor.

"What are you doing!" yelled Jean-Claude. "I want that."

The captain shot a look that left no doubt about his opinion of Jean-Claude's mental state.

"For stock," Jean-Claude said. "You know, soup."

The captain's look did not change when he handed Jean-Claude the head and bones.

Driving back to Madison, I turned to Jean-Claude and said, "We are going to have a night of fish."

"How are we going to cook them?" he said.

I thought about that question as I drove along I-95. When we lived in France, Jean-Claude would never have asked such a thing. There were only a few things to do with fish: poach, sauté, or bake and dress with one of the classical sauces. Now I found myself without a pat answer to Jean-Claude's simple question. From a culinary point of view, the decisions we faced showed just how far we had come since we had stepped off our respective ocean liners four decades earlier.

MAMAN, WHO IS still going strong as she nears ninety, scolds me whenever I visit her at the retirement community near Lyon. She loves my cooking, but it is no longer French, she says. Maman has a point.

My cooking today is certainly not purely French — or purely anything. It is a modern American cuisine with strong French influences. My tastes have remained simple. I like straightforward food that is well seasoned and elegantly presented, without fuss or deception. I like caviar, roast squab, steamed lobster, and sweet, hard caramel custard, but I am equally enthralled by simpler dishes. For me, there is nothing better than a chunk of crunchy, thick-crusted bread with its light, airy, elastic insides spread with the greatest farm butter available. A thin, firm, crackling *ficelle* (a skinny loaf of French bread) with a bar of dark chocolate works like a madeleine for me, taking me back to my youth and the French *quatre heure,* or small snack, that my brothers and I enjoyed in the late afternoon after school.

Leek and potato soup will always be a standard at my house. I have a fondness for eggs. Large, fresh organic eggs, each with a thick, deep-yellow-orange yolk and a spongy white, pan-fried in good butter along with a piece of *jambon à l'os,* or boiled ham on the bone, is a royal treat. Then there is the small, twisted potato that we call *ratte* in French. Similar to fingerlings, these yellow, waxy, and dense potatoes are best sautéed in butter and peanut oil in a skillet. Maman always grows a few *rattes* in her garden and keeps some of the plants for me to enjoy when I visit — and they are worth the trip! About an hour before we want to eat them, usually for lunch, she takes her four-pronged gardening fork and unearths one or two. She washes them under cold water and scrapes them with a paring knife to remove most of the skin. Finally, she fries them until they are mahogany brown and crisp on the outside. While the potatoes are cooking, she makes a white curly endive salad, *une frisée,* and seasons it with a dressing made of diced garlic, mustard, red wine vinegar, peanut oil, and salt and pepper.

That simple combination is still one of the greatest feasts that I can evoke in my gastronomic memory.

I am mad about charcuterie. Pig's feet, headcheese, blood sausage, and *andouillettes* (chitterling sausages) are among my favorites. I have eaten termites and worms with the Bushmen of East Africa and rotten fish with the fishermen of West Africa. I have consumed eggs fertilized with chick embryos in Vietnam and China, as well as rattlesnake and "gator" meat in Florida. I am not a skittish eater. While I do enjoy the esoteric, refined food of the great restaurants, I eat that food only occasionally. My everyday tastes tend to a fare of roast chicken, braised pork, sautéed whiting, and tomato salad. I love chocolate desserts and custards and remember with great fondness the large, bluish, juicy cherries of my aunt's garden and the extraordinary deep-orange apricots from the Rhône Valley, still warm from the summer sun and sticky with natural sugar and ripeness. I like copious glasses of wine with my food, and I do not like to eat alone. I need family and friends to enjoy the dishes and the pleasure of dining.

The future is indeed very bright and exciting for anyone entering this business. I'm delighted that the Pépin family will continue to participate for at least another generation. Claudine recently announced that she plans to get married — to a chef, of course — and open a restaurant in Oregon.

～～～

SO WHAT DID Jean-Claude and I do with our wonderful catch?

We smoked some of the bluefish fillets, because that brings out the best in this oily, thoroughly American fish, and we garnished them with a mustard potato salad seasoned with dill. Drawing on influences of both the Far East and nouvelle cuisine, we took some of the striped bass and made carpaccio flavored with sesame seed oil and soy sauce. We grilled the blackfish, adding just a little oil, salt, pepper, and lemon juice and also prepared a seviche from the same fish, flavored with hot pepper, cilantro, mint, and lime juice. As the pièce de résistance, we poached some of the striped bass fillets in Champagne and white wine and accompanied them with a cream sauce that included mushrooms and shallots, a dish that I prepared back at Le Pavillon when I first came to this country.

The next morning, I helped Jean-Claude load his Subaru station wagon with several coolers of bones, heads, and trimmings. He made me promise to come up to Hunter when the snow started flying. We'd cook something good in the fish stock and maybe sneak in a day or two of skiing, which I have recently been able to resume. Jean-Claude climbed behind the wheel and started the car.

"I'm not sure whether I enjoyed catching those fish or cooking them more," he said.

I felt the same way.

Seviche of Scallops

YIELD: 6 FIRST-COURSE SERVINGS

I NEVER SERVED ANY FISH or shellfish raw until I came to America, and I certainly didn't do so at Le Pavillon. I discovered gravlax, seviche, and fish carpaccio when I encountered nouvelle cuisine in the early 1970s, and these uncooked fish dishes — along with dozens of variations I've done through the years — have become favorites at our house. There are many ingredients in this recipe, but it is easily put together. The seviche is best prepared about 2 hours ahead of serving (so the ingredients can marinate together) and refrigerated; the scallops will get mushy, however, if the dish is assembled more than 8 hours ahead. Be sure your scallops are scrupulously fresh.

$\frac{1}{2}$ cup sun-dried tomatoes (about 1 ounce)

1 pound sea scallops

$1\frac{1}{2}$ cups diced (1-inch pieces) cucumber, from 1 peeled, seeded cucumber

$\frac{3}{4}$ cup coarsely chopped red onion

$\frac{1}{2}$ cup diced ($\frac{1}{2}$ inch) scallion

1 teaspoon chopped garlic

$\frac{1}{2}$ cup (loosely packed) coarsely chopped fresh cilantro leaves

$\frac{1}{4}$ cup (loosely packed) coarsely chopped fresh mint leaves

About 1 tablespoon finely chopped serrano or jalapeño pepper (more or less, depending on your tolerance for hot flavors)

1 teaspoon grated key lime rind (or rind from a regular lime)

$\frac{1}{4}$ cup key lime juice (or juice from a regular lime)

$\frac{1}{4}$ cup extra-virgin olive oil

1 1/2 teaspoons salt

2 tablespoons sweet mirin (sweet rice wine), or 2 tablespoons
rice vinegar and 1 teaspoon sugar

1/2 teaspoon Tabasco hot pepper sauce

6 large Boston lettuce leaves

Cover the dried tomatoes with hot water, and let them soak for 10 minutes, or until softened. Meanwhile, cut the scallops into 1/4-inch slices, and put them in a large bowl. When the tomatoes have softened, remove them from the water, cut them into 1/2-inch pieces, and add them to the bowl. Then mix in all the remaining ingredients except the lettuce.

At serving time, arrange the lettuce leaves in martini glasses or on plates, and spoon the seviche into them. Serve.

Index

A

Abraham and Strauss, 228–29
acacia flowers
    Locust Flower (Acacia) Fritters, 284–85
African American chefs, 242
African American culture
    offal and, 144
    Pépin's appreciation of, 153–55
Aicardi, M., 114–16, 119, 251
air raids, 5–6, 9, 20
Algerian War, 106, 108
    Szurdak's service in, 121
Alssid, Rebecca, 245
America. *See also specific cities and towns*
    decision to go to, 128–29
    Jeanne Pépin's visit to, 190–92
    shift in eating habits in, Pépin's and Franey's role in, 155–58
American attitudes, Pépin's learning of, 189–90

American food
    cooptation into Pépin's French repertoire, 235–36
    culinary revolution in, 155–58, 164–65
    with French influences, as Pépin's cooking today, 289–90
    Pépin's changing view of, 164–65
    Pépin's discoveries during travels, 235–36
    Pépin's early experiences with, 140–41
    Pépin's favorites among, 141
ananas voilé en surprise, 101
apple cider, fermenting and bottling of, 202–3
apples
    Maman's Apple Tart, 132–33
apprenticeship, Pépin's, 46–63
    beginning of, 46
    end of, 63
    first solo meal prepared during, 60–62

parties hosted by, 170–77,
191–92
Pépin's and Franey's writing
assistance to, 250–52
as restaurant reviewer, 256
sexual orientation of, 257,
258
using crystal flutes for picnic, 171–72
clam chowder, at Howard Johnson's, 156–57
clams
New England Clam Chow-
der, 166–67
Clark, Patrick, 242
Classical French Cooking
(Claiborne), Pépin's and
Franey's assistance with,
250–52
Coca-Cola, interest in La
Potagerie, 219
Columbia University, studies at,
139–40, 163–64, 189–90,
211–12
Combe, Charlotte, 232, 235
commis
as first, at Le Plaza Athénée,
96–98
job of, 89–90
as second, at Le Plaza
Athénée, 88–96
commis entremetier, position as,
80–81
cookbooks. *See also* writing
by Child, 182

by Claiborne, 250–52
by Curnonsky, 115
by Pellaprat, 115
by Pépin, 252, 253–54, 255
Le Répertoire de la cuisine, 99
cooking demonstrations, 228
cooking lessons. *See* teaching
cooking schools
apprenticeship compared
with, 242–43
Cordon Bleu, 115
emergence of, 231
French Culinary Institute,
241–43
Great Chefs of France, 231
growth of, 234–35
coque, 7
Cordon Bleu school of cooking, 115
corned beef
Reuben Sandwich, 148–50
corporal punishment, at Lycée
St. Louis, 16–17
La Côte Basque (New York restaurant), 138
coupe Mont Blanc, 69
La Coupole (Lyon restaurant),
72
cowherding, 3–4
crabs, Pépin's enjoyment of,
235
Crampette, Chef, 81–84
la crasse du beurre, 8
Creel, Harry, 257–58
Cross, Billy, 231

food (*cont.*)
>   preparation for Howard
>   Johnson's, 156–58
>   served by Franey and
>   Pépin, 159–60
>   learning about through
>   senses, 59–60
>   at Lycée St. Louis, 17
>   nouvelle cuisine and, 177–
>   79
>   prepared by Jeanne Pépin
>   during World War II, 6–9
>   preserved, prepared by Glo-
>   ria, 202
>   for Roland's first commun-
>   ion, 18–19
>   served at Le Pavillon, differ-
>   ence from foods served in
>   Paris, 138–39
food stylists, 250–51
food writing. *See* writing
foraging
>   fishing for trout, 214
>   fishing on la Turdine, 35–38
>   fishing on Long Island
>   Sound, 287–88
>   for lobsters, 173
>   for mushrooms, 33–34, 209–
>   10, 275
>   for Pépin's and Gloria's en-
>   gagement party, 191
>   on seacoast, 275–76
>   for shrimp, 85
>   for snails, 232–33

foreign cuisines, Pépin's expo-
>   sure to, 236–38
Fouquet's (Paris restaurant),
>   99–100
Fournou's Oven (San Fran-
>   cisco restaurant), 231
France. *See also specific cities*
>   1967 visit to, with Gloria,
>   192–93
>   return visit to, 160–62
>   war with Algeria, 106, 108
>   Szurdak's service in, 121
France gastronomique, 115
Franey, Betty, 141
Franey, Pierre, 160, 168, 256
>   attempt to obtain and pre-
>   pare calf's head, 174–76
>   career of, 137
>   culinary revolution and,
>   155–58, 164–65
>   end of writing relationship
>   with Claiborne, 257
>   friendship with Claiborne,
>   169, 170
>   frozen foods served by, 159
>   job offer from, 152–54
>   at Le Pavillon, 136–37, 138
>   Pépin's and Gloria's wed-
>   ding party and, 191
>   preparation of Claudine's
>   christening party by, 205
>   Soulé's treatment of, 145
>   visits to, 141
Freiberg, Bo, 236

Heller, Susie, 264

High Tree Farm, 232

home cooks, professionals compared with, 245–46

Hopkins, Tom, 255

L'Hôtel d'Albion (Aix-les-Bains restaurant), traineeship at, 66–68

Hôtel L'Amour (Neyron restaurant), 23–26, 34

L'Hôtel Matignon (prime minister's residence), as chef at, 113–25

L'Hôtel Restaurant de la Paix (Bellegarde restaurant), employment at, 69–71

L'Hôtel Terminus (Lyon restaurant), 49

House Beautiful, McCully's food column in, 179, 181, 252

Howard Johnson Company culinary revolution and, 155–58, 164–65

after death of Howard D. Johnson, 210–11

early career at, 154–60

job offer from, 145, 151, 152–54

resignation from, 216

work during 1960s at, 164–65

Hunter, New York cider fermenting and bottling in, 202–3

mushroom foraging in, 209–10

Pépin family's move from, 272–73

preserved foods prepared by Gloria in, 202

purchase of house in, 200–201

renovation of house in, 202

as year-round weekend retreat, 203

I

Iliad (Homer), food in, 245

J

James, Michael, 231

Jamet, Louis, 201

Jamet, Lucien, 201

Jauget, Chef, 71 characteristics of, 54

Pépin's initiation by, 48–50

Pépin's relationship with, 54–56, 62

Jerusalem artichokes, Pépin's dislike of, 7

Jeudy, Jean-Michel, 231–32

Johnny Carson, 267

Johnson, Howard B., changes made by, 210–11

Johnson, Howard Deering friendship with, 162–63

Howard Johnson's after death of, 210–11

job offer from, 145, 151

personality of, 162–63

preparation of Claudine's christening party by, 205

Jones, Judith, 255, 256

attempt to return to work at,
following accident, 227
menu at, 218–19
popularity of, 219
prices at, 218
relationship with partners of,
219–20
Poulet à la Crème, 64–65
poulet à l'estragon, solo preparation during apprentice-
ship, 60–62
poulet Pavillon, 138–39
prime minister of France, as
chef for, 113–25
prix de l'Arc de Triomphe celebration, 100–101
professional cooks, home
cooks compared with,
245–46
punishment, at Lycée St. Louis,
16–17
"The Purposeful Cook"
(Pépin), 257

Q

Quadrangle Books, 253–54

R

rabbit
Braised Rabbit en Cocotte
with Mustard Sauce, 247–
49
Raimo, M., 90
Ramadier, Paul, 112

Ramequins au Fromage, 74–75
rattes, 289–90
à la recherche de l'orange perdue,
266
recipes. *See* Recipes, page 318,
and names of specific recipes
red beans
Gloria's Pork Ribs and Red
Beans, 198–99
Red Coach Grill (restaurant
chain), 158
René, André, 230
Le Répertoire de la cuisine, 99
Le Restaurant de la Gare
(L'Arbresle restaurant),
34–35, 38, 39
restaurants. *See also specific restaurants*
chain, culinary revolution
and, 155–58, 164–65
Claiborne as reviewer of, 256
of Jeanne Pépin, 23–26, 34–
35, 38, 39–40. *See also* Le
Pélican
Reuben Sandwich, 148–50
Ripert, Chef, 80, 81
Roast Leg of Lamb Provençal,
126–27
Robert Mondavi Winery, Great
Chefs of France cooking
school at, 231
Roman Gnocchi, 104–5
La Rotonde (Paris restaurant),
82

Roussillon, Georges, 110–13, 131, 190

S

Sailhac, Alain, at French Culinary Institute, 242
Sailland, Maurice Edmond, 115
St.-Jean-de-Maurienne, summer in, 11–14
Saint-Oyant, Mme., 69
salads
    Chicken Salad à la Danny Kaye, 259–61
    Pissenlit, 282–84
    Semi-Dry Tomatoes and Mozzarella Salad, 270–71
sandwiches
    at Le Restaurant de la Gare, 38
    Reuben Sandwich, 148–50
Sanger, Arnold, 229
sardines, canned, Pépin's love of, 11
Sartre, Jean-Paul, 82
Saturday Night Live (television show), 267
sauce making, at Le Plaza Athénée, 96–98
saucisson (dry salami sausage), 18–19
sauerkraut
    Reuben Sandwich, 148–50

scallops
    Seviche of Scallops, 292–93
seafood. See also fish
    foraging for, 85, 173, 275
    Moules Ravigote, 183–84
    New England Clam Chowder, 166–67
    Seviche of Scallops, 292–93
secretary of the Treasury (French), as chef for, 110–13
Semi-Dry Tomatoes and Mozzarella Salad, 270–71
Séoul, Félix (le père Félix), 98
Seranne, Ann, 256
Seviche of Scallops, 292–93
Shalit, Gene, 219
shrimping, 85
Silber, John, 244, 245
Simon and Schuster, 252–53
"60-Minute Gourmet" (Franey's column in New York Times), 257
skiing, 185–87
Sky-Dive (New York restaurant), 231
Smoked Trout Gloria, 214–15
snails, gathering of, 232–33
Snyder, Tom, 265, 266
la Société des cuisiniers de Paris, 77–79, 99, 106
Soler, Jean, 245
Soltner, André, 159–60, 201, 202–3

What's My Line? (television
show), appearance on,
219
wild mushrooms
Cèpes aux Lardons, 213–14
foraging for, 33–34, 209–10,
275
Windows on the World (New
York restaurant), 229–31
consultation on, 229
opening of, 230
wine
Claudine's career in, 266–67
Jean-Victor's bottling of, 29–
32
Pépin's childhood experi-
ence with, 30–31, 32–33
WJCT-TV, 264
World Trade Center restaurants, 229–31
World War II
air raids during, 5–6, 9, 20

cheesemaking during, 13–14
end of, 20
Pépin family's flight from
Bourg during, 9–10
summers on farms during,
1–4, 11–14
writing, 250–56, 258. *See also*
House Beautiful; literature;
New York Times
of *The Art of Cooking,* 255–56
assistant hired for, 254–55
of first cookbooks, 252–54
for *House Beautiful* food column, 252
impetus for, 252
introduction to, 250–52

Z

Zimmerman, Gloria ("Zim"),
278, 279–80
Zizi. *See* Pépin, Roland (Zizi)
Zraly, Kevin, 231

Recipes

Spring
Dinner

Mussels + clams Belgica
Style
Coq au Vin Gloria
Potato Mousseline
Garlic Salad
Cheese
Strawberry
Shortcake

Sancerre 78
Château la Cardonne 76

Cognac